KNOWING GOD

J. I. Packer

InterVarsity Press
Downers Grove
Illinois 60515

For Kit

InterVarsity Press is the
book publishing division of
Inter-Varsity Christian Fellowship.

ISBN Cloth: 0-87784-867-X
ISBN Paper: 0-87784-770-3
Library of Congress Catalog
Card Number: 73-81573

Printed in the United
States of America

Foreword

As clowns yearn to play Hamlet, so I have wanted to write a treatise on God. This book, however, is not it. Its length might suggest that it is trying to be, but anyone who takes it that way will be disappointed. It is at best a string of beads: a series of small studies of great subjects, most of which first appeared in the *Evangelical Magazine*. They were conceived as separate messages, but are now presented together because they seem to coalesce into a single message about God and our living. It is their practical purpose that explains both the selection and omission of topics and the manner of treatment.

In *A Preface to Christian Theology*, John Mackay illustrated two kinds of interest in Christian things by picturing persons sitting on the high front balcony of a Spanish house watching travellers go by on the road below. The 'balconeers' can overhear the travellers' talk and chat with them; they may comment critically on the way that the travellers walk; or they may discuss questions about the road, how it can exist at all or lead anywhere, what might be seen from different points along it, and so forth; but they are onlookers, and their problems are theoretical only. The travellers, by contrast, face problems which, though they have their theoretical angle, are essentially practical — problems of the 'which-way-to-go' and 'how-to-make-it' type, problems which call not merely for comprehension but for decision and action too. Balconeers and travellers may think over the same area, yet their problems differ. Thus (for instance) in relation to *evil*, the balconeer's problem is to find a theoretical explanation of how evil can consist with God's sovereignty and goodness, but the traveller's problem is how to master evil and bring good out of it. Or again, in relation to *sin*, the balconeer asks whether racial sinfulness and personal perversity are really credible, while the traveller, knowing sin from within, asks what hope there is of deliverance. Or take the problem of the *Godhead;* while the balconeer is asking how one God can conceivably be three, what sort of unity three could have, and how three who make one can be persons, the traveller wants to know how to show proper honour, love and trust towards the three persons who are now together at work to bring him out of sin to glory. And so we might go on. Now this is a book for travellers, and it is with travellers' questions that it deals.

The conviction behind the book is that ignorance of God—ignorance both of his ways and of the practice of communion with him—lies at the root of much of the church's weakness today. Two unhappy trends seem to have produced this state of affairs.

Trend one is that *Christian minds have been conformed to the modern spirit:* the spirit, that is, that spawns great thoughts of man and leaves room for only small thoughts of God. The modern way with God is to set him at a distance, if not to deny him altogether; and the irony is that modern Christians, preoccupied with maintaining religious practices in an irreligious world, have themselves allowed God to become remote. Clear-sighted persons, seeing this, are tempted to withdraw from the churches in something like disgust to pursue a quest for God on their own. Nor can one wholly blame them, for churchmen who look at God, so to speak, through the wrong end of the telescope, so reducing him to pigmy proportions, cannot hope to end up as more than pigmy Christians, and clear-sighted people naturally want something better than this. Furthermore, thoughts of death, eternity, judgment, the greatness of the soul, and the abiding consequences of temporal decisions are all 'out' for moderns, and it is a melancholy fact that the Christian church, instead of raising its voice to remind the world of what is being forgotten, has formed a habit of playing down these themes in just the same way. But these capitulations to the modern spirit are really suicidal so far as Christian life is concerned.

Trend two is that *Christian minds have been confused by the modern scepticism.* For more than three centuries the naturalistic leaven in the Renaissance outlook has been working like a cancer in Western thought. Seventeenth-century Arminians and Deists, like sixteenth-century Socinians, came to deny, as against Reformation theology, that God's control of his world was either direct or complete, and theology, philosophy and science have for the most part combined to maintain that denial ever since. As a result, the Bible has come under heavy fire, and many landmarks in historical Christianity with it. The foundation-facts of faith are

6

called in question. Did God meet Israel at Sinai? Was Jesus more than a very spiritual man? Did the gospel miracles really happen? Is not the Jesus of the gospels largely an imaginary figure?—and so on. Nor is this all. Scepticism about both divine revelation and Christian origins has bred a wider scepticism which abandons all idea of a unity of truth, and with it any hope of unified human knowledge; so that it is now commonly assumed that my religious apprehensions have nothing to do with my scientific knowledge of things external to myself, since God is not 'out there' in the world, but only 'down here' in the psyche. The uncertainty and confusion about God which marks our day is worse than anything since Gnostic theosophy tried to swallow Christianity in the second century.

It is often said today that theology is stronger than it has ever been, and in terms of academic expertise and the quantity and quality of books published this is probably true; but it is a long time since theology has been so weak and clumsy at its basic task of holding the church to the realities of the gospel. Ninety years ago C. H. Spurgeon described the wobblings he then saw among the Baptists on Scripture, atonement and human destiny as 'the down-grade'; could he survey Protestant thinking about God at the present time, I guess he would speak of 'the nose-dive'!

'Stand ye in the way and see, and ask for the old paths, where is the good way, and walk therein, and ye shall find rest for your souls' (Jeremiah 6:16). Such is the invitation which this book issues. It is not a critique of new paths, except indirectly, but rather a straightforward recall to old ones, on the ground that 'the good way' is still what it used to be. I do not ask my readers to suppose that I know very well what I am talking about. 'Those like myself', wrote C. S. Lewis, 'whose imagination far exceeds their obedience are subject to a just penalty; we easily imagine conditions far higher than any we have really reached. If we describe what we have imagined we may make others, and make ourselves, believe that we have really been there'—and so fool both them and ourselves (*The Four Loves*, Fontana ed., p. 128). All readers and writers of devotional literature do well to weigh Lewis's words. Yet 'since we have the same spirit of faith as he had who wrote, "I believed, and so I spoke," we too believe, and so we speak' (2 Corinthians 4:13, RSV)—and if what is written here helps anyone in the way that the meditations behind the writing helped me, the work will have been abundantly worth while.

Trinity College, Bristol   J.I.P.
July 1972

I
KNOW
THE
LORD

II
BEHOLD
YOUR
GOD!

III
IF GOD
BE
FOR US . . .

I
KNOW
THE
LORD

CHAPTER I

The Study of God

I

On 7 January 1855 the minister of New Park Street Chapel, Southwark, opened his morning sermon as follows:

It has been said by someone that 'the proper study of mankind is man'. I will not oppose the idea, but I believe it is equally true that the proper study of God's elect is God; the proper study of a Christian is the Godhead. The highest science, the loftiest speculation, the mightiest philosophy, which can ever engage the attention of a child of God, is the name, the nature, the person, the work, the doings, and the existence of the great God whom he calls his Father.

There is something exceedingly *improving to the mind* in a contemplation of the Divinity. It is a subject so vast, that all our thoughts are lost in its immensity; so deep, that our pride is drowned in its infinity. Other subjects we can compass and grapple with; in them we feel a kind of self-content, and go our way with the thought, 'Behold I am wise'. But when we come to this master-science, finding that our plumb-line cannot sound its depth, and that our eagle eye cannot see its height, we turn away with the thought that vain man would be wise, but he is like a wild ass's colt; and with solemn exclamation, 'I am but of yesterday, and know nothing'. No subject of contemplation will tend more to humble the mind, than thoughts of God . . .

But while the subject *humbles* the mind, it also *expands* it. He who often thinks of God, will have a larger mind than the man who simply plods around this narrow globe . . . The most

13

excellent study for expanding the soul, is the science of Christ, and Him crucified, and the knowledge of the Godhead in the glorious Trinity. Nothing will so enlarge the intellect, nothing so magnify the whole soul of man, as a devout, earnest, continued investigation of the great subject of the Deity.

And, whilst humbling and expanding, this subject is eminently *consolatory*. Oh, there is, in contemplating Christ, a balm for every wound; in musing on the Father, there is a quietus for every grief; and in the influence of the Holy Ghost, there is a balsam for every sore. Would you lose your sorrow? Would you drown your cares? Then go, plunge yourself in the Godhead's deepest sea; be lost in his immensity; and you shall come forth as from a couch of rest, refreshed and invigorated. I know nothing which can so comfort the soul; so calm the swelling billows of sorrow and grief; so speak peace to the winds of trial, as a devout musing upon the subject of the Godhead. It is to that subject that I invite you this morning . . .

These words, spoken over a century ago by C. H. Spurgeon (at that time, incredibly, only twenty years old) were true then, and they are true now. They make a fitting preface to a series of studies on the nature and character of God.

II

'But wait a minute,' says someone, 'tell me this. Is our journey really necessary? In Spurgeon's day, we know, people found theology interesting, but I find it boring. Why need anyone take time off today for the kind of study you propose? Surely a layman, at any rate, can get on without it? After all, this is 1972, not 1855!'

A fair question! — but there is, I think, a convincing answer to it. The questioner clearly assumes that a study of the nature and character of God will be unpractical and irrelevant for life. In fact, however, it is the most practical project anyone can engage in. Knowing about God is crucially important for the living of our lives. As it would be cruel to an Amazonian tribesman to fly him to London, put him down without explanation in Trafalgar Square and leave him, as one who knew nothing of English or England, to fend for himself, so we are cruel to ourselves if we try to live in this world without knowing about the God whose world it is and who runs it. The world becomes a strange, mad, painful place, and life in it a disappointing and unpleasant business, for those who do not know about God. Disregard the study of God, and you sentence yourself to stumble and blunder through life

The Study of God

blindfold, as it were, with no sense of direction and no understanding of what surrounds you. This way you can waste your life and lose your soul.

Recognising, then, that the study of God is worth while, we prepare to start. But where shall we start from? Clearly, we can only start from where we are. That, however, means setting out in a storm, for the doctrine of God is a storm-centre today. The so-called 'debate about God', with its startling slogans—'our image of God must go'; 'God is dead'; 'we can sing the Creed, but we can't say it'—is raging all round us. We are told that 'God-talk', as Christians have historically practised it, is a refined sort of nonsense, and knowledge about God is strictly a non-entity. Types of teaching which profess such knowledge are written off as outmoded—'Calvinism', 'fundamentalism', 'Protestant scholasticism', 'the old orthodoxy'. What are we to do? If we postpone our journey till the storm dies down, we may never get started at all. My proposal is this. You will know how Bunyan's pilgrim, when called back by his wife and children from the journey on which he was setting out, 'put his fingers in his ears, and ran on crying, Life, Life, Eternal Life'. I ask you for the moment to stop your ears to those who tell you there is no road to knowledge about God, and come a little way with me and see. After all, the proof of the pudding is in the eating, and anyone who is actually following a recognised road will not be too worried if he hears non-travellers telling each other that no such road exists.

Storm or no storm, then, we are going to start. But how do we plot our course?

Five basic truths, five foundation-principles of the knowledge about God which Christians have, will determine our course throughout. They are as follows:

1 God has spoken to man, and the Bible is His Word, given to us to make us wise unto salvation.
2 God is Lord and King over His world; He rules all things for His own glory, displaying His perfections in all that He does, in order that men and angels may worship and adore Him.
3 God is Saviour, active in sovereign love through the Lord Jesus Christ to rescue believers from the guilt and power of sin, to adopt them as His sons, and to bless them accordingly.
4 God is Triune; there are within the Godhead three persons, the Father, the Son and the Holy Ghost; and the work of salvation is one in which all three act together, the Father purposing redemption, the Son securing it, and the Spirit applying it.

15

5 Godliness means responding to God's revelation in trust and obedience, faith and worship, prayer and praise, submission and service. Life must be seen and lived in the light of God's Word. This, and nothing else, is true religion.

In the light of these general and basic truths, we are now going to examine in detail what the Bible shows us of the nature and character of the God of whom we have been speaking. We are in the position of travellers who, after surveying a great mountain from afar, travelling round it, and observing how it dominates the landscape and determines the features of the surrounding country-side, now approach it directly, with the intention of climbing it.

III

What is the ascent going to involve? What are the themes that will occupy us?

We shall have to deal with the *Godhead* of God, the qualities of Deity which set God apart from men and mark the difference and distance between the Creator and His creatures: such qualities as His self-existence, His infinity, His eternity, His unchangeable-ness. We shall have to deal with the *powers* of God: His almighti-ness, His omniscience, His omnipresence. We shall have to deal with the *perfections* of God, the aspects of His moral character which are manifested in His words and deeds—His holiness, His love and mercy, His truthfulness, His faithfulness, His goodness, His patience, His justice. We shall have to take note of what pleases Him, what offends Him, what awakens His wrath, what affords Him satisfaction and joy.

For many of us, these are comparatively unfamiliar themes. They were not always so to the people of God. There was a time when the subject of God's attributes (as it was called) was thought so important as to be included in the Catechism which all children in the churches were taught and all adult members were expected to know. Thus, to the fourth question in the Westminster Shorter Catechism, 'What is God?' the answer read as follows: 'God is a Spirit, infinite, eternal, and unchangeable in His being, wisdom, power, holiness, justice, goodness, and truth'—a statement which the great Charles Hodge described as 'probably the best definition of God ever penned by man'. Few children today, however, are brought up on the Westminster Shorter Catechism, and few modern worshippers will ever have heard a course of sermons covering the doctrine of the Divine character in the way that Charnock's massive *Discourses on the Existence and Attributes of*

God (1682) did. Few, too, will ever have read anything simple and straightforward on the subject of the nature of God, for scarcely any such writing exists at the present time. We can expect, therefore, that an exploration of the themes mentioned above will give us much that is new to think about, and many fresh ideas to ponder and digest.

IV

For this very reason we need, before we start to ascend our mountain, to stop and ask ourselves a very fundamental question — a question, indeed, that we always ought to put to ourselves whenever we embark on any line of study in God's holy Book. The question concerns our own motives and intentions as students. We need to ask ourselves: what is my ultimate aim and object in occupying my mind with these things? What do I intend to *do* with my knowledge about God, once I have got it? For the fact that we have to face is this: that if we pursue theological knowledge for its own sake, it is bound to go bad on us. It will make us proud and conceited. The very greatness of the subject-matter will intoxicate us, and we shall come to think of ourselves as a cut above other Christians because of our interest in it and grasp of it; and we shall look down on those whose theological ideas seem to us crude and inadequate, and dismiss them as very poor specimens. For, as Paul told the conceited Corinthians, 'knowledge puffeth up . . . if any man thinketh that he knoweth anything, he knoweth not yet as he ought to know' (1 Cor. 8: 1 f., RV). To be preoccupied with getting theological knowledge as an end in itself, to approach Bible study with no higher a motive than a desire to know all the answers, is the direct route to a state of self-satisfied self-deception. We need to guard our hearts against such an attitude, and pray to be kept from it. As we saw earlier, there can be no spiritual health without doctrinal knowledge; but it is equally true that there can be no spiritual health with it, if it is sought for the wrong purpose and valued by the wrong standard. In this way, doctrinal study really can become a danger to spiritual life, and we today, no less than the Corinthians of old, need to be on our guard here.

But, says someone, is it not a fact that a love for God's revealed truth, and a desire to know as much of it as one can, is natural to every person who has been born again? Look at Psalm 119 — 'teach me thy statutes'; 'open thou mine eyes, that I may behold wondrous things out of thy law'; 'O how I love thy law'; 'how sweet are thy words unto my taste! yea, sweeter than honey to my mouth!'; 'give me understanding, that I may know thy testimonies' (verses 12, 18, 97, 103, 125). Does not every child of God long, with the psalmist, to know just as much about his heavenly Father as he can learn? Is not, indeed, the fact that he has 'received . . . the love of the truth' in this way one proof that he has been born again? (see 2 Thess. 2: 10). And is it not right that he should seek to satisfy this God-given desire to the full?

Yes, of course it is. But if you look back to Psalm 119 again, you will see that the psalmist's concern to get knowledge about God was not a theoretical, but a practical concern. His supreme desire was to know and enjoy God Himself, and he valued knowledge about God simply as a means to this end. He wanted to understand God's truth in order that his heart might respond to it and his life be conformed to it. Observe the emphasis of the opening verses. 'Blessed are the undefiled in the way, who *walk in the law of the Lord*. Blessed are they that keep his testimonies, and that *seek him with the whole heart*. . . . O that *my ways were directed to keep thy statutes!*' (verses 1, 2, 5). He was interested in truth and orthodoxy, in biblical teaching and theology, not as ends in themselves, but as means to the further ends of life and godliness. His ultimate concern was with the knowledge and service of the great God whose truth he sought to understand.

And this must be our attitude too. Our aim in studying the Godhead must be to know God Himself the better. Our concern must be to enlarge our acquaintance, not simply with the doctrine of God's attributes, but with the living God whose attributes they are. As He is the subject of our study, and our helper in it, so He must Himself be the end of it. We must seek, in studying God, to be led to God. It was for this purpose that revelation was given, and it is to this use that we must put it.

V

How are we to do this? How can we turn our knowledge *about* God into knowledge *of* God? The rule for doing this is demanding, but simple. It is that we turn each truth that we learn *about* God into matter for meditation *before* God, leading to prayer and praise *to* God.

We have some idea, perhaps, what prayer is, but what is meditation? Well may we ask; for meditation is a lost art today, and Christian people suffer grievously from their ignorance of the practice. Meditation is the activity of calling to mind, and thinking over, and dwelling on, and applying to oneself, the various things that one knows about the works and ways and purposes and promises of God. It is an activity of holy thought, consciously performed in the presence of God, under the eye of God, by the help of God, as a means of communion with God. Its purpose is to clear one's mental and spiritual vision of God, and to let His truth make its full and proper impact on one's mind and heart. It is a matter of talking to oneself about God and oneself; it is, indeed, often a matter of arguing with oneself, reasoning oneself out of moods of doubt and unbelief into a clear apprehension of God's power and grace. Its effect is ever to humble us, as we contemplate God's greatness and glory, and our own littleness and sinfulness, and to encourage and reassure us — 'comfort' us, in the old, strong, Bible sense of the word — as we contemplate the unsearchable riches of divine mercy displayed in the Lord Jesus Christ. These were the points stressed by Spurgeon in the passage which we quoted at the beginning, and they are true. And it is as we enter more and more deeply into this experience of being humbled and exalted that our knowledge of God increases, and with it our peace, our strength, and our joy. God help us, then, to put our knowledge about God to this use, that we all may in truth 'know the Lord'.

CHAPTER 2

The People who Know their God

I

I walked in the sunshine with a scholar who had effectively forfeited his prospects of academic advancement by clashing with church dignitaries over the gospel of grace. 'But it doesn't matter,' he said at length, 'for I've known God and they haven't.' The remark was a mere parenthesis, a passing comment on something I had said, but it has stuck with me, and set me thinking.

Not many of us, I think, would ever naturally say that we have known God. The words imply a definiteness and matter-of-factness of experience to which most of us, if we are honest, have to admit that we are still strangers. We claim, perhaps, to have a testimony, and can rattle off our conversion story with the best of them; we say that we *know* God — this, after all, is what evangelicals are expected to say; but would it occur to us to say, without hesitation, and with reference to particular events in our personal history, that we *have known* God? I doubt it, for I suspect that with most of us experience of God has never become so vivid as that.

Nor, I think, would many of us ever naturally say that in the light of the knowledge of God which we have come to enjoy past disappointments and present heartbreaks, as the world counts heartbreaks, *don't matter*. For the plain fact is that to most of us they do matter. We live with them as our 'crosses' (so we call them). Constantly we find ourselves slipping into bitterness and apathy and gloom as we reflect on them, which we frequently do. The attitude we show to the world is a sort of dried-up stoicism, miles removed from the 'joy unspeakable and full of glory' which Peter took for granted that his readers were displaying (1 Peter 1:8). 'Poor souls,' our friends say of us, 'how they've *suffered*' — and that is just what we feel about ourselves! But these private mock heroics have no place at all in the minds of those who really know God. They never brood on might-have-beens; they never think of the things they have missed, only of what they have gained. 'What things were gain to me, these have I counted loss for Christ,' wrote Paul. 'Yea verily, and I count all things to be loss for the excellency of the knowledge of Christ Jesus my Lord: for whom I suffered the loss of all things, and do count them but dung, that I may gain Christ, and be found in him . . . that I may know him . . .' (Philippians 3: 7-10). When Paul says he counts the things he lost 'dung', he means not merely that he does not think of them as having any value, but also that he does not live with them constantly in his mind: what normal person spends his time nostalgically dreaming of manure? Yet this, in effect, is what many of us do. It shows how little we have in the way of true knowledge of God.

We need frankly to face ourselves at this point. We are, perhaps, orthodox evangelicals. We can state the gospel clearly, and can smell unsound doctrine a mile away. If anyone asks us how men may know God, we can at once produce the right formulae—that we come to know God through Jesus Christ the Lord, in virtue of His cross and mediation, on the basis of His word of promise, by the power of the Holy Spirit, via a personal exercise of faith. Yet the gaiety, goodness, and unfetteredness of spirit which are the marks of those who have known God are rare among us—rarer, perhaps, than they are in some other Christian circles where, by comparison, evangelical truth is less clearly and fully known. Here, too, it would seem that the last may prove to be first, and the first last. A little knowledge of God is worth more than a great deal of knowledge about Him.

To focus this point further, let me say two things:

First, *one can know a great deal about God without much knowledge of Him*. I am sure that many of us have never really grasped this. We find in ourselves a deep interest in theology (which is, of course, a most fascinating and intriguing subject—in the seventeenth century it was every gentleman's hobby). We read books of theological exposition and apologetics. We dip into Christian history, and study the Christian creed. We learn to find our way around in the Scriptures. Others appreciate our interest in these things, and we find ourselves asked to give our opinion in public on this or that Christian question, to lead study groups, to give papers, to write articles, and generally to accept responsibility, informal if not formal, for acting as teachers and arbiters of orthodoxy in our own Christian circle. Our friends tell us how much they value our contribution, and this spurs us to further explorations of God's truth, so that we may be equal to the demands made upon us. All very fine—yet interest in theology, and knowledge about God, and the capacity to think clearly and talk well on Christian themes, is not at all the same thing as knowing Him. We may know as much about God as Calvin knew—indeed, if we study his works diligently, sooner or later we shall—and yet all the time (unlike Calvin, may I say) we may hardly know God at all.

Second, *one can know a great deal about godliness without much knowledge of God*. It depends on the sermons one hears, the books one reads, and the company one keeps. In this analytical and technological age there is no shortage of books on the church bookstalls, or sermons from the pulpits, on how to pray, how to witness, how to read our Bibles, how to tithe our money, how to be a young Christian, how to be an old Christian, how to be a happy Christian, how to get consecrated, how to lead men to Christ, how to receive the baptism of the Holy Spirit (or, in some cases, how to avoid receiving it), how to speak with tongues (or, how to explain away Pentecostal manifestations), and generally how to go through all the various motions which the teachers in question associate with being a Christian believer. Nor is there any shortage of biographies delineating the experiences of Christians in past days for our interested perusal. Whatever else may be said about this state of affairs, it certainly makes it possible to learn a great deal at second-hand about the practice of Christianity. Moreover, if one has been given a good bump of common sense one may frequently be able to use this learning to help floundering Christians of less stable temperament to regain their footing and develop a sense of proportion about their troubles, and in this way one may gain for oneself a reputation for being quite a pastor. Yet one can have all this and hardly know God at all.

We come back, then, to where we started. The question is not whether we are good at theology, or 'balanced' (horrible, self-conscious word!) in our approach to problems of Christian living; the question is, can we say, simply, honestly, not because we feel that as evangelicals we ought to, but because it is plain matter of fact, that we have known God, and that because we have known God the unpleasantness we have had, or the pleasantness we have not had, through being Christians does not matter to us? If we really knew God, this is what we would be saying, and if we are not saying it, that is a sign that we need to face ourselves more sharply with the difference between knowing God and merely knowing about Him.

II

We have said that when a man knows God, losses and 'crosses' cease to matter to him; what he has gained simply banishes these things from his mind. What other effects does knowledge of God have on a man? Various sections of Scripture answer this question from different points of view, but perhaps the most clear and striking answer of all is provided by the book of Daniel. We may summarise its witness in four propositions.

1. *Those who know God have great energy for God.*
In one of the prophetic chapters of Daniel we read: 'the people that know their God shall be strong, and do exploits' (11:32). RSV renders thus: 'the people who know their God shall *stand firm and take action.*' In the context, this statement is introduced by 'but', and set in contrast to the activity of the 'vile person' (verse 21) who sets up 'the abomination that maketh desolate', and corrupts by smooth and flattering talk those whose loyalty to God's covenant has failed (verses 31–2). This shows us that the action taken by those who know God is their *reaction* to the anti-God trends which they see operating around them. While their God is being defied or disregarded, they cannot rest; they feel they must do something; the dishonour done to God's name goads them into action.

This is exactly what we see happening in the narrative chapters of Daniel, where we are told of the 'exploits' of Daniel and his three friends. They were men who knew God, and who in consequence felt compelled from time to time actively to stand out against the conventions and dictates of irreligion and false religion. Daniel in particular appears as one who would not let a situation of that sort slide, but felt bound openly to challenge it. Rather than risk possible ritual defilement through eating palace food, he insisted on a vegetarian diet, to the consternation of the prince of the eunuchs (1:8–16). When Nebuchadnezzar suspended the practice of prayer for a month, on pain of death, Daniel not merely went on praying three times a day, but did so in front of an open window, so that everyone might see what he was doing (6:10 f.). One recalls Bishop Ryle leaning forward in his stall at St. Paul's Cathedral so that everyone might see that he did not turn east for the Creed! Such gestures must not be misunderstood. It is not that Daniel, or for that matter Bishop Ryle, was an awkward, cross-grained fellow who luxuriated in rebellion and could only be happy when he was squarely 'agin' the government. It is simply that those who know their God are sensitive to situations in which God's truth and honour are being directly or tacitly jeopardized, and rather than let the matter go by default will force the issue on men's attention and seek thereby to compel a change of heart about it—even at personal risk.

Nor does this energy for God stop short with public gestures. Indeed, it does not start there. Men who know their God are before anything else men who pray, and the first point where their zeal and energy for God's glory come to expression is in their prayers. In Daniel 9 we read how, when the prophet 'understood by the books' that the foretold time of Israel's captivity was drawing to an end, and when at the same time he realised that the nation's sin was still such as to provoke God to judgment rather than mercy, he set himself to seek God 'by prayer and supplications, with fasting, and sackcloth, and ashes' (verse 3), and prayed for the restoring of Jerusalem with a vehemence and passion and agony of spirit to which most of us are complete strangers. Yet the invariable fruit of true knowledge of God is energy to pray for God's cause—energy, indeed, which can only find an outlet and a relief of inner tension when channelled into such prayer—and the more knowledge, the more energy! By this we may test ourselves. Perhaps we are not in a position to make public gestures against ungodliness and apostasy. Perhaps we are old, or ill, or otherwise limited by our physical situation. But we can all pray about the ungodliness and apostasy which we see in everyday life all around us. If, however, there is in us little energy for such prayer, and little consequent practice of it, this is a sure sign that as yet we scarcely know our God.

2. *Those who know God have great thoughts of God.*
There is not space enough here to gather up all that the book of Daniel tells us about the wisdom, might, and truth of the great God who rules history and shows His sovereignty in acts of judgment and mercy towards individuals and nations according to His own good pleasure. Suffice it to say that there is, perhaps, no more vivid or sustained presentation of the many-sided reality of God's sovereignty in the whole Bible.

In face of the might and splendour of the Babylonian empire which had swallowed up Palestine, and the prospect of further great world-empires to follow, dwarfing Israel by every standard of human calculation, the book as a whole forms a dramatic reminder that the God of Israel is King of Kings and Lord of Lords, that 'the heavens do rule' (4:6), that God's hand is on history at every point, that history, indeed, is no more than 'His story', the unfolding of His eternal plan, and that the kingdom which will triumph in the end is God's.

The central truth which Daniel taught Nebuchadnezzar in chapters 2 and 4, and of which he reminded Belshazzar in chapter 5 (verses 18–23), and which Nebuchadnezzar acknowledged in chapter 4 (verses 34–37), and which Darius confessed in chapter 6 (verses 25–27), and which was the basis of Daniel's prayers in chapters 2 and 9, and of his confidence in defying authority in chapters 1 and 6, and of his friends' confidence in defying authority in chapter 3, and which formed the staple substance of all the disclosures which God made to Daniel in chapters 2, 4, 7, 8, 10, and 11–12, is the truth that 'the most High ruleth in the kingdom of men' (4:25, cf. 5:21). He knows, and foreknows, all things, and His foreknowledge is foreordination; He, therefore, will have the last word, both in world history and in the destiny of every man; His kingdom and righteousness will triumph in the end, for neither men nor angels shall be able to thwart Him.

These were the thoughts of God which filled Daniel's mind, as witness his prayers (always the best evidence for a man's view of God): 'Blessed be the name of God for ever and ever: for wisdom and might are his: and he changeth the times and the seasons: he removeth kings, and setteth up kings: he giveth wisdom . . . he knoweth what is in the darkness, and the light dwelleth with him . . .' (2: 20 ff.); 'O Lord, the great and dreadful God, keeping covenant and mercy to them that love him, and to them that keep his commandments . . . O Lord, righteousness belongeth unto thee . . . To the Lord our God belong mercies and forgivenesses . . . the LORD our God is righteous in all his works which he doeth . . .' (9:4, 7, 9, 14). Is this how we think of God? Is this the view of God which our own praying expresses? Does this tremendous sense of His holy majesty, His moral perfection, and His gracious faithfulness keep us humble and dependent, awed and obedient, as it did Daniel? By this test, too, we may measure how much, or how little, we know God.

3 *Those who know God show great boldness for God.*

Daniel and his friends were men who stuck their necks out. This was not foolhardiness. They knew what they were doing. They had counted the cost. They had measured the risk. They were well aware what the outcome of their actions would be unless

God miraculously intervened, as in fact He did. But these things did not move them. Once they were convinced that their stand was *right*, and that loyalty to their God required them to take it, then, in Oswald Chambers's phrase, they 'smilingly washed their hands of the consequences'. 'We ought to obey God rather than men,' said the apostles (Acts 5: 29). 'Neither count I my life dear unto myself, so that I might finish my course with joy,' said Paul (Acts 20: 24). This was precisely the spirit of Daniel, Shadrach, Meshach, and Abed-nego. It is the spirit of all who know God. They may find the determination of the right course to take agonisingly difficult, but once they are clear on it they embrace it boldly and without hesitation. It does not worry them that others of God's people see the matter differently, and do not stand with them. (Were Shadrach, Meshach, and Abed-nego the only Jews who declined to worship Nebuchadnezzar's image? Nothing in their recorded words suggests that they either knew, or, in the final analysis, cared. They were clear as to what they personally had to do, and that was enough for them.) By this test also we may measure our own knowledge of God.

4 *Those who know God have great contentment in God*.
There is no peace like the peace of those whose minds are possessed with full assurance that they have known God, and God has known them, and that this relationship guarantees God's favour to them in life, through death, and on for ever. This is the peace of which Paul speaks in Romans 5:1—'being justified by faith, we have peace with God through our Lord Jesus Christ'— and whose substance he analyses in full in Romans 8. 'There is therefore now no condemnation to them which are in Christ Jesus . . . the Spirit itself beareth witness with our spirit, that we are the children of God, and if children, then heirs . . . we know that all things work together for good to them that love God . . . whom he justified, then he also glorified . . . if God be for us, who can be against us? . . . Who shall lay anything to the charge of God's elect? . . . Who shall separate us from the love of Christ? . . . I am persuaded that neither death, nor life . . . nor things present, nor things to come . . . shall be able to separate us from the love of God, which is in Christ Jesus our Lord' (verses 1, 16 f., 28, 30, 33, 35 ff.). This is the peace which Shadrach, Meshach, and Abed-nego knew; hence the calm contentment with which they stood their ground in face of Nebuchadnezzar's ultimatum— 'if ye worship not, ye shall be cast the same hour into the midst of a burning fiery furnace; and who is that God that shall deliver you

out of my hands?' Their reply (3:16–18) is classic. 'O Nebuchadnezzar, we are not careful to answer thee in this matter.' (No panic!) 'If it be so, our God whom we serve is able to deliver us ... and he will deliver us out of thine hand, O king.' (Courteous, but unanswerable—they knew their God!) 'But if not'—if no deliverance comes—'be it known unto thee, O king, that we will not serve thy gods.' (It doesn't matter! It makes no difference! Live or die, they are content.)

> *Lord, it belongs not to my care*
> *Whether I die or live;*
> *To love and serve Thee is my share,*
> *And this Thy grace must give.*

> *If life be long, I will be glad,*
> *That I may long obey;*
> *If short—then why should I be sad*
> *To soar to endless day?*

The comprehensiveness of our contentment is another measure whereby we may judge whether we really know God.

III

Do we desire such knowledge of God? Then—

First, we must recognise how much we lack knowledge of God. We must learn to measure ourselves, not by our knowledge about God, not by our gifts and responsibilities in the church, but by how we pray and what goes on in our hearts. Many of us, I suspect, have no idea how impoverished we are at this level. Let us ask the Lord to show us.

Second, we must seek the Saviour. When He was on earth, He invited men to company with Him; thus they came to know Him, and in knowing Him to know His Father. The Old Testament records pre-incarnate manifestations of the Lord Jesus doing the same thing—companying with men, in character as the angel of the Lord, in order that men might know Him. The book of Daniel tells us of what appear to be two such instances—for who was the fourth man, 'like a son of the gods' (3:25, RSV), who walked with Daniel's three friends in the furnace? and who was the angel whom God sent to shut the lions' mouths when Daniel was in their den (6:22)? The Lord Jesus Christ is now absent from us in body, but spiritually it makes no difference; still we may find and know God through seeking and finding His company. It is those who have sought the Lord Jesus till they have found Him—for the promise is that when we seek Him with all our hearts, we shall surely find Him—who can stand before the world to testify that they have known God.

CHAPTER 3

Knowing and Being Known

I

What were we made for? To know God. What aim should we set ourselves in life? To know God. What is the 'eternal life' that Jesus gives? Knowledge of God. 'This is life eternal, that they might know thee, the only true God, and Jesus Christ, whom thou hast sent' (John 17:3). What is the best thing in life, bringing more joy, delight, and contentment, than anything else? Knowledge of God. 'Thus saith the LORD, Let not the wise man glory in his wisdom, neither let the mighty man glory in his might, let not the rich man glory in his riches; but let him that glorieth glory in this, that he understandeth and knoweth me' (Jer. 9:23 f.). What, of all the states God ever sees man in, gives Him most pleasure? Knowledge of Himself. 'I desire . . . the knowledge of God more than burnt offerings,' says God (Hos. 6:6).

In these few sentences we have said a very great deal. Our point is one to which every Christian heart will warm, though the person whose religion is merely formal will not be moved by it. (And by this very fact his unregenerate state may be known.) What we have said provides at once a foundation, shape, and goal for our lives, plus a principle of priorities and a scale of values. Once you become aware that the main business that you are here for is to know God, most of life's problems fall into place of their own accord. The world today is full of sufferers from the wasting disease which Albert Camus focused as Absurdism ('life is a bad joke'), and from the complaint which we may call Marie Antoinette's fever, since she found the phrase that describes it ('nothing tastes'). These disorders blight the whole of life: everything becomes at once a problem and a bore, because nothing seems worth while. But Absurdist tapeworms and Antoinette's fever are ills from which, in the nature of the case, Christians are immune, except for occasional spells of derangement when the power of temptation presses their mind out of shape—and these, by God's mercy, do not last. What makes life worth while is having a big enough objective, something which catches our imagination and lays hold of our allegiance; and this the Christian has, in a way that no other man has. For what higher, more exalted, and more compelling goal can there be than to know God?

From another standpoint, however, we have not as yet said very much. When we speak of knowing God, we are using a verbal formula, and formulae are like cheques; they are no use unless we know how to cash them. What are we talking about when we use the phrase 'knowing God'? A special sort of emotion? Shivers down the back? A dreamy, off-the-ground, floating feeling? Tingling thrills and exhilaration, such as drug-takers seek? Or is knowing God a special sort of intellectual experience? Does one hear a voice? see a vision? find strange trains of thought coursing through one's mind? or what? These matters need discussing, especially since, according to Scripture, this is a region in which it is easy to be fooled, and to think you know God when you do not. We pose the question, then: what sort of activity, or event, is it that can properly be described as 'knowing God'?

II

It is clear, to start with, that 'knowing' God is of necessity a more complex business than 'knowing' a fellow-man, just as 'knowing' my neighbour is a more complex business than 'knowing' a house, or a book, or a language. The more complex the object, the more complex is the knowing of it. Knowledge of something abstract, like a language, is acquired by learning; knowledge of something inanimate, like Ben Nevis or the British Museum, comes by inspection and exploration. These activities, though demanding in terms of concentrated effort, are relatively simple to describe. But when one gets to living things, knowing them becomes a good deal more complicated. One does not know a living thing till one knows, not merely its past history, but how it is likely to react and behave under specific circumstances. A person who says 'I know this horse' normally means, not just 'I have seen it before' (though, the way we use words, he might only mean that); more probably, however, he means 'I know how it behaves, and can tell you how it ought to be handled.' Such knowledge only comes through some prior acquaintance with the horse, seeing it in action, and trying to handle it oneself.

In the case of human beings, the position is further complicated by the fact that, unlike horses, people cover up, and do not show everybody all that is in their hearts. A few days are enough to get to know a horse as well as you will ever know it, but you may spend months and years doing things in company with another person and still have to say at the end of that time, 'I don't really *know* him at all.' We recognise degrees in our knowledge of our fellow-men; we know them, we say, 'well', 'not very well', 'just to shake hands with', 'intimately', or perhaps 'inside-out', according to how much, or how little, they have opened up to us when we met them.

Thus, the quality and extent of our knowledge of them depends more on them than on us. Our knowing them is more directly the result of their allowing us to know them than of our attempting to get to know them. When we meet, our part is to give them our attention and interest, to show them good-will and to open up in a friendly way from our side. From that point, however, it is they, not we, who decide whether we are going to know them or not.

Imagine, now, that we are going to be introduced to someone whom we feel to be 'above' us — whether in rank, or intellectual distinction, or professional skill, or personal sanctity, or in some other respect. The more conscious we are of our own inferiority, the more we shall feel that our part is simply to attend to him respectfully and let him take the initiative in the conversation. (Think of meeting the Queen, or the Duke of Edinburgh.) We would like to get to know this exalted person, but we fully realise that this is a matter for him to decide, not us. If he confines himself to courteous formalities with us, we may be disappointed, but we do not feel able to complain; after all, we had no claim on his friendship. But if instead he starts at once to take us into his confidence, and tells us frankly what is in his mind on matters of common concern, and if he goes on to invite us to join him in particular undertakings he has planned, and asks us to make ourselves permanently available for this kind of collaboration whenever he needs us, then we shall feel enormously privileged, and it will make a world of difference to our general outlook. If life seemed footling and dreary hitherto, it will not seem so any more, now that the great man has enrolled us among his personal assistants. Here is something to write home about! — and something to live up to!

Now this, so far as it goes, is an illustration of what it means to know God. Well might God say through Jeremiah, 'Let him that glorieth glory in this, that he understandeth and knoweth me' —

for knowing God is a relationship calculated to thrill a man's heart. What happens is that the almighty Creator, the Lord of hosts, the great God before whom the nations are as a drop in a bucket, comes to him and begins to talk to him, through the words and truths of Holy Scripture. Perhaps he has been acquainted with the Bible and Christian truth for many years, and it has meant nothing to him; but one day he wakes up to the fact that God is actually speaking to him—him!—through the biblical message. As he listens to what God is saying, he finds himself brought very low; for God talks to him about his sin, and guilt, and weakness, and blindness, and folly, and compels him to judge himself hopeless and helpless, and to cry out for forgiveness. But this is not all. He comes to realise as he listens that God is actually opening His heart to him, making friends with him, and enlisting him a colleague—in Barth's phrase, a *covenant partner*. It is a staggering thing, but it is true—the relationship in which sinful human beings know God is one in which God, so to speak, takes them on to His staff, to be henceforth His fellow-workers (see I Cor. 3:9) and personal friends. The action of God in taking Joseph from prison to become Pharaoh's prime minister is a picture of what He does to every Christian: from being Satan's prisoner, he finds himself transferred to a position of trust in the service of God. At once life is transformed. Whether being a servant is matter for shame or for pride depends on whose servant one is. Many have said what pride they felt in rendering personal service to Sir Winston Churchill during the Second World War. How much more should it be a matter of pride and glorying to know and serve the Lord of heaven and earth!

What, then, does the activity of knowing God involve? Holding together the various elements involved in this relationship, as we have sketched it out, we must say that knowing God involves, first, listening to God's word and receiving it as the Holy Spirit interprets it, in application to oneself; second, noting God's nature and character, as His word and works reveal it; third, accepting His invitations, and doing what He commands; fourth, recognising, and rejoicing in, the love that He has shown in thus approaching one and drawing one into this divine fellowship.

III

The Bible puts flesh on these bare bones of ideas by using pictures and analogies, and telling us that we know God in the manner of a son knowing his father, a wife knowing her husband, a subject knowing his king, and a sheep knowing its shepherd (these are the four main analogies employed). All four analogies point to a relation in which the knower 'looks up' to the one known, and the latter takes responsibility for the welfare of the former. This is part of the biblical concept of knowing God, that those who know Him—that is, those by whom He allows Himself to be known—are loved and cared for by Him. We shall say more of this in a moment.

Then the Bible adds the further point that we know God in this way only through knowing Jesus Christ, who is Himself God manifest in the flesh.'. . . Hast thou not known me. . . ? he that hath seen me hath seen the Father': 'no man cometh to the Father but by me' (John 14:9, 6). It is important, therefore, that we should be clear in our minds as to what 'knowing' Jesus Christ means.

For His earthly disciples, knowing Jesus was directly comparable to knowing the great man in our illustration. The disciples were ordinary Galileans, with no special claims on the interest of Jesus. But Jesus, the rabbi who spoke with authority, the prophet who was more than a prophet, the master who evoked in them increasing awe and devotion till they could not but acknowledge him as their God, found them, called them to Himself, took them into His confidence, and enrolled them as His agents to declare to the world the kingdom of God. 'He appointed twelve, to be with him, and to be sent out to preach . . .' (Mark 3:14, RSV). They recognised the one who had chosen them and called them friends as 'the Christ, the Son of the living God' (Matt. 16:16), the man born to be king, the bearer of 'the words of eternal life' (John 6:68), and the sense of allegiance and privilege which this knowledge brought transformed their whole lives.

Now, when the New Testament tells us that Jesus Christ is risen, one of the things it means is that the victim of Calvary is now, so to speak, loose and at large, so that any man anywhere can enjoy the same kind of relationship with Him as the disciples had in the days of His flesh. The only differences are that, first, His presence with the Christian is spiritual, not bodily, and so invisible to our physical eyes; second, the Christian, building on the New Testament witness, knows from the start those truths about the deity and atoning sacrifice of Jesus which the original disciples only grasped gradually, over a period of years; and, third, that Jesus's way of speaking to us now is not by uttering fresh words, but rather by applying to our consciences those words of His that are recorded in the gospels, together with the rest of the biblical testimony to Himself. But knowing Jesus Christ still remains as definite a relation of personal discipleship as it was for the twelve when He was on earth. The Jesus who walks through the gospel story walks with Christians now, and knowing Him involves going with Him, now as then.

'My sheep hear my voice,' says Jesus, 'and I know them, and they follow me' (John 10:27). His 'voice' is His claim, His promise, and His call. 'I am the bread of life . . . the door of the sheep . . . the good shepherd . . . the resurrection' (John 6:35; 10: 7, 14; 11:25). 'He who does not honour the Son does not honour the Father who sent him. Truly, truly, I say to you, he who hears my word and believes him who sent me, has eternal life' (John 5:23 f., RSV). 'Come unto me, all ye that labour, and are heavy laden, and I will give you rest. Take my yoke upon you, and learn of me . . . and ye shall find rest . . .' (Matt. 11:28 f.). Jesus's voice is 'heard' when Jesus's claim is acknowledged, His promise trusted, and His call answered. From then on, Jesus is known as shepherd, and those who trust Him He knows as His own sheep. '. . . I know them, and they follow me; and I give unto them eternal life; and they shall never perish, neither shall any man pluck them out of my hand' (John 10:27 f.). To know Jesus is to be saved by Jesus, here and hereafter, from sin, and guilt, and death.

IV

Standing back, now, to survey what we have said that it means to 'know thee, the only true God, and Jesus Christ, whom thou hast sent', we may underline the following points.

First, knowing God is a matter of *personal dealing*, as is all direct acquaintance with personal beings. Knowing God is more than knowing about Him; it is a matter of dealing with Him as He opens up to you, and being dealt with by Him as He takes knowledge of you. Knowing about Him is a necessary precondition of trusting in Him ('how could they have faith in one they had never heard of?' [Rom. 10:14, NEB]), but the width of our knowledge about Him is no gauge of the depth of our knowledge of him. John Owen and John Calvin knew more theology than John Bunyan or Billy Bray, but who would deny that the latter pair knew their God every bit as well as the former? (All four, of course, were beavers for the Bible, which counts for far more anyway than a formal theological training.) If the decisive factor was notional correctness, then obviously the most learned biblical scholars would know God better than anyone else. But it is not; you can have all the right notions in your head without ever tasting in your heart the realities to which they refer; and a simple Bible-

34

reader and sermon-hearer who is full of the Holy Ghost will develop a far deeper acquaintance with his God and Saviour than more learned men who are content with being theologically correct. The reason is that the former will *deal with God* regarding the practical application of truth to his life, whereas the latter will not.

Second, knowing God is a matter of *personal involvement*, in mind, will, and feeling. It would not, indeed, be a fully personal relationship otherwise. To get to know another person, you have to commit yourself to his company and interests, and be ready to identify yourself with his concerns. Without this, your relationship with him can only be superficial and flavourless. 'O taste and see that the Lord is good,' says the psalmist (Psalm 34:8). To 'taste' is, as we say, to 'try' a mouthful of something, with a view to appreciating its flavour. A dish may look good, and be well recommended by the cook, but we do not know its real quality till we have tasted it. Similarly, we do not know another person's real quality till we have 'tasted' the experience of friendship with him. Friends are, so to speak, communicating flavours to each other all the time, by sharing their attitudes both towards each other (think of people in love) and towards everything else that is of common concern. As they thus open their hearts to each other by what they say and do, each 'tastes' the quality of the other, for sorrow or for joy. They have identified themselves with, and so are personally and emotionally involved in, each other's concerns. They feel for each other, as well as thinking of each other. This is an essential aspect of the knowledge which friends have of each other; and the same applies to the Christian's knowledge of God, which, as we have seen, is itself a relationship between friends.

The emotional side of knowing God is often played down these days, for fear of encouraging a maudlin self-absorption. It is true that there is nothing more irreligious than self-absorbed religion, and that it is constantly needful to stress that God does not exist for our 'comfort', or 'happiness', or 'satisfaction', or to provide us with 'religious experiences', as if these were the most interesting and important things in life. It is also necessary to stress that anyone who, on the basis of 'religious experiences', 'saith, I know him, and keepeth not his commandments, is a liar, and the truth is not in him' (1 John 2:4; cf. verses 9, 11, 3:6, 11, 4:20). But, for all this, we must not lose sight of the fact that knowing God is an emotional relationship, as well as an intellectual and volitional one, and could not indeed be a deep relation between persons were it not so. The believer is, and must be, emotionally involved in the victories and vicissitudes of God's cause in the world, just as Sir

Winston's personal staff were emotionally involved in the ups and downs of the war. The believer rejoices when his God is honoured and vindicated, and feels the acutest distress when he sees God flouted. Barnabas, when he came to Antioch, 'and had seen the grace of God, was glad' (Acts 11:23); by contrast, the psalmist wrote: 'rivers of waters run down my eyes, because they keep not thy law' (Psalm 119: 136). Equally, the Christian feels shame and grief when convicted of having failed his Lord (see, for instance, Psalm 51, and Luke 22:61 f.), and from time to time knows transports of delight as God brings home to him in one way or another the glory of the everlasting love with which he has been loved ('transported with a joy too great for words' [1 Pet. 1:8, NEB.]). This is the emotional and experiential side of friendship with God. Ignorance of it argues that, however true a man's thoughts of God may be, he does not yet know the God of whom he is thinking.

Then, third, knowing God is a matter of *grace*. It is a relationship in which the initiative throughout is with God—as it must be, since God is so completely above us and we have so completely forfeited all claim on His favour by our sins. *We* do not make friends with *God; God* makes friends with *us*, bringing us to know Him by making His love known to us. Paul expresses this thought of the priority of grace in our knowledge of God when he writes to the Galatians, 'now that you have come to know God, *or rather to be known by God . . .*' (Gal. 4: 9). What comes to the surface in this qualifying clause is the apostle's sense that grace came first, and remains fundamental, in his readers' salvation. Their knowing God was the consequence of God's taking knowledge of them. They know Him by faith because He first singled them out by grace.

'Know', when used of God in this way, is a sovereign-grace word, pointing to God's initiative in loving, choosing, redeeming, calling, and preserving. That God is fully aware of us, 'knowing us through and through' as we say, is certainly part of what is meant, as appears from the contrast between our imperfect knowledge of God and His perfect knowledge of us in 1 Corinthians 13: 12. But it is not the main meaning. The main meaning comes out in passages like the following,

'And the LORD said unto Moses . . . thou hast found grace in my sight, and *I know thee by name*' (Exod. 33:17). 'Before I formed thee (Jeremiah) in the belly *I knew thee;* and before thou camest forth out of the womb I sanctified thee' (Jer. 1:5). 'I am the good shepherd, *and know my sheep*, and am known of mine . . . and I lay down my life for the sheep . . . My sheep hear my voice, *and I*

36

know them . . . and they shall never perish' (John 10: 14 f., 27 f.). Here God's knowledge of those who are His is associated with His whole purpose of saving mercy. It is a knowledge that implies personal affection, redeeming action, covenant faithfulness, and providential watchfulness, towards those whom God knows. It implies, in other words, salvation, now and for ever, as we hinted before.

V

What matters supremely, therefore, is not, in the last analysis, the fact that I know God, but the larger fact which underlies it—the fact that *He knows me*. I am graven on the palms of His hands. I am never out of His mind. All my knowledge of Him depends on His sustained initiative in knowing me. I know Him, because He first knew me, and continues to know me. He knows me as a friend, one who loves me; and there is no moment when His eye is off me, or His attention distracted from me, and no moment, therefore, when His care falters.

This is momentous knowledge. There is unspeakable comfort—the sort of comfort that energises, be it said, not enervates—in knowing that God is constantly taking knowledge of me in love, and watching over me for my good. There is tremendous relief in knowing that His love to me is utterly realistic, based at every point on prior knowledge of the worst about me, so that no discovery now can disillusion him about me, in the way I am so often disillusioned about myself, and quench His determination to bless me. There is, certainly, great cause for humility in the thought that He sees all the twisted things about me that my fellow-men do not see (and am I glad!), and that He sees more corruption in me than that which I see in myself (which, in all conscience, is enough). There is, however, equally great incentive to worship and love God in the thought that, for some unfathomable reason, He wants me as His friend, and desires to be my friend, and has given His Son to die for me in order to realise this purpose. We cannot work these thoughts out here, but merely to mention them is enough to show how much it means to know, not merely that we know God, but that He knows us.

CHAPTER 4

The Only True God

I

What does the word 'idolatry' suggest to your mind? Savages grovelling before a totem-pole? Cruel-faced statues in Hindu temples? The dervish-dance of the priests of Baal around Elijah's altar? These things are certain idolatrous, in a very obvious way; but we need to realise that there are more subtle forms of idolatry as well.

Look at the second commandment. It runs as follows, 'Thou shalt not make unto thee any graven image, or any likeness of any thing that is in heaven above, or that is in the earth beneath, or that is in the water under the earth: thou shalt not bow down thyself to them, nor serve them: for I the Lord thy God am a jealous God . . .' (Exod. 20:4 f.). What is this commandment talking about?

If it stood alone, it would be natural to suppose that it refers to the worship of images of gods other than Jehovah—the Babylonian idol-worship, for instance, which Isaiah derided (Isa. 44:9 ff.; 46:1 f.), or the paganism of the Graeco-Roman world of Paul's day, of which he wrote in Romans 1: 23, 25, 'they changed the glory of the uncorruptible God into an image made like to corruptible man, and to birds, and fourfooted beasts, and creeping things . . . (they) changed the truth of God into a lie, and worshipped and served the creature more than the Creator. . . .' But in its context the second commandment can hardly be referring to this sort of idolatry, for if it were it would simply be repeating the thought of the first commandment without adding anything to it.

Accordingly, we take the second commandment—as in fact it

has always been taken—as pointing us to the principle that (to quote Charles Hodge) 'idolatry consists not only in the worship of false gods, but also in the worship of the true God by images'. In its Christian application, this means that we are not to make use of visual or pictorial representations of the Triune God, or of any person of the Trinity, for the purposes of Christian worship. The commandment thus deals, not with the object of our worship, but with the manner of it; what it tells us is that statues and pictures of the One whom we worship are not to be used as an aid to worshipping Him.

It may seem strange at first sight that such a prohibition should find a place among the ten basic principles of biblical religion, for at first sight it does not seem to have much point. What harm is there, we ask, in the worshipper surrounding himself with statues and pictures, if they help him to lift his heart to God? We are accustomed to treat the question of whether these things should be used or not as a matter of temperament and personal taste. We know that some people have crucifixes and pictures of Christ in their rooms, and they tell us that looking at these objects helps them to focus their thoughts on Christ when they pray. We know that many claim to be able to worship more freely and easily in churches that are filled with such ornaments than they can in churches that are bare of them. Well, we say, what is wrong with that? What harm can these things do? If people really do find them helpful, what more is there to be said? What point can there be in prohibiting them? In face of this perplexity, some would suggest that the second commandment only applies to immoral and degrading representations of God, borrowed from pagan cults, and to nothing more.

But the very wording of the commandment rules out such a limiting exposition. God says quite categorically, 'thou shalt not make *any* likeness of *any* thing' for use in worship. This categorical statement rules out, not simply the use of pictures and statues which depict God as an animal, but also the use of pictures and statues which depict Him as the highest created thing we know—a man. It also rules out the use of pictures and statues of Jesus Christ as a man, although Jesus Himself was and remains Man; for all pictures and statues are necessarily made after the 'likeness' of ideal manhood as we conceive it, and therefore come under the ban which the commandment imposes. Historically, Christians have differed as to whether the second commandment forbids the use of pictures of Jesus for purposes of teaching and instruction (in Sunday-school classes for instance), and the question is not an easy one to settle; but there is no room for doubting that the commandment obliges us to dissociate our worship, both in public and in private, from all pictures and statues of Christ, no less than from pictures and statues of His Father.

But what, in that case, is the point of this comprehensive prohibition? From the emphasis given to the commandment itself, with the frightening sanction attached to it (the proclaiming of God's jealousy, and His severity in punishing transgressors), one would suppose that this must really be a matter of crucial importance. But is it? The answer is *yes*. The Bible shows us that the glory of God and the spiritual well-being of man are both directly bound up with it. Two lines of thought are set before us which together amply explain why this commandment should have been stressed so emphatically. These lines of thought relate, not to the real or supposed helpfulness of images, but to the *truth* of them. They are as follows:

1 Images *dishonour* God, for they obscure His glory. The likeness of things in heaven (sun, moon, stars), and in earth (men, animals, birds, insects), and in the sea (fishes, mammals, crustaceans), is precisely *not* a likeness of their Creator. 'A true image of God', wrote Calvin, 'is not to be found in all the world; and hence. . . His glory is defiled, and His truth corrupted by the lie, whenever He is set before our eyes in a visible form . . . Therefore, to devise any image of God is itself impious; because by this corruption His majesty is adulterated, and He is figured to be other than He is.' The point here is not just that an image represents God as having body and parts, whereas in reality He has neither. If this were the only ground of objection to images, representations of Christ would be blameless. But the point really goes much deeper. The heart of the objection to pictures and images is that they inevitably conceal most, if not all, of the truth about the personal nature and character of the divine Being whom they represent.

To illustrate: Aaron made a golden calf (that is, a bull-image). It was meant as a visible symbol of Jehovah, the mighty God who had brought Israel out of Egypt. No doubt the image was thought to honour Him, as being a fitting symbol of His great strength. But it is not hard to see that such a symbol in fact insults Him: for what idea of His moral character, His righteousness, goodness, and patience, could one gather from looking at a statue of Him as a bull? Thus Aaron's image hid Jehovah's glory. In a similar way, the pathos of the crucifix obscures the glory of Christ, for it hides the fact of His deity, His victory on the cross, and His present kingdom. It displays His human weakness, but it conceals His divine strength; it depicts the reality of His pain, but keeps out of our sight the reality of His joy and His power. In both these cases, the symbol is unworthy most of all because of what it fails to display. And so are all other visible representations of Deity.

Whatever we may think of religious art from a cultural standpoint, we should not look to pictures of God to show us His glory and move us to worship; for His glory is precisely what such pictures can never show us. And this is why God added to the second commandment a reference to Himself as 'jealous' to avenge Himself on those who disobey Him: for God's 'jealousy' in the Bible is His zeal to maintain His own glory, which is jeopardised when images are used in worship. In Isaiah 40:18, after vividly declaring God's immeasurable greatness, the Scripture asks us: 'To whom then will ye liken God? or what likeness will ye compare unto him?' The question does not expect an answer, only a chastened silence. Its purpose is to remind us that it is as absurd as it is impious to think that an image modelled, as images must be, upon some creature could be an acceptable likeness of the Creator.

Nor is this the only reason why we are forbidden to use images in worship.

2 Images *mislead men.* They convey false ideas about God. The very inadequacy with which they represent Him perverts our thoughts of Him, and plants in our minds errors of all sorts about His character and will. Aaron, by making an image of God in the form of a bull-calf, led the Israelites to think of Him as a Being who could be worshipped acceptably by frenzied debauchery. Hence the 'feast to the LORD' which Aaron organised (Exod. 32:5) became a shameful orgy. Again, it is a matter of historical fact that the use of the crucifix as an aid to prayer has encouraged people to equate devotion with brooding over Christ's bodily sufferings; it has made them morbid about the spiritual value of physical pain, and it has kept them from knowledge of the risen Saviour.

These examples show how images will falsify the truth of God in the minds of men. Psychologically, it is certain that if you habitually focus your thoughts on an image or picture of the One to whom you are going to pray, you will come to think of Him, and pray to Him, as the image represents Him. Thus you will in this sense 'bow down' and 'worship' your image; and to the extent to which the image fails to tell the truth about God, to that extent you will fail to worship God in truth. That is why God forbids you and me to make use of images and pictures in our worship.

II

The realisation that images and pictures of God affect our thoughts of God points to a further realm in which the prohibition of the second commandment applies. Just as it forbids us to manufacture molten images of God, so it forbids us to dream up mental images of Him. Imagining God in our heads can be just as real a breach of the second commandment as imagining Him by the work of our hands. How often do we hear this sort of thing: 'I *like to think* of God as the great Architect (or, Mathematician; or, Artist).' 'I don't think of God as a Judge; I *like to think* of Him simply as a Father.' We know from experience how often remarks of this kind serve as the prelude to a denial of something that the Bible tells us about God. It needs to be said with the greatest possible emphasis that those who hold themselves free to think of God *as they like* are breaking the second commandment. At best, they can only think of God in the image of man—as an ideal man, perhaps, or a super-man. But God is not any sort of man. We were made in His image, but we must not think of Him as existing in ours. To think of God in such terms is to be ignorant of Him, not to know Him. All speculative theology, which rests on philosophical reasoning rather than biblical revelation, is at fault here. Paul tells us where this sort of theology ends: 'the world by wisdom knew not God' (1 Cor. 1:21). To follow the imagination of one's heart in the realm of theology is the way to remain ignorant of God, and to become an idol-worshipper—the idol in this case being a false mental image of God, 'made unto thee' by speculation and imagination.

In the light of this, the positive purpose of the second commandment becomes plain. Negatively, it is a warning against ways of worship and religious practice that lead us to dishonour God and to falsify His truth. Positively, it is a summons to us to recognise that God the Creator is transcendent, mysterious, and inscrutable, beyond the range of any imagining or philosophical guesswork of which we are capable; and hence a summons to us to humble ourselves, to listen and learn of Him, and to let Him teach us what He is like and how we should think of Him. 'My thoughts are not your thoughts,' He tells us, 'neither are your ways my ways . . . For as the heavens are higher than the earth, so are my ways higher than your ways, and my thoughts than your thoughts' (Isa. 55:8 f.). Paul speaks in the same vein 'O the depth of the riches both of the wisdom and knowledge of God! how unsearchable are his judgments, and his ways past finding out! For who hath known the mind of the Lord?' (Rom. 11:33 f.).

God is not the sort of person that we are; His widom, His aims,

His scale of values. His mode of procedure, differs so vastly from our own that we cannot possibly guess our way to them by intuition or infer them by analogy from our notion of ideal manhood. We cannot know Him unless He speaks and tells us about Himself. But in fact He has spoken. He has spoken to and through His prophets and apostles, and He has spoken in the words and deeds of His own Son. Through this revelation, which is made available to us in Holy Scripture, we may form a true notion of God; without it we never can. Thus it appears that the positive force of the second commandment is that it compels us to take our thoughts of God from His own holy Word, and from no other source whatsoever.

That this is the commandment's positive thrust seems plain from the very form in which it is stated. Having forbidden the making and worshipping of images, God declares Himself 'jealous' to punish, not image-worshippers as such, but all who 'hate' Him, in the sense of disregarding His commandments as a whole. The natural and expected thing in the context would be a specific threat to image-users; why, instead, is God's threat generalised? Surely this is in order to make us realise that those who make images and use them in worship, and thus inevitably take their theology from them, will in fact tend to neglect God's revealed will at every point. The mind that takes up with images is a mind that has not yet learned to love and attend to God's Word. Those who look to man-made images, material or mental, to lead them to God are not likely to take any part of His revelation as seriously as they should.

In Deuteronomy 4, Moses himself expounds the prohibition of images in worship along exactly these lines, opposing the making of images to the heeding of God's word and commandments as if these two things were completely exclusive of each other. He reminds the people that at Sinai, though they saw tokens of God's presence, they saw no visible representation of God Himself, but only heard His word, and he exhorts them to continue to live, as it were, at the foot of the mount, with God's own word ringing in their ears to direct them and no supposed image of God before their eyes to distract them.

The point is clear. God did not show them a visible symbol of Himself, but spoke to them; therefore they are not now to seek visible symbols of God, but simply to obey His word. If it be said that Moses was afraid of the Israelites borrowing designs for images from the idolatrous nations around them, our reply is that undoubtedly he was, and this is exactly the point: all man-made images of God, whether molten or mental, are really borrowings from the stock-in-trade of a sinful and ungodly world, and are bound therefore to be out of accord with God's own holy Word. To make an image of God is to take one's thoughts of Him from a human source, rather than from God Himself; and this is precisely what is wrong with image-making.

III

The question which arises for us all from the line of thought which we have been pursuing is this: how far are we keeping the second commandment? Granted, there are no bull-images in the churches we attend, and probably we have not got a crucifix in the house (though we may have some pictures of Christ on our walls that we ought to think twice about); but are we sure that the God whom we seek to worship is the God of the Bible, the Triune Jehovah? Do we worship the one true God in truth? or are our ideas of God such that in reality we do not believe in the *Christian* God, but in some other, just as the Moslem or Jew or Jehovah's Witness does not believe in the Christian God, but in some other?

You may say: how can I tell? Well, the test is this. The God of the Bible has spoken in His Son. The light of the knowledge of His glory is given to us in the face of Jesus Christ. Do I look habitually to the person and work of the Lord Jesus Christ as showing me the final truth about the nature and the grace of God? Do I see all the purposes of God as centring upon Him?

If I have been enabled to see this, and in mind and heart to go to Calvary and lay hold of the Calvary solution, then I can know that I truly worship the true God, and that He is my God, and that I am even now enjoying eternal life, according to our Lord's own definition, 'this is life eternal, that they might know thee the only true God, and Jesus Christ, whom thou hast sent' (John 17:3).

CHAPTER 5

God Incarnate

I

It is no wonder that thoughtful people find the gospel of Jesus Christ hard to believe, for the realities with which it deals pass man's understanding. But it is sad that so many make faith harder than it need be, by finding difficulties in the wrong places.

Take the atonement, for instance. Many feel difficulty there. How, they ask, can we believe that the death of Jesus of Nazareth — one man, expiring on a Roman gibbet—put away a world's sins? How can that death have any bearing on God's forgiveness of our sins today? Or take the resurrection, which seems to many a stumbling-block. How, they ask, can we believe that Jesus rose physically from the dead? Granted, it is hard to deny that the tomb was empty—but surely the difficulty of believing that Jesus emerged from it into unending bodily life is even greater? Is not any form of the theory of temporary resuscitation after a faint, or of the stealing of the body, easier to credit than the Christian doctrine of the resurrection? Or, again, take the virgin birth, which has been widely denied among Protestants in this century. How, people ask, can one possibly believe in such a biological anomaly? Or take the gospel miracles; many find a source of difficulty here. Granted, they say, that Jesus healed (it is hard, on the evidence, to doubt that he did, and in any case history has known other healers); how can one believe that He walked on the water, or fed the five thousand, or raised the dead? Stories like that are surely quite incredible. With these and similar problems many minds on the fringes of faith are deeply perplexed today.

But in fact the real difficulty, because the supreme mystery with which the gospel confronts us, does not lie here at all. It lies, not in the Good Friday message of atonement, nor in the Easter message of resurrection, but in the Christmas message of incarnation. The really staggering Christian claim is that Jesus of Nazareth was God made man—that the second person of the Godhead became the 'second man' (1 Cor. 15:47), determining human destiny, the second representative head of the race, and that He took humanity without loss of deity, so that Jesus of Nazareth was as truly and fully divine as He was human. Here are two mysteries for the price of one—the plurality of persons within the unity of God, and the union of Godhead and manhood in the person of Jesus. It is here, in the thing that happened at the first Christmas, that the profoundest and most unfathomable depths of the Christian revelation lie. 'The Word was made flesh' (John 1:14); God became man; the divine Son became a Jew; the Almighty appeared on earth as a helpless human baby, unable to do more than lie and stare and wriggle and make noises, needing to be fed and changed and taught to talk like any other child. And there was no illusion or deception in this: the babyhood of the Son of God was a reality. The more you think about it, the more staggering it gets. Nothing in fiction is so fantastic as is this truth of the incarnation.

This is the real stumbling-block in Christianity. It is here that Jews, Moslems, Unitarians, Jehovah's Witnesses, and many of those who feel the difficulties above-mentioned (about the virgin birth, the miracles, the atonement, and the resurrection), have come to grief. It is from misbelief, or at least inadequate belief, about the incarnation that difficulties at other points in the gospel story usually spring. But once the incarnation is grasped as a reality, these other difficulties dissolve.

If Jesus had been no more than a very remarkable, godly man, the difficulties in believing what the New Testament tells us about his life and work would be truly mountainous. But if Jesus was the same person as the eternal Word, the Father's agent in creation, 'through whom also he made the worlds' (Heb. 1:2, RV), it is no wonder if fresh acts of creative power marked His coming into this world, and His life in it, and His exit from it. It is not strange that He, the author of life, should rise from the dead. If He was truly God the Son, it is much more startling that He should die than that He should rise again. ''Tis mystery all! The Immortal dies,' wrote Wesley; but there is no comparable mystery in the Immortal's resurrection. And if the immortal Son of God did really submit to taste death, it is not strange that such a death should have saving significance for a doomed race. Once we grant that

Jesus was divine, it becomes unreasonable to find difficulty in any of this; it is all of a piece, and hangs together completely. The incarnation is in itself an unfathomable mystery, but it makes sense of everything else that the New Testament contains.

II

The gospels of Matthew and Luke tell us in some detail how the Son of God came to this world. He was born outside a small hotel in an obscure Jewish village in the great days of the Roman Empire. The story is usually prettyfied when we tell it Christmas by Christmas, but it is really rather beastly and cruel. The reason why Jesus was born outside the hotel is that it was full and nobody would offer a bed to a woman in labour, so that she had to have her baby in the stables, and cradle him in a cattle-trough. The story is told dispassionately and without comment, but no thoughtful reader can help shuddering at the picture of callousness and degradation that it draws. It is not, however, to draw moral lessons from this that the evangelists tell the story. For them the point of the story lies not in the circumstances of the birth (save in the one respect that it fulfilled prophecy, by taking place in Bethlehem: see Matthew 2:1–6), but rather in the identity of the baby. About this the New Testament has two thoughts to convey. We have indicated them already; now let us look at them in more detail.

1 *The baby born at Bethlehem was God.*

More precisely, putting it in Bible language. He was *the Son of God*, or, as Christian theology regularly expresses it, *God the Son*. *The* Son, note, not *a* Son: as John says four times in the first three chapters of his gospel, in order to make quite sure that his readers understand the uniqueness of Jesus, He was the *'only-begotten'* Son of God (see John 1:14, 18; 3:16, 18). Accordingly, the Christian Church confesses: 'I believe in God the Father . . . and in Jesus Christ, *His only Son*, our Lord.'

Christian apologists sometimes talk as if the statement that Jesus is the only-begotten Son of God were the final and complete answer to all questions about His identity. But this is hardly so, for the phrase itself raises questions, and can easily be misunderstood. Does the statement that Jesus is God's Son mean that there are really two gods? Is Christianity then polytheistic, as Jews and Mohammedans maintain? Or does the phrase 'Son of God' imply that Jesus, though in a class by Himself among created beings, was not personally divine in the same sense as the Father is? In the early church, the Arians held this, and in modern times

Unitarians, Jehovah's Witnesses, Christadelphians and others have taken the same line. Is it right? What *does* the Bible mean when it calls Jesus the Son of God?

These questions have puzzled some, but the New Testament does not really leave us in doubt as to how they should be answered. In principle, they were all raised and solved together by the apostle John in the Prologue to his gospel. He was writing, it seems, for readers of both Jewish and Greek background. He wrote, as he tells us, in order that they 'might know that Jesus is ... the Son of God; and ... believing ... might have life through his name' (John 20:31). It is as Son of God that he presents Jesus throughout the gospel. However, John knew that the phrase 'Son of God' was tainted with misleading associations in the minds of his readers. Jewish theology used it as a title for the expected (human) Messiah. Greek mythology told of many 'sons of gods', supermen born of a union between a god and a human woman. In neither of these cases did the phrase convey the thought of personal deity; in both, indeed, it excluded it. John wanted to make sure that when he wrote of Jesus as the Son of God he would not be understood (that is, misunderstood) in such senses as these, and to make it clear from the outset that the Sonship which Jesus claimed, and which Christians ascribed to Him, was precisely a matter of personal deity and nothing less. Hence this famous Prologue (John 1:1–18). The Church of England reads it annually as the gospel for Christmas Day, and rightly so. Nowhere in the New Testament is the nature and meaning of Jesus's divine Sonship so clearly explained as here.

See how carefully and conclusively John expounds his theme.

He does not bring the term 'Son' into his opening sentences at all; instead, he speaks first of the Word. There was no danger of this being misunderstood; Old Testament readers would pick up the reference at once. God's Word in the Old Testament is His creative utterance, His power in action fulfilling His purpose. The Old Testament depicted God's utterance, the actual statement of His purpose, as having power in itself to effect the thing purposed. Genesis 1 tells us how at creation 'God said, *Let there be* ... and *there was* ...' (Gen. 1:3). 'By the word of the LORD were the heavens made ... he spake, and it was done' (Ps. 33:6, 9). The Word of God is thus God at work.

John takes up this figure and proceeds to tell us seven things about the divine Word.

(i) '*In the beginning was* the Word' (verse 1). Here is the Word's *eternity.* He had no beginning of His own; when other things began, He—*was*.

(ii) 'And the Word was *with God*' (verse 1). Here is the Word's *personality.* The power that fulfils God's purposes is the power of a distinct personal being, who stands in an eternal relation to God of active fellowship (this is what the phrase means).

(iii) 'And the Word *was God*' (verse 1). Here is the Word's *deity.* Though personally distinct from the Father, He is not a creature; He is divine in Himself, as the Father is. The mystery with which this verse confronts us is thus the mystery of personal distinctions within the unity of the Godhead.

(iv) '*All things were made* by him' (verse 3). Here is the Word *creating.* He was the Father's agent in every act of making that the Father has ever performed. All that was made was made through Him. (Here, incidentally, is further proof that He, the maker, does not belong to the class of things made, any more than the Father does.)

(v) 'In him was *life*' (verse 4). Here is the Word *animating.* There is no physical life in the realm of created things save in and through Him. Here is the Bible answer to the problem of the origin and continuance of life, in all its forms: life is given and maintained by the Word. Created things do not have life in themselves, but life in the Word, the second person of the Godhead.

(vi) 'And the life was *the light of men*' (verse 4). Here is the Word *revealing.* In giving life, He gives light too; that is to say, every man receives intimations of God from the very fact of his being alive in God's world, and this, no less than the fact that he is alive, is due to the work of the Word.

(vii) 'And the Word *became flesh*' (verse 14). Here is the Word *incarnate.* The baby in the manger at Bethlehem was none other than the eternal Word of God.

And now, having shown us who and what the Word is—a divine Person, author of all things—John indicates an identification. The Word, he tells us, was revealed by the incarnation to be God's *Son.* 'We beheld his glory, the glory *as of the only begotten of the Father*' (verse 14). The identification is confirmed in verse 18, 'The only begotten Son, which is in the bosom of the Father . . .' Thus John establishes the point at which he was aiming throughout. He has now made it clear what is meant by calling Jesus the Son of God. The Son of God is the Word of God; we see what the Word is; well, that is what the Son is. Such is the Prologue's message.

When, therefore, the Bible proclaims Jesus as the Son of God, the statement is meant as an assertion of His distinct personal deity. The Christmas message rests on the staggering fact that the child in the manger was—*God*.

But this is only half the story.

2 *The baby born at Bethlehem was God made man.*

The Word had become flesh: a real human baby. He had not ceased to be God; He was no less God then than before; but He had begun to be man. He was not now God *minus* some elements of His deity, but God *plus* all that He had made His own by taking manhood to Himself. He who made man was now learning what it felt like to be man. He who made the angel who became the devil was now in a state in which He could be tempted—could not, indeed, avoid being tempted—by the devil; and the perfection of His human life was only achieved by conflict with the devil. The Epistle to the Hebrews, looking up to Him in His ascended glory, draws great comfort from this fact. 'In all things it behoved him to be made like unto his brethren . . . For in that he himself hath suffered being tempted, *he is able to help them that are tempted.*' 'We have not an high priest which cannot be touched with the feeling of our infirmities, but was in all points tempted like as we are, yet without sin. Let us *therefore* come boldly unto the throne of grace, that we may obtain mercy, and find grace to help in time of need' (Heb. 2:17 f., 4:15 f.).

The mystery of the incarnation is unfathomable. We cannot explain it; we can only formulate it. Perhaps it has never been formulated better than in the words of the Athanasian Creed. 'Our Lord Jesus Christ, the Son of God, is God and man; . . . perfect God, and perfect man: . . . who although he be God and man: yet he is not two, but one Christ; one, not by conversion of the Godhead into flesh: but by taking of the manhood into God.' Our minds cannot get beyond this. What we see in the manger is, in Charles Wesley's words,

> *Our God contracted to a span;*
> *Incomprehensibly made man.*

Incomprehensibly—we shall be wise to remember this, to shun speculation, and contentedly to adore.

III

How are we to think of the incarnation? The New Testament does not encourage us to puzzle our heads over the physical and psychological problems that it raises, but to worship God for the love that was shown in it. For it was a great act of condescension and self-humbling. 'He, Who had always been God by nature,' writes Paul, 'did not cling to His prerogatives as God's equal, but stripped Himself of all privilege by consenting to be a slave by nature and being born as mortal man. And, having become man, He humbled Himself by living a life of utter obedience, even to the extent of dying, *and the death he died was the death of a common criminal*' (Phil. 2:6 ff., Phillips). And all this was for our salvation.

Theologians have sometimes toyed with the idea that the incarnation was originally and basically intended for the perfecting of the created order, and that its redemptive significance was, so to speak, God's afterthought; but, as James Denney rightly insisted, 'the New Testament knows nothing of an incarnation which can be defined apart from its relation to atonement . . . Not Bethlehem, but Calvary, is the focus of revelation, and any construction of Christianity which ignores or denies this distorts Christianity by putting it out of focus' (*The Death of Christ*, 1902, p. 235 f.). The crucial significance of the cradle at Bethlehem lies in its place in the sequence of steps down that led the Son of God to the cross of Calvary, and we do not understand it till we see it in this context. The key text in the New Testament for interpreting the incarnation is not, therefore, the bare statement in John 1:14, 'the Word became flesh, and dwelt among us', but rather the more comprehensive statement of 2 Corinthians 8:9, 'ye know the grace of our Lord Jesus Christ, that, though he was rich, yet for your sakes he became poor, that ye through his poverty might become rich'. Here is stated, not the fact of the incarnation only, but also its meaning; the taking of manhood by the Son is set before us in a way which shows us how we should set it before ourselves and ever view it—not simply as a marvel of nature, but rather as a wonder of grace.

IV

Here, however, we must pause to consider a different use which some make of the texts from Paul that we have cited. In Philippians 2:7, the phrase translated by Phillips as 'stripped Himself of all privilege' and by the Authorised Version as 'made himself of no reputation' is literally 'emptied himself' (so RV). Does not this (it is asked), together with the statement in 2 Corinthians 8:9 that Jesus 'became poor', throw some light on the nature of the incarnation itself? Does it not imply that a certain reduction of the Son's deity was involved in His becoming man?

51

This is the so-called kenosis theory, *kenosis* being the Greek word for 'emptying'. The idea behind it in all its forms is that, in order to be fully human, the Son had to renounce some of His divine qualities, otherwise He could not have shared the experience of being limited in space, time, knowledge, and consciousness which is essential to truly human life. The theory has been formulated in different ways. Some have argued that the Son put off only His "metaphysical" attributes (omnipotence, omnipresence, omniscience), retaining the 'moral' ones (justice, holiness, truthfulness, love); others have maintained that when He became man He renounced all His specifically divine powers, and His divine self-consciousness too, though in the course of His earthly life He reacquired the latter.

In England, the kenosis theory was first broached by Bishop Gore in 1889, to explain why our Lord was ignorant of what the nineteenth-century higher critics thought they knew about the errors of the Old Testament. Gore's thesis was that in becoming man the Son had given up His divine knowledge of matters of fact, though retaining full divine infallibility on moral issues. In the realm of historical fact, however, He was limited to current Jewish ideas, which He accepted without question, not knowing that they were not all correct. Hence His treatment of the Old Testament as verbally inspired and wholly true, and His ascription of the Pentateuch to Moses and Psalm 110 to David—views which Gore thought untenable. Many have followed Gore at this point, seeking justification for rejecting Christ's estimate of the Old Testament.

But the kenosis theory will not stand. For, in the first place, it is a speculation to which the texts quoted for it do not give the least support. When Paul talks of the Son as having emptied Himself and become poor, what he has in mind, as the context in each case shows, is the laying aside, not of divine powers and attributes, but of divine glory and dignity, 'the glory which I had with thee before the world was', as Christ put it in His great high-priestly prayer (John 17:5). The Phillips and AV renderings of Philippians 2:7 are correct interpretations of Paul's meaning. There is no Scripture support for the idea of the Son shedding any aspects of His deity.

Also, the theory raises great and insoluble problems of its own. How can we say that the man Christ Jesus was fully God, if He lacked some of the qualities of deity? How can we say that He perfectly revealed the Father, if some of the Father's powers and attributes were not in Him? Moreover, if, as the theory supposes, true manhood on earth was incompatible with unreduced deity, it must presumably be so in heaven too; so it follows that 'the man in the glory' has lost some of His divine powers for all eternity. If, as the Anglican Article 2 says, 'Godhead and Manhood' were at the incarnation 'joined together in one Person, never to be divided', it would seem to be inescapable, on this theory, that at the incarnation the Godhead of the Son forfeited certain divine attributes, never to be recovered. Yet the New Testament seems clear and emphatic on the omnipotence and omnipresence and omniscience of the risen Christ (Matt. 28:18, 20; John 21:17; Eph. 4:10). But if, in face of this, advocates of the kenosis theory should deny that these attributes are incompatible with true humanity in heaven, what reason can they give for believing this incompatibility to have existed on earth?

Furthermore, Gore's use of the theory to justify the ascribing of error to part of Christ's teaching, while maintaining the divine authority of the rest, is not possible. Christ claimed in comprehensive and categorical terms that all His teaching was from God: that He was never more than His Father's messenger. 'My doctrine is not mine, but his that sent me', 'as my Father hath taught me, I speak these things', 'I have not spoken of myself; but the Father which sent me, he gave me a commandment, what I should say ... whatsoever I speak therefore, even as the Father said unto me, so I speak' (John 7:16; 8:28; 12:49 f.). He declared Himself to be 'a man that hath told you the truth, which I have heard of God' (John 8: 40).

In face of these claims, only two courses are open: either we accept them, and ascribe full divine authority to all that Jesus taught, including His declarations of the inspiration and authority of the Old Testament, or else we reject them, and call in question the divine authority of His teaching at every point. If Gore really wished to maintain the authority of Jesus's moral and spiritual teaching, he should not have queried the truth of His teaching about the Old Testament; if, on the other hand, he was really determined to disagree with Jesus about the Old Testament, he should have been consistent, and taken the view that, since Jesus's claims for His teaching cannot be accepted as they stand, we are under no obligation to agree with Jesus about anything. If the kenosis theory is used for the purpose for which Gore used it, it proves too much: it proves that Jesus, having renounced His divine knowledge, was fallible at every point, and that when He claimed that all His teaching was from God he was fooling both Himself and us. If we would maintain the divine authority of

Jesus as a teacher, according to His claim, we must reject the kenosis theory, or at any rate we must reject this application of it.

In fact, the gospel narratives themselves present evidence against the kenosis theory. It is true that Jesus's knowledge of things both human and divine was sometimes limited. He asks occasionally for information — 'Who touched my clothes?' 'How many loaves have ye?' (Mark 5:30; 6:38). He declares that He shares the ignorance of the angels as to the day appointed for His return (Mark 13:32). But at other times He displayed supernatural knowledge. He knows the Samaritan woman's shady past (John 4:17 f.). He knows that when Peter goes fishing, the first fish he catches will have a coin in its mouth (Matt. 17: 27). He knows, without being told, that Lazarus is dead (John 11:11–13). Similarly, from time to time He displays supernatural power in miracles of healing, feeding, and resuscitating the dead. The impression of Jesus which the gospels give is not that He was wholly bereft of divine knowledge and power, but that He drew on both intermittently, while being content for much of the time not to do so. The impression, in other words, is not so much one of deity reduced as of divine capacities restrained.

How are we to account for this restraint? Surely, in terms of the truth of which John's gospel in particular makes so much, the entire submission of the Son to the Father's will. Part of the revealed mystery of the Godhead is that the three persons stand in a fixed relation to each other. The Son appears in the gospels, not as an independent divine person, but as a dependent one, who thinks and acts only and wholly as the Father directs. 'The Son can do nothing of himself', 'I can of mine own self do nothing' (John 5:19, 30). 'I came down from heaven, not to do mine own will, but the will of him that sent me' (John 6:38). 'I do nothing of myself . . . I do always those things that please him' (John 8:28 f.). It is the nature of the second person of the Trinity to acknowledge the authority and submit to the good pleasure of the first. That is why He declares Himself to be the Son, and the first person to be His Father. Though co-equal with the Father in eternity, power, and glory, it is natural to Him to play the Son's part, and find all His joy in doing His Father's will, just as it is natural to the first person of the Trinity to plan and initiate the works of the Godhead and natural to the third person to proceed from the Father and the Son to do their joint bidding. Thus the obedience of the God-man to the Father while He was on earth was not a new relationship occasioned by the incarnation, but the continuation in time of the eternal relationship between the Son and the Father in heaven. As in heaven, so on earth, the Son was utterly dependent upon the Father's will.

But if this is so, all is explained. The God-man did not know independently, any more than He acted independently. Just as He did not do all that He could have done, because certain things were not His Father's will (see Matt. 26:53 f.), so He did not consciously know all that He might have known, but only what the Father willed Him to know. His knowing, like the rest of His activity, was bounded by His Father's will. And therefore the reason why He was ignorant of (for instance) the date of His return was not because He had given up the power to know all things at the incarnation, but because the Father had not willed that He should have this particular piece of knowledge while on earth, prior to His Passion. Calvin was surely right to comment on Mark 13:32 as follows, 'until he had fully discharged his (mediatorial) office, that information was not given to him which he received after his resurrection.' So Jesus's limitation of knowledge is to be explained, not in terms of the mode of the incarnation, but with reference to the will of the Father for the Son while on earth. And therefore we conclude that, just as there are some facts in the gospels which contradict the kenosis theory, so there are no facts in the gospels which are not best explained without it.

IV

We see now what it meant for the Son of God to empty Himself and become poor. It meant a laying aside of glory (the real kenosis); a voluntary restraint of power; an acceptance of hardship, isolation, ill-treatment, malice, and misunderstanding; finally, a death that involved such agony—spiritual, even more than physical—that His mind nearly broke under the prospect of it. (See Luke 12:50, and the Gethsemane story.) It meant love to the uttermost for unlovely men, who 'through his poverty, might become rich'. The Christmas message is that there is hope for a ruined humanity—hope of pardon, hope of peace with God, hope of glory—because at the Father's will Jesus Christ became poor, and was born in a stable so that thirty years later He might hang on a cross. It is the most wonderful message that the world has ever heard, or will hear.

We talk glibly of the 'Christmas spirit', rarely meaning more by this than sentimental jollity on a family basis. But what we have said makes it clear that the phrase should in fact carry a tremendous weight of meaning. It ought to mean the reproducing in human lives of the temper of Him who for our sakes became poor at the first Christmas. And the Christmas spirit itself ought to be the mark of every Christian all the year round.

It is our shame and disgrace today that so many Christians—I will be more specific: so many of the soundest and most orthodox Christians—go through this world in the spirit of the priest and the Levite in our Lord's parable, seeing human needs all around them, but (after a pious wish, and perhaps a prayer, that God might meet them) averting their eyes, and passing by on the other side. That is not the Christmas spirit. Nor is it the spirit of those Christians—alas, they are many—whose ambition in life seems limited to building a nice middle-class Christian home, and making nice middle-class Christian friends, and bringing up their children in nice middle-class Christian ways, and who leave the sub-middle-class sections of the community, Christian and non-Christian, to get on by themselves.

The Christmas spirit does not shine out in the Christian snob. For the Christmas spirit is the spirit of those who, like their Master, live their whole lives on the principle of making themselves poor—spending and being spent—to enrich their fellow-men, giving time, trouble, care and concern, to do good to others—and not just their own friends—in whatever way there seems need. There are not as many who show this spirit as there should be. If God in mercy revives us, one of the things He will do will be to work more of this spirit in our hearts and lives. If we desire spiritual quickening for ourselves individually, one step we should take is to seek to cultivate this spirit. 'Ye know the grace of our Lord Jesus Christ, that, though he was rich, yet for your sakes he became poor, that ye through his poverty might be rich.' 'Let this mind be in you, which was also in Christ Jesus.' *I will run the way of thy commandments, when thou shalt enlarge my heart'* (Ps. 119:32).

CHAPTER 6

He Shall Testify

I

'Glory be to the Father,' sings the church, 'and to the Son, and to the Holy Ghost.' What is this? we ask; praise to three gods? No—praise to one God in three persons; as the hymn puts it—

> *Jehovah! Father, Spirit, Son!*
> *Mysterious Godhead! Three in One!*

This is the God whom Christians worship—the Triune Jehovah. The heart of Christian faith in God is the revealed mystery of the Trinity. *Trinitas* is a Latin word meaning three-ness. Christianity rests on the doctrine of the *trinitas*, the three-ness, the tri-personality, of God.

It is often assumed that the doctrine of the Trinity, just because it is mysterious, is a piece of theological lumber that we can get on very happily without. Our practice certainly seems to reflect this assumption. The Prayer Book of the Church of England prescribes thirteen occasions each year when the Athanasian Creed, the classic statement of this doctrine, should be recited in public worship, but it is rare today to find it used on even one of these. The average Anglican clergyman never preaches on the Trinity save, perhaps, on Trinity Sunday; the average nonconformist minister, who does not observe Trinity Sunday, never preaches on it at all. One wonders what the apostle John would say, were he here to comment on our practice. For according to him the doctrine of the Trinity is an essential part of the Christian gospel.

In the opening sentences of his gospel, as we saw in our last chapter, John introduces us to the mystery of two distinct persons within the unity of the Godhead. This is the deep end of theology, no doubt, but John throws us straight into it. 'In the beginning was the Word, and the Word was *with* God, and the Word *was* God.' The Word was a person in fellowship with God, and the Word was Himself personally and eternally divine. He was, as John proceeds to tell us, the only Son of the Father. John sets this mystery of one God in two persons at the head of his gospel because he knows that nobody can make head or tail of the words and works of Jesus of Nazareth till he has grasped the fact that this Jesus is in truth God the Son.

But this is not all that John means us to learn about the plurality of persons in the Godhead. For, in his account of our Lord's last talk to His disciples, he reports how the Saviour, having explained that He was going to prepare a place for them in His Father's house, went on to promise them the gift of 'another Comforter' (John 14:16). Note this phrase; it is full of meaning. It denotes a person, and a remarkable person too. A *Comforter* — the richness of the idea is seen from the variety of renderings in different translations, 'counsellor' (RSV), 'helper' (Moffatt), 'advocate' (Weymouth), one 'to befriend you' (Knox). The thoughts of encouragement, support, assistance, care, and the shouldering of responsibility for another's welfare, are all conveyed by this word. *Another* Comforter — yes, because Jesus was their original Comforter, and the newcomer's task was to continue this side of His ministry. It follows, therefore, that we can only appreciate all that our Lord meant when He spoke of 'another Comforter' as we look back over all that He Himself had done in the way of love, and care, and patient instruction, and provision for the disciple's well-being, during His own three years of personal ministry to them. He will care for you, Christ was saying in effect, in the way that I have cared for you. Truly a remarkable person!

Our Lord went on to name the new Comforter. He is 'the Spirit', 'the Holy Ghost' (14:17, 26). This name denoted deity. In the Old Testament, God's *Word* and God's *Spirit* are parallel figures. God's Word is His almighty speech; God's Spirit is His almighty breath. Both phrases convey the thought of His power in action. The speech and the breath of God appear together in the record of creation. 'The Spirit *(breath)* of God moved upon the face of the waters. And God *said* ... and there *was* ...' (Gen. 1:2 f.). 'By the *word* of the LORD were the heavens made; and all the host of them by the *breath* (Spirit) of His mouth' (Ps. 33:6). John told us in the Prologue that the divine Word spoken of here is a person. Our Lord now gives parallel teaching, to the effect that the divine

Spirit is also a person. And He confirms His witness to the deity of this personal Spirit by calling him the *holy* Spirit, as later He was to speak of the *holy* Father (17:11).

Note how Christ related the Spirit's mission to the will and purpose of the Father and the Son. In one place, it is the Father who will send the Spirit, as it was the Father who had sent the Son (see 5:23, etc.). The Father will send the Spirit, says our Lord, 'in my name' — that is, as Christ's deputy, doing Christ's will and acting as His representative and with His authority (14:26). Just as Jesus had come in His Father's name (5:43), acting as the Father's agent, speaking the Father's words (12:49 f.), doing the Father's works (10:25, cf. 17:12), and bearing witness throughout to the One whose emissary he was, so the Spirit would come in Jesus's name, to act in the world as the agent and witness of Jesus. The Spirit 'proceedeth from (*para*: from the side of) the Father' (15:26), just as previously the Son had 'come forth from *(para)* the Father' (16:27). Having sent the eternal Son into the world, the Father now recalls Him to glory and sends the Spirit to take His place.

But this is only one way of looking at the matter. In another place, it is the Son who will send the Spirit 'from the Father' (15:26). As the Father sent the Son into the world, so the Son will send the Spirit into the world (16:7). The Spirit is sent by the Son, as well as by the Father. Thus we have the following set of relationships:

1 The Son is subject to the Father, for the Son is sent by the Father in His (the Father's) name.

2 The Spirit is subject to the Father, for the Spirit is sent by the Father in the Son's name.

3 The Spirit is subject to the Son as well as to the Father, for the Spirit is sent by the Son as well as by the Father. (Compare 20:22, 'he breathed on them, and saith unto them, Receive ye the Holy Ghost.')

Thus John records our Lord's disclosure of the mystery of the Trinity: three persons, and one God, the Son doing the will of the Father and the Spirit doing the will of the Father and the Son. And the point stressed is that the Spirit, who comes to Christ's disciples 'that he may abide with you for ever' (14:16), is coming to exercise the ministry of a Comforter in Christ's stead. If, therefore, the ministry of Christ the Comforter was important, the ministry of the Holy Ghost the Comforter can scarcely be less

59

important. If the work that Christ did matters to the Church the work that the Spirit does must matter also.

II

But you would not get that impression from reading Church history, nor from looking at the Church today.

It is startling to see how differently the biblical teaching about the second and third persons of the Trinity respectively is treated. The person and work of Christ have been, and remain, subjects of constant debate within the Church; yet the person and work of the Holy Spirit are consistently ignored. The doctrine of the Holy Spirit is the Cinderella of Christian doctrines. Very few seem to be interested in it. Many excellent books have been written on the person and work of Christ, but the number of books worth reading on the person and work of the Holy Spirit can almost be counted on the fingers of one hand. Christian people are not in doubt as to the work that Christ did; they know that He redeemed men by His atoning death, even if they differ among themselves as to what exactly this involved. But the average Christian is in a complete fog as to what work the Holy Spirit does. Some talk of the Spirit of Christ in the way that one would talk of the Spirit of Christmas — as a vague cultural pressure making for bonhomie and religiosity. Some think of the Spirit as inspiring the moral convictions of unbelievers like Gandhi, or the theosophical mysticism of a Rudolf Steiner. But most, perhaps, do not think of the Holy Spirit at all, and have no positive ideas of any sort about what He does. They are for practical purposes in the same position as the disciples who Paul met at Ephesus — 'We have not so much as heard whether there be any Holy Ghost' (Acts 19:2).

It is an extraordinary thing that those who profess to care so much about Christ should know and care so little about the Holy Spirit. Christians are aware of the difference it would make if, after all, it transpired that there had never been an incarnation or an atonement. They know that then they would be lost, for they would have no Saviour. But many Christians have really no idea what difference it would make if there were no Holy Spirit in the world. Whether in that case they, or the Church, would suffer in any way they just do not know. Surely something is amiss here. How can we justify neglecting the ministry of Christ's appointed agent in this way? Is it not a hollow fraud to say that we honour Christ when we ignore, and by ignoring dishonour, the one whom Christ has sent to us as His deputy, to take His place, and care for us on His behalf? Ought we not to concern ourselves more about the Holy Spirit than we do?

III

But is the work oft he Holy Spirit really important?

Important! Why, were it not for the work of the Holy Spirit there would be no gospel, no faith, no Church, no Christianity in the world at all.

In the first place: without the Holy Spirit there would be *no gospel, and no New Testament.*

When Christ left the world, He committed His cause to His disciples. He made them responsible for going and making disciples of all the nations. 'Ye . . . shall bear witness,' He told them in the upper room (John 15: 27). 'Ye shall be witnesses unto me . . . unto the uttermost part of the earth,' were His parting words to them on Olivet, before He ascended (Acts 1:8). Such was their appointed task. But what sort of witnesses were they likely to prove? They had never been good pupils; they had consistently failed to understand Christ, and missed the point of His teaching, throughout His earthly ministry; how could they be expected to do better now He had gone? Was it not morally certain that, with the best will in the world, they would soon get the truth of the gospel inextricably mixed up with a mass of well-meant misconceptions, and their witness would rapidly be reduced to a twisted, garbled, hopeless muddle?

The answer to this question is no; because Christ sent the Holy Spirit to them, to teach them all truth and so save them from all error, to remind them of what they had been taught already, and to reveal to them the rest of what their Lord meant them to learn. 'The Comforter . . . shall teach you all things, and bring all things to your remembrance, whatsoever I have said unto you' (John 14:26). 'I have yet many things to say unto you, but ye cannot bear them now. Howbeit when he, the Spirit of truth, is come, he will guide you into all truth: for he shall not speak of himself; but whatsoever he shall hear, that shall he speak' (i.e., He would make known to them all that Christ would instruct Him to tell them, just as Christ had made known to them all that the Father had instructed Him to tell them: see John 12:49f., 17:8, 14), 'and he will show you things to come. He shall glorify me: for he shall receive of mine, and shall show it unto you' (16:12–14). In this way 'he shall testify of me (to you, my disciples, to whom I send Him): and (equipped and enabled by His testifying work) ye also shall bear witness . . .' (15:26 f.). The promise was that, taught by the Spirit, these original disciples should be enabled to speak as so many mouths of Christ so that, just as the Old Testament prophets had been able to introduce their sermons with the words, 'Thus saith the Lord Jehovah,' so the New Testament apostles might with equal truth be able to say of their teaching, oral or written, 'Thus saith the Lord Jesus Christ.'

And the thing happened. The Spirit came to the disciples, and testified to them of Christ and His salvation, according to the promise. Speaking of the glories of this salvation ('the things which God hath prepared for them that love him'), Paul writes, 'God hath revealed them unto us by His Spirit: . . . we have received . . . the Spirit which is of God; that we might know the things that are freely given to us of God. Which things also we speak' (and, he might have added, write), 'not in the words which man's wisdom teacheth, but which the Holy Ghost teacheth' (1 Cor. 2:9–13). The Spirit testified to the apostles by revealing to them all truth and inspiring them to communicate it with all truthfulness. Hence the gospel, and hence the New Testament. But the world would have had neither without the Holy Spirit.

Nor is this all. In the second place: without the Holy Spirit there would be *no faith and no new birth*—in short, *no Christians.*

The light of the gospel shines; but 'the god of this world hath blinded the minds of them which believe not' (2 Cor. 4:4), and the blind do not respond to the stimulus of light. As Christ told Nicodemus, 'except a man be born again, he cannot see the kingdom of God . . . he cannot enter into the kingdom of God' (John 3:3,5). Speaking corporately for Himself and His disciples to Nicodemus and to the whole class of unregenerate religious people to which Nicodemus belonged, Christ went on to explain that the inevitable consequence of unregeneracy is unbelief—'Ye receive not our witness' (verse 11). The gospel produces no conviction in them; unbelief holds them fast.

What follows, then? Should we conclude that preaching the gospel is a waste of time, and write off evangelism as a hopeless enterprise, foredoomed to fail? No; because the Spirit abides with the Church to testify of Christ. To the apostles, He testified by *revealing* and *inspiring*, as we saw. To the rest of men, down the ages, He testifies by *illuminating:* opening blinded eyes, restoring spiritual vision, enabling sinners to see that the gospel is indeed God's truth, and Scripture is indeed God's Word, and Christ is indeed God's Son. 'When he (the Spirit) comes,' our Lord promised, 'he will convince the world of sin and of righteousness and of judgment' (16:7, RSV). It is not for us to imagine that we can prove the truth of Christianity by our own arguments; nobody can prove the truth of Christianity save the Holy Spirit, by His own almighty work of renewing the blinded heart. It is the sovereign prerogative of Christ's Spirit to convince men's consciences of the truth of Christ's gospel; and Christ's human witnesses must learn to ground their hopes of success, not on clever presentation of the truth by man, but on powerful demonstration of the truth by the Spirit. Paul points the way here — 'When I came to you, brethren, I did not come proclaiming to you the testimony of God in lofty words or wisdom . . . my speech and my message were not in plausible words of wisdom, *but in demonstration of the Spirit and power*, that your faith might not rest in the wisdom of men, but in the power of God' (1 Cor. 2:1–5, RSV). And because the Spirit does bear witness in this way, men come to faith when the gospel is preached. But without the Spirit there would not be a Christian in the world.

<h1 style="text-align:center">IV</h1>

Do we honour the Holy Spirit by recognising and relying on His work? Or do we slight Him by ignoring it, and thereby dishonour, not merely the Spirit, but the Lord who sent Him? In our faith: do we acknowledge the authority of the Bible, the prophetic Old Testament and the apostolic New Testament which He inspired? Do we read and hear it with the reverence and receptiveness that are due to the Word of God? If not, we dishonour the Holy Spirit. In our life: do we apply the authority of the Bible, and live by the Bible, whatever men may say against it, recognising that God's Word cannot but be true, and that what God has said He certainly means, and will stand to? If not, we dishonour the Holy Spirit, who gave us the Bible. In our witness: do we remember that the Holy Spirit alone, by His witness, can authenticate our witness, and look to Him to do so, and trust Him to do so, and show the reality of our trust, as Paul did, by eschewing the gimmicks of human cleverness? If not, we dishonour the Holy Spirit. Can we doubt that the present barrenness of the Church's life is God's judgment on us for the way in which we have dishonoured the Holy Spirit? And, in that case, what hope have we of its removal till we learn in our thinking and our praying and our practice to honour the Holy Spirit? 'He shall testify . . .'

'*He that hath an ear, let him hear what the Spirit saith unto the churches.*'

II

BEHOLD YOUR GOD!

CHAPTER 7

God Unchanging

I

They tell us that the Bible is the Word of God—a lamp to our feet, and a light to our path. They tell us that we shall find in it the knowledge of God, and of His will for our lives. We believe them; rightly, for what they say is true. So we take our Bibles and start to read them. We read steadily and thoughtfully, for we are in earnest; we really do want to know God. But as we read, we get more and more puzzled. Though fascinated, we are not being fed. Our reading is not helping us; it leaves us bewildered and, if the truth be told, somewhat depressed. We find ourselves wondering whether Bible-reading is worth going on with.

What is our trouble? Well, basically it is this. Our Bible-reading takes us into what, for us, is quite a new world—namely, the Near Eastern world as it was thousands of years ago, primitive and barbaric, agricultural and unmechanised. It is in that world that the action of the Bible story is played out. In that world, we meet Abraham, and Moses, and David, and the rest, and watch God dealing with them. We hear the prophets denouncing idolatry and threatening judgment upon sin. We see the Man of Galilee, doing miracles, arguing with the Jews, dying for sinners, rising from death and ascending to heaven. We read letters from Christian teachers directed against strange errors which, so far as we know, do not now exist. It is all intensely interesting, but it all seems very far away. It all belongs to *that* world, not to *this* world. We feel that we are, so to speak, on the outside of the Bible world, looking in. We are mere spectators, and that is all. Our unspoken thought is—'Yes, God did all that then, and very wonderful it was for the people involved, but how does it touch us now? We don't live in the same world. How can the record of God's words and deeds in Bible times, the record of His dealings with Abraham and Moses and David and the rest, help us, who have to live in the space age?' We cannot see how the two worlds link up, and hence again and again we find ourselves feeling that the things we read about in the Bible can have no application for us. And when, as so often, these things are in themselves thrilling and glorious, our sense of being excluded from them depresses us considerably.

Most Bible-readers have known this feeling. Not all know how to counter it. Some Christians seem to resign themselves to following afar off, believing the Bible record, indeed, but neither seeking nor expecting for themselves such intimacy and direct dealing with God as the men of the Bible knew. Such an attitude, all too common today, is in effect a confession of failure to see a way through this problem.

But how can this sense of the remoteness from us of the biblical experience of God be overcome? Many things might be said, but the crucial point is surely this. The sense of remoteness is an illusion which springs from seeking the link between our situation and that of the various Bible characters in the wrong place. It is true that in terms of space, time, and culture, they, and the historical epoch to which they belonged, are a very long way away from us. But the link between them and us is not found at that level. The link is God Himself. For the God with whom they had to do is the same God with whom we have to do. We could sharpen the point by saying, *exactly* the same God; for God does not change in the least particular. Thus it appears that the truth on which we must dwell in order to dispel this feeling that there is an unbridgeable gulf between the position of men in Bible times and our own, is the truth of God's *immutability*.

II

God does not change. Let us draw out this thought.

1 God's *life* does not change.
He is 'from everlasting' (Ps. 93:2), 'an everlasting King' (Jer. 10:10), 'incorruptible' (Rom. 1:23), 'who only hath immortality' (1 Tim. 6:16). 'Before the mountains were brought forth, or ever thou hadst formed the earth and the world, even from everlasting to everlasting thou art God' (Ps. 90:2). Earth and heaven, says the psalmist, 'shall perish, but thou shalt endure: yea, all of them shall wax old like a garment; as a vesture shalt thou change them, and they shall be changed: but *thou art the same*, and thy years shall have no end'

68

(Ps. 102:26 f.). 'I am the first,' says God. 'I am also the last' (Isa. 48:12). Created things have a beginning and an ending, but not so their Creator. The answer to the child's question, 'who made God?', is simply that God did not need to be made, for He was always there. He exists for ever; and He is always the same. He does not grow older. His life does not wax or wane. He does not gain new powers, nor lose those that He once had. He does not mature or develop. He does not get stronger, or weaker, or wiser, as time goes by. 'He cannot change for the better,' wrote A. W. Pink, 'for he is already perfect; and being perfect. He cannot change for the worse.' The first and fundamental difference between the Creator and His creatures is that they are mutable and their nature admits of change, whereas God is immutable and can never cease to be what He is. As the hymn puts it,

> *We blossom and flourish as leaves on the tree,*
> *And wither and perish — but* nought changeth Thee.

Such is the power of God's own 'endless life' (cf. Heb. 7:16).

2 God's *character* does not change.
Strain, or shock, or a leucotomy, can alter the character of a man, but nothing can alter the character of God. In the course of a human life, tastes and outlook and temper may change radically: a kind, equable man may turn bitter and crotchety; a man of good-will may grow cynical and callous. But nothing of this sort happens to the Creator. He never becomes less truthful, or merciful, or just, or good, than He used to be. The character of God is today, and always will be, exactly what it was in Bible times.

It is instructive in this connection to bring together God's two disclosures of His 'name' in the book of Exodus. God's revealed 'name' is, of course, more than a label; it is a revelation of what He is, in relation to men. In Exodus 3, we read how God announced His name to Moses as 'I am that I am' (verse 14)—a phrase of which 'Yahweh' (Jehovah, 'the LORD') is, in effect, a shortened form (verse 15). This 'name' is not a description of God, but simply a declaration of His self-existence, and His eternal changelessness; a reminder to mankind that He has life in Himself, and that what He is now, He is eternally. In Exodus 34, however, we read how God 'proclaimed the name of the LORD' to Moses by listing the various facets of His holy character. 'The LORD, the LORD (Yahweh), a God merciful and gracious, slow to anger, and abounding in steadfast love and faithfulness, keeping steadfast love for thousands, forgiving iniquity and transgression and sin, but who will by no means clear the guilty, visiting the iniquity of the fathers upon the children . . .' (verses 5 ff. RSV). This proclamation supplements that of Exodus 3 by telling us what in fact Yahweh is; and that of Exodus 3 supplements this by telling us that God is for ever what at that moment, three thousand years ago, He told Moses that He was. God's moral character is changeless. So James, in a passage that deals with God's goodness and holiness, His generosity to men and His hostility to sin, speaks of God as one 'with whom there is no variation or shadow due to change' (James 1:17, RSV).

3 God's *truth* does not change.

Men sometimes say things that they do not really mean, simply because they do not know their own mind; also, because their views change, they frequently find that they can no longer stand to things that they said in the past. All of us sometimes have to recall our words, because they have ceased to express what we think; sometimes we have to eat our words, because hard facts refute them. The words of men are unstable things. But not so the words of God. They stand for ever, as abidingly valid expressions of His mind and thought. No circumstances prompt Him to recall them; no changes in His own thinking require Him to amend them. Isaiah writes, 'All flesh is grass . . . the grass withereth . . . but the word of our God shall stand for ever' (Isa. 40:6 ff.). Similarly, the psalmist says, 'For ever, O LORD, thy word is settled in heaven.' 'All thy commandments are truth . . . thou hast founded them for ever' (Ps. 119:89, 152). The word translated 'truth' in the last verse carries with it the idea of stability. When we read our Bibles, therefore, we need to remember that God still stands to all the promises, and demands, and statements of purpose, and words of warning, that are there addressed to New Testament believers. These are not relics of a bygone age, but an eternally valid revelation of the mind of God towards His people in all generations, so long as this world lasts. As our Lord Himself has told us, 'The Scripture cannot be broken' (John 10:35). Nothing can annul God's eternal truth.

4 God's *ways* do not change.

He continues to act towards sinful men in the way that He does in the Bible story. Still He shows His freedom and lordship by discriminating between sinners, causing some to hear the gospel while others do not hear it, and moving some of those who hear it to repentance while leaving others in their unbelief; thus teaching His saints that He owes mercy to none, and that it is entirely of His grace, not at all through their own effort, that they themselves have found life. Still He blesses those on whom He sets His love in a way that humbles them, so that all the glory may be His alone. Still He hates the sins of His people, and uses all kinds of inward and outward pains and griefs to wean their hearts from compromise and disobedience. Still He seeks the fellowship of His people, and sends them both sorrows and joys in order to detach their love from other things and attach it to Himself. Still He teaches the believer to value His promised gifts by making him wait for them, and compelling him to pray persistently for them, before He bestows them. So we read of Him dealing with His people in the Scripture record, and so He deals with them still. His aims and principles of action remain consistent; He does not at any time act out of character. Man's ways, we know, are pathetically inconstant — but not God's.

5 God's *purposes* do not change.
'The Strength of Israel will not lie nor repent,' declared Samuel, 'for he is not a man, that he should repent' (1 Sam. 15:29). Balaam had said the same, 'God is not a man, that he should lie; neither the son of man, that he should repent; hath he said, and shall he not do it? or hath he spoken, and shall he not make it good?' (Num. 23:19). Repenting means revising one's judgment, and changing one's plan of action. God never does this; He never needs to, for His plans are made on the basis of a complete knowledge and control which extend to all things past, present, and future, so that there can be no sudden emergencies or unlooked-for developments to take Him by surprise. 'One of two things causes a man to change his mind and reverse his plans: want of foresight to anticipate everything, or lack of foresight to execute them. But as God is both omniscient and omnipotent there is never any need for Him to revise His decrees' (A. W. Pink). 'The counsel of the LORD standeth sure, the thoughts of his heart to all generations' (Ps. 33:11). What He does in time, He planned from eternity. And all that He planned in eternity He carries out in time. And all that He has in His word committed Himself to do will infallibly be done. Thus, we read of 'the immutability of his counsel' to bring believers into full enjoyment of their promised inheritance, and of the immutable oath by which He confirmed this counsel to Abraham, the archetypal believer, both for Abraham's

own assurance and for ours too (Heb. 6:17 f.). So it is with all God's announced intentions. They do not change. No part of His eternal plan changes.

It is true that there is a group of texts (Gen. 6: 6 f.; 1 Sam. 15:11; 2 Sam. 24:16; Jonah 3:10; Joel 2:13 f.) which speak of God as repenting. The reference in each case is to a reversal of God's previous treatment of particular men, consequent upon their reaction to that treatment. But there is no suggestion that this reaction was not foreseen, or that it took God by surprise, and was not provided for in His eternal plan. No change in His eternal purpose is implied when He begins to deal with a man in a new way.

6 God's *Son* does not change.

Jesus Christ is 'the same yesterday, and today, and for ever' (Heb. 13:8), and His touch has still its ancient power. It still remains true that 'he is able also to save them to the uttermost that come unto God by him, seeing he ever liveth to make intercession for them' (Heb. 7:25). He never changes. This fact is the strong consolation of all God's people.

III

Where is the sense of distance and difference, then, between believers in Bible times and ourselves? It is excluded. On what grounds? On the grounds that God does not change. Fellowship with Him, trust in His word, living by faith, 'standing on the promises of God', are essentially the same realities for us today as they were for Old and New Testament believers. This thought brings comfort as we enter into the perplexities of each day: amid all the changes and uncertainties of life in a nuclear age, God and His Christ remain the same—almighty to save. But the thought brings a searching challenge too. If our God is the same as the God of New Testament believers, how can we justify ourselves in resting content with an experience of communion with Him, and a level of Christian conduct, that falls so far below theirs? *If God is the same, this is not an issue that any one of us can evade.*

CHAPTER 8

The Majesty of God

I

Our word 'majesty' comes from the Latin; it means *greatness*. When we ascribe majesty to someone, we are acknowledging greatness in that person, and voicing our respect for it: as, for instance, when we speak of 'Her Majesty' the Queen.

Now, 'majesty' is a word which the Bible uses to express the thought of the greatness of God, our Maker and our Lord. 'The Lord reigneth, he is clothed with *majesty* . . . Thy throne is established of old' (Ps. 93:1 f.). 'I will speak of the glorious honour of thy *majesty*, and of thy wondrous works' (Ps. 145:5). Peter, recalling his vision of Christ's royal glory at the Transfiguration, says, 'we . . . were eyewitnesses of his *majesty*' (2 Pet. 1:16). In Hebrews, the phrase 'the majesty' twice does duty for 'God'; Christ, we are told, at His ascension sat down 'on the right hand of *the majesty* on high', 'on the right hand of the throne of *the majesty* in the heavens' (Heb. 1:3; 8:1). The word 'majesty', when applied to God, is always a declaration of His greatness and an invitation to worship The same is true when the Bible speaks of God as being 'on high' and 'in heaven'; the thought here is not that God is far distant from us in space, but that He is far above us in greatness, and therefore is to be adored. 'Great is the LORD, and greatly to be praised' (Ps. 48:1). 'The LORD is a great God, and a great King . . . O come, let us worship and bow down' (Ps. 95:3, 6). The Christian's instincts of trust and worship are stimulated very powerfully by knowledge of the greatness of God.

But this is knowledge which Christians today largely lack: and that is one reason why our faith is so feeble and our worship so flabby. We are modern men, and modern men, though they cherish great thoughts of man, have as a rule small thoughts of God. When the man in the Church, let alone the man in the street, uses the word 'God', the thought in his mind is rarely of divine *majesty*. A recent book was called *Your God Is Too Small;* it was a timely title. We are poles apart from our evangelical forefathers at this point, even when we confess our faith in their words. When you start reading Luther, or Edwards, or Whitefield, though your doctrine may be theirs, you soon find yourself wondering whether you have any acquaintance at all with the mighty God whom they knew so intimately.

Today, vast stress is laid on the thought that God is *personal*, but this truth is so stated as to leave the impression that God is a person of the same sort as we are—weak, inadequate, ineffective, a little pathetic. But this is not the God of the Bible! Our personal life is a finite thing: it is limited in every direction, in space, in time, in knowledge, in power. But God is not so limited. He is eternal, infinite, and almighty. He has us in His hands; but we never have Him in ours. Like us. He is personal, but unlike us He is *great*. In all its constant stress on the reality of God's personal concern for His people, and on the gentleness, tenderness, sympathy, patience, and yearning compassion that He shows towards them, the Bible never let us lose sight of His majesty, and His unlimited dominion over all His creatures.

II

For illustration of this, we do not have to look further than the opening chapters of Genesis. Right from the start of the Bible story, through the wisdom of divine inspiration, the narrative is told in such a way as to impress upon us the twin truths that the God to whom we are being introduced is both *personal* and *majestic*. Nowhere else in the Bible is the personal nature of God expressed in more vivid terms. He deliberates with Himself, 'Let us . . .' (Gen. 1:26). He brings the animals to Adam to see what Adam will call them (2:19). He walks in the garden, calling to Adam (3:8 f.). He asks people questions (3: 11 ff., 4:9, 16:8). He comes down from heaven in order to find out what men are doing (11:5, 18:20 ff.). He is so grieved by human wickedness that He repents of making man (6:6 f.). Representations of God like these are meant to bring home to us the fact that the God with whom we have to do is not a mere cosmic principle, impersonal and indifferent, but a living Person, thinking, feeling, active, approving of good, disapproving of evil, and interested in His creatures all the time.

But we are not to gather from these passages that God's knowledge and power are limited, or that He is normally absent, and so unaware of what is going on in the world except when He comes specially to investigate. These same chapters rule out all such ideas by setting before us a presentation of God's greatness no less vivid than that of His personality. The God of Genesis is the Creator, bringing order out of chaos, calling life into being by His word, making Adam from earth's dust and Eve from Adam's rib (chs. 1–2). And He is Lord of all that He has made. He curses the ground and subjects mankind to physical death, thus changing His original perfect world-order (3:17 ff.); He floods the earth in judgment, destroying all life save that in the Ark (chs. 6–8); He confounds human language, and scatters the builders of Babel (11: 7 ff.); He overthrows Sodom and Gomorrah by (apparently) a volcanic eruption (19:24 ff.). Abraham truly calls him 'the Judge of all the earth' (18: 25), and rightly adopts Melchizedek's name for Him, 'God Most High, maker of heaven and earth' (14:19–22, RSV). He is present everywhere, and observes everything: Cain's murder (4:9 ff.), mankind's corruption (6:5), Hagar's destitution (16:7 ff.). Well did Hagar name Him *El roi*, 'a God that seeth', and call her son Ishmael, 'God hears' for God does in truth both hear and see, and nothing escapes Him. His own name for Himself is *El Shaddai*, 'God Almighty', and all His actions illustrate the omnipotence which this name proclaims. He promises Abraham and his wife a son in their nineties, and rebukes Sarah for her incredulous — and, as it proved, unjustified — laughter: 'Is anything too hard for the LORD?' (18:14). And it is not only at isolated moments that God takes control of events, either; all history is under His sway. Proof of this is given by His detailed predictions of the tremendous destiny which He purposed to work out for Abraham's seed (12:1–3, 13:14–17, 15:13–21, etc.). Such, in brief, is the majesty of God, according to the first chapters of Genesis.

III

How may we form a right idea of God's greatness? The Bible teaches us two steps that we must take. The first is to *remove from our thoughts of God limits that would make Him small*. The second is to *compare Him with powers and forces which we regard as great*.

For an example of what the *first* step involves, look at Psalm 139, where the psalmist meditates on the infinite and unlimited nature of God's presence, and knowledge, and power, in relation to men. Man, he says, is always in God's presence; you can cut yourself off from your fellow-men, but you cannot get away from your Creator. 'Thou hast beset me behind and before . . . Whither shall I go from thy spirit? or whither shall I flee from thy presence?' If I should go up into heaven (the sky), or down into hell (i.e., the underworld), or away to the world's end, I still could not escape from the presence of God—'behold, thou art there' (verse 5 ff.). Nor can darkness, which hides me from human sight, shield me from God's gaze' (verse 11 ff.).

And just as there are no bounds to His presence with me, so there are no limits to His knowledge of me. Just as I am never left alone, so I never go unnoticed. 'O LORD, thou hast searched me and know me. Thou knowest my downsitting and mine uprising (all my actions and movements), thou understandest my thought (all that goes on in my mind) afar off . . . and art acquainted with all my ways (all my habits, plans, aims, desires, as well as all my life to date). For there is not a word in my tongue (spoken, or meditated), but lo, O LORD, thou knowest it altogether' (verse 1 ff.). I can hide my heart, and my past, and my future plans, from men, but I cannot hide anything from God. I can talk in a way that deceives my fellow-creatures as to what I really am, but nothing I say or do can deceive God. He sees through all my reserve and pretence; He knows me as I really am, better indeed than I know myself. A God whose presence and scrutiny I could evade would be a small and trivial deity. But the true God is great and terrible, just because He is always with me and His eye is always upon me. Living becomes an awesome business when you realise that you spend every moment of your life in the sight and company of an omniscient, omnipresent Creator.

Nor is this all. The all-seeing God is also God almighty, the resources of whose power are already revealed to me by the amazing complexity of my own physical body, which He made for me. Confronted with this, the psalmist's meditations turn to worship. 'I will praise thee; for I am fearfully and wonderfully made: marvellous are thy works . . .' (verse 14).

Here, then, is the first step in apprehending the greatness of God: to realise how unlimited are His wisdom, and His presence, and His power. Many other passages of Scripture teach the same lesson: notably, Job 38–41, the chapters in which God Himself takes up Elihu's recognition that 'with God is terrible majesty' (37:22), and sets before Job a tremendous display of His wisdom and power in Nature, and asks Job if he can match such 'majesty' as this (40:10), and convinces him that, since he cannot, he should not presume to find fault with God's handling of Job's own case, which also goes far beyond Job's understanding. But we cannot dwell further on this now.

IV

For an example of what the *second* step involves, look at Isaiah 40:12 ff. Here God speaks to people whose mood is the mood of many Christians today — despondent people, cowed people, secretly despairing people; people against whom the tide of events has been running for a very long time; people who have ceased to believe that the cause of Christ can ever prosper again. Now see how God through His prophet reasons with them.

Look at the *tasks* I have done, He says. Could you do them? Could any man do them? 'Who hath measured the waters in the hollow of his hand, and meted out heaven with the span, and comprehended the dust of the earth in a measure, and weighed the mountains in scales, and the hills in a balance?' (verse 12). Are you wise enough, and mighty enough, to do things like that? But I am; or I could not have made this world at all. 'Behold your God!'

Look now at the *nations*, the prophet continues: the great national powers, at whose mercy you feel yourselves to be. Assyria, Egypt, Babylon — you stand in awe of them, and feel afraid of them, so vastly do their armies and resources exceed yours. But now consider how God stands related to those mighty forces which you fear so much. 'Behold, the nations are as a drop of a bucket, and are counted as small dust of the balance . . . All nations before him are as nothing; and they are counted to him less than nothing, and vanity (emptiness)' (verse 15 ff.). You tremble before the nations, because you are much weaker than they; but God is so much greater than the nations that they are as nothing to Him. 'Behold your God!'

Look next at the *world*. Consider the size of it, the variety and complexity of it; think of the three thousand-odd millions who populate it, and of the vast sky above it. What puny figures you and I are, by comparison with the whole planet on which we live! Yet what is this whole mighty planet by comparison with God? 'It is he that sitteth upon (above) the circle of the earth, and the inhabitants thereof are as grasshoppers; that stretcheth out the heavens as a curtain, and spreadeth them out as a tent to dwell in' (verse 22). The world dwarfs us all, but God dwarfs the world. The world is His footstool, above which He sits secure. He is greater than the world, and all that is in it; so that all the feverish activity of its three thousand bustling millions does no more to affect Him than the chirping and jumping of grasshoppers in the summer sun does to affect us. 'Behold your God!'

Look, fourthly, at the world's *great men*—the governors whose laws and policies determine the welfare of millions; the would-be world-rulers, the dictators and empire-builders, who have it in their power to plunge the globe into war. Think of Sennacherib and Nebuchadnezzar; think of Alexander, Napoleon, Hitler. Think, today, of Kosygin, Nixon, and Mao Tse-tung. Do you suppose that it is really these great men who determine which way the world shall go? Think again; for God is greater than the world's great men. He 'bringeth the princes to nothing; he maketh the judges (rulers) of the earth as vanity' (verse 23). He is, as the Prayer Book says, 'the only ruler of princes'. 'Behold your God!'

But we have not finished yet. Look, lastly, at the *stars*. The most universally awesome experience that mankind knows is to stand alone on a clear night and look at the stars. Nothing gives a greater sense of remoteness and distance; nothing makes one feel more strongly one's own littleness and insignificance. And we, who live on the threshold of the space age, can supplement this universal experience with our scientific knowledge of the actual factors involved—millions of stars in number, billions of light-years in distance. Our minds reel; our imaginations cannot grasp it; when we try to conceive of unfathomable depths of outer space, we are left mentally numb and dizzy. But what is this to God?' 'Lift up your eyes on high, and behold who hath created these things, that bringeth out their host (the stars) by number: he calleth them all by names by the greatness of his might, for that he is strong in power; not one faileth' (verse 26). It is God who brings out the stars; it was God who first set them in space; He is their Maker and Master: they are all in his hands, and subject to His will. Such are His power and His majesty. 'Behold your God!'

V

Let Isaiah now apply to us the Bible doctrine of the majesty of God, by asking us the three questions which he here puts in God's name to disillusioned and downcast Israelites.

1 'To whom then will ye compare me, that I should be like him? says the Holy One' (verse 25, RSV). This question rebukes *wrong thoughts about God.* 'Your thoughts of God are too human,' said Luther to Erasmus. This is where most of us go astray. Our thoughts of God are not great enough; we fail to reckon with the reality of His limitless wisdom and power. Because we ourselves

are limited and weak, we imagine that at some points God is too, and find it hard to believe that He is not. We think of God as too much like what we are. Put this mistake right, says God; learn to acknowledge the full majesty of your incomparable God and Saviour.

2 'Why sayest thou, O Jacob, and speakest, O Israel, My way is hid from the Lord and my judgment is passed away from my God?' (verse 27, RV). This question rebukes *wrong thoughts about ourselves*. God has not abandoned us any more than He abandoned Job. He never abandons anyone on whom He has set His love; nor does Christ, the good shepherd, ever lose track of His sheep. It is as false as it is irreverent to accuse God of forgetting, or overlooking, or losing interest in, the state and needs of His own people. If you have been resigning yourself to the thought that God has left you high and dry, seek grace to be ashamed of yourself. Such unbelieving pessimism deeply dishonours our great God and Saviour.

3 'Hast thou not known? hast thou not heard, that the everlasting God, the LORD, the creator of the ends of the earth, fainteth not, neither is weary?' (verse 28). This question rebukes *our slowness to believe in God's majesty*. God would shame us out of our unbelief. What is the trouble? He asks: have you been imagining that I, the Creator, have grown old and tired? Has nobody ever told you the truth about Me? The rebuke is well deserved by many of us. How slow we are to believe in God *as God*, sovereign, all-seeing and almighty! How little we make of the majesty of our Lord and Saviour Christ! The need for us is to 'wait upon the LORD' in meditations of His majesty, till we find our strength renewed through the writing of these things upon our hearts.

CHAPTER 9

God Only Wise

I

What does the Bible mean when it calls God *wise*? In Scripture wisdom is a moral as well as an intellectual quality, more than mere intelligence or knowledge, just as it is more than mere cleverness or cunning. To be truly wise, in the Bible sense, one's intelligence and cleverness must be harnessed to a right end. Wisdom is the power to see, and the inclination to choose, the best and highest goal, together with the surest means of attaining it.

Wisdom is, in fact, the practical side of moral goodness. As such, it is found in its fulness only in God. He alone is naturally and entirely and invariably wise. 'His wisdom ever waketh,' says the hymn, and it is true. God is never other than wise in anything that He does. Wisdom, as the old theologians used to say, is His *essence*, just as power, and truth, and goodness, are His *essence* — integral elements, that is, in His character.

Wisdom in men can be frustrated by circumstantial factors outside the wise man's control. Ahithophel, David's turncoat counsellor, gave sound advice when he urged Absalom to finish David off at once, before he had recovered from the first shock of Absalom's revolt; but Absalom stupidly took a different line, and Ahithophel, seething with wounded pride, foreseeing, no doubt, that the revolt was now sure to fail, and unable to forgive himself for being such a fool as to join it, went home in despair and committed suicide (2 Sam. 17).

But God's wisdom cannot be frustrated in the way that Ahithophel's 'good counsel' (verse 14) was, for it is allied to omnipotence. Power is as much God's essence as wisdom is. Omniscience governing omnipotence, infinite power ruled by infinite wisdom, is a basic biblical description of the divine character. 'He is *wise* in heart, and *mighty* in strength' (Job 9:4). 'With him is *wisdom and strength*' (12:13). 'He is mighty in *strength and wisdom*' (36:5). 'He is strong in *power* . . . there is no searching of his *understanding*' (Isa. 40:26, 28). '*Wisdom and might* are his' (Dan. 2:20). The same conjunction appears in the New Testament: 'Now to him that is of *power* to establish you according to my gospel . . . God only *wise* . . .' (Rom. 16:25, 27). Wisdom without power would be pathetic, a broken reed; power without wisdom would be merely frightening; but in God boundless wisdom and endless power are united, and this makes him utterly worthy of our fullest trust.

God's almighty wisdom is always active, and never fails. All His works of creation and providence and grace display it, and until we can see it in them we just are not seeing them straight. But we cannot recognise God's wisdom unless we know the end for which He is working. Here many go wrong. Misunderstanding what the Bible means when it says that God is love (see 1 John 4:8–10), they think that God intends a trouble-free life for all, irrespective of their moral and spiritual state, and hence they conclude that anything painful and upsetting (illness, accident, injury, loss of job, the suffering of a loved one) indicates either that God's wisdom, or power, or both, have broken down, or that God, after all, does not exist. But this idea of God's intention is a complete mistake. God's wisdom is not, and never was, pledged to keep a fallen world happy, or to make ungodliness comfortable. Not even to Christians has He promised a trouble-free life; rather the reverse. He has other ends in view for life in this world than simply to make it easy for everyone.

What is He after, then? What is His goal? What does He aim at? When He made man, His purpose was that man should love and honour Him, praising Him for the wonderfully ordered complexity and variety of His world, using it according to His will, and so enjoying both it and Him. And though man has fallen, God has not abandoned His first purpose. Still He plans that a great host of mankind should come to love and honour Him. His ultimate objective is to bring them to a state in which they please Him entirely and praise Him adequately, a state in which He is all in all to them, and He and they rejoice continually in the knowledge of each other's love—men rejoicing in the saving love of God, set upon them from all eternity, and God rejoicing in the responsive love of men, drawn out of them by grace through the gospel.

This will be God's 'glory', and man's 'glory' too, in every sense which that weighty word can bear. But it will only be fully realised in the next world, in the context of a transformation of the whole created order. Meanwhile, however, God works steadily towards it. His immediate objectives are to draw individual men and women into a relationship of faith, hope, and love, towards Himself, delivering them from sin and showing forth in their lives the power of His grace; to defend His people against the forces of evil; and to spread throughout the world the gospel by means of which He saves. In the fulfilment of each part of this purpose the Lord Jesus Christ is central, for God has set Him forth both as Saviour from sin, whom men must trust, and as Lord of the church, whom men must obey. We have dwelt on the way in which divine wisdom was manifested in Christ's incarnation and cross. We would add now that it is in the light of the complex purpose which we have outlined that the wisdom of God in His dealings with individual men is to be seen.

II

Bible biography helps us here. No clearer illustrations of the wisdom of God ordering human lives can be found than in some of the scriptural narratives. Take, for instance, the life of Abraham. Abraham was capable of repeated shabby deceptions, which actually endangered his wife's chastity (Gen. 12:10 ff., 20). Plainly, then, he was by nature a man of little moral courage, altogether too anxious about his own personal security (12:12 f., 20:11). Also, he was vulnerable to pressure; at his wife's insistence, he fathered a child upon her maid, Hagar, and when Sarai reacted to Hagar's pride in her pregnancy with hysterical recriminations he let Sarai drive Hagar out of the house (verse 16). Plainly, then, Abraham was not by nature a man of strong principle, and his sense of responsibility was somewhat deficient. But God in wisdom dealt with this easy-going unheroic figure to such good effect that not merely did he faithfully fulfil his appointed role on the stage of church history, as pioneer occupant of Canaan, first recipient of God's covenant (verse 17), and father of Isaac, the miracle-child; he also became a new man.

What Abraham needed most of all was to learn the practice of *living in God's presence*, seeing all life in relation to Him, and looking to Him, and Him alone, as Commander, Defender and Rewarder. This was the great lesson which God in wisdom concentrated on teaching him. 'Fear not, Abram: I am thy *shield*, and thy exceeding great *reward*' (15:1). 'I am God Almighty; *walk before me*, and be thou *perfect* (single-eyed and sincere)' (17:1). Again and again God confronted Abraham with Himself, and so led Abraham to the point where his heart could say, with the psalmist, 'Whom have I in heaven but Thee? and there is none upon earth that I desire beside Thee . . . God is the strength of my heart, and my portion for ever' (Ps. 73:25 f.). And as the story proceeds, we see in Abraham's life the results of his learning this lesson. The old weaknesses still sometimes reappear, but alongside it there emerges a new nobility and independence, the outworking of Abraham's developed habit of walking with God, resting in His revealed will, relying on Him, waiting for Him, bowing to His providence, and obeying Him even when he commands something odd and unconventional. From being a man of the world, Abraham becomes a man of God.

Thus, as he responds to God's call, leaves home, and travels through the land which his descendants are to possess (12:7) — though not he himself, note; Abraham never possessed any more of Canaan than a grave (verse 23) — we observe in him a new meekness, as he declines to claim his due precedence over his nephew Lot (13:8 f.). We see also a new courage, as he sets off with a mere three hundred men to rescue Lot from the combined forces of four kings (14:14 ff.). We see a new dignity, as he deprecates keeping the recaptured booty, lest it should seem to have been the king of Sodom, rather than God most High, who made him rich (14:2 2f.). We see a new patience, as he waits a quarter of a century, from the age of seventy-five to a hundred, for the birth of his promised heir (12:4, 21:5). We see him becoming a man of prayer, an importunate intercessor burdened with a sense of responsibility before God for others' welfare (18:23 ff.). We see him at the end so utterly devoted to God's will, and so confident that God knows what He is doing, that he is willing at God's command to kill his own son, the heir for whose birth he had waited so long (22). How wisely God had taught him his lesson! And how well Abraham had learned it!

Jacob, Abraham's grandson, needed different treatment: Jacob was a self-willed mother's boy, blessed (or cursed) with all the opportunist instincts and amoral ruthlessness of the go-getting business man. God in His wisdom had planned that Jacob, though he was the younger son, should have the firstborn's birthright and blessing, and so become the bearer of the covenant promise (cf. 28:13 ff.); also, He had planned that Jacob should marry his cousins Leah and Rachel and become the father of the twelve patriarchs, to whom the promise was to be passed on (cf. 48, 49).

But God in His wisdom had also resolved to instil true religion into Jacob himself. Jacob's whole attitude to life was ungodly, and needed changing; Jacob must be weaned away from trust in his own cleverness to dependence upon God, and must be made to abhor the unscrupulous double-dealing which came so natural to him. Jacob, therefore, must be made to feel his own utter weakness and foolishness, and brought to such complete self-distrust that he would no longer try to get on by exploiting others. Jacob's self-reliance must go, once and for all. With patient wisdom (for God always waits for the right time) God led Jacob to the point at which He could stamp the required sense of impotent helplessness indelibly and decisively on Jacob's soul. It is instructive to trace the steps by which He did this.

First, over a period of some twenty years, God let Jacob have his head in weaving complex webs of deceit, with their inevitable consequences — mutual mistrust, friendships turned to enmity, and the isolation of the deceiver. The consequences of Jacob's cleverness were themselves God's curse upon it. When Jacob had filched Esau's birthright and blessing (25:29 ff.; 27), Esau turned against him (naturally!) and Jacob had to leave home in a hurry. He went to his uncle Laban, who proved to be as tricky a customer as Jacob himself. Laban exploited Jacob's position and bamboozled him into marrying, not only his pretty daughter, whom Jacob wanted, but also the plain one with bad eyes, for whom he would otherwise have found it hard to get a good husband (29:15–30).

Jacob's experience with Laban was a case of the biter bit; God used it to show Jacob what it was like to be at the receiving end of a swindle — something that Jacob needed to learn, if he was ever to fall out of love with his own previous way of life. But Jacob was not cured yet. His immediate reaction was to give tit for tat; he manipulated the breeding of Laban's sheep so astutely, with such profit to himself and loss to his employer, that Laban grew furious, and Jacob felt it prudent to leave with his family for Canaan, before active reprisals began (30:25 — chap. 31). And God, who had hitherto borne Jacob's dishonesty without rebuke, encouraged him to go (30:11 ff., cf. 32:1 f., 9 f.); for He knew what He would do before the journey ended. As Jacob went, Laban chased after him, and made it perfectly clear that he did not want to see Jacob come back (chap. 31).

When Jacob's caravan reached the border of Esau's country, Jacob sent his brother a polite message to tell him of their arrival. But the news that came back made him think that Esau was bringing an armed force against him, to avenge the stolen blessing of twenty years before. Jacob was thrown into complete despair. And now God's time had come. That night, as Jacob stood alone by the river Jabbok, God met him (32: 24 ff.). There were hours of desperate, agonised conflict, spiritual and, as it seemed to Jacob, physical also. Jacob had hold of God; he wanted a blessing, an assurance of divine favour and protection in this crisis, but he could not get what he sought. Instead, he grew ever more conscious of his own state—utterly helpless and, without God, utterly hopeless. He felt the full bitterness of his unscrupulous, cynical ways, now coming home to roost. He had hitherto been self-reliant, believing himself to be more than a match for anything that might come, but now he felt his complete inability to handle things, and knew with blinding, blazing certainty that never again dare he trust himself to look after himself and to carve out his destiny. Never again dare he try to live by his wits.

To make this doubly clear to Jacob, as they wrestled God *lamed* him (verse 25), putting his thigh out of joint to be a perpetual reminder in his flesh of his own spiritual weakness, and his need to lean always upon God, just as for the rest of his life he had to walk leaning on a stick. Jacob abhorred himself; with all his heart he found himself for the first time hating, really hating, that fancied cleverness of his. It had set Esau against him (justly!), not to mention Laban, and now it had made his God unwilling, as it seemed, to bless him any more. 'Let me go . . .' said the One with whom he wrestled; it seemed as though God meant to abandon him. But Jacob held tight, 'I will not let thee go, except thou bless me' (verse 26). And now at last God spoke the word of blessing: for Jacob was now weak and despairing, and humble and dependent enough to be blessed. 'He weakened my strength in the way,' said the psalmist (Ps. 102:23); that was what God had done to Jacob. There was no particle of self-reliance left in Jacob by the time God had finished with him. The nature of Jacob's 'prevailing' with God (verse 28) was simply that he had held on to God while God weakened him, and wrought in him the spirit of submission and self-distrust; that he had desired God's blessing so much that he clung to God through all this painful humbling, till he came low enough for God to raise him up by speaking peace to him and assuring him that he need not fear about Esau any more. True, Jacob did not become a plaster saint overnight; he was not completely straight with Esau the next day (33:14–17); but in principle God had won His battle with Jacob, and won it for good. Jacob never lapsed back into his old ways. Limping Jacob had learned his lesson. The wisdom of God had done its work.

One more example from Genesis, different again: that of Joseph. Young Joseph's brothers sold him into slavery in Egypt where, traduced by Potiphar's venomous wife, he was imprisoned; though afterwards he rose to eminence. For what purpose did God in His wisdom plan that? So far as Joseph personally was concerned, the answer is given in Psalm 105:19 — 'the word of the Lord *tried* him.' Joseph was being tested, refined, and matured; he was being taught during his spell as a slave, and in prison, to stay himself upon God, to keep cheerful and charitable in frustrating circumstances, and to wait patiently for the Lord. God uses sustained hardship to teach these lessons very frequently. So far as the life of God's people was concerned, Joseph himself gave the answer to our question when he revealed his identity to his distracted brothers. 'God sent me before you to preserve you a posterity in the earth, and to save your lives by a great deliverance. So now it was not you that sent me hither, but God ...' (45: 7 f.). Joseph's theology was as sound as his charity was deep. Once again, we are confronted with the wisdom of God ordering the events of a human life for a double purpose: the man's own personal sanctification, and the fulfilling of his appointed ministry and service in the life of the people of God. And in the life of Joseph, as in that of Abraham and of Jacob, we see that double purpose triumphantly fulfilled.

III

These things are written for our learning: for the same wisdom which ordered the paths which God's saints trod in Bible times orders the Christian's life today. We should not, therefore, be too taken aback when unexpected and upsetting and discouraging things happen to us now. What do they mean? Why, simply that God in His wisdom means to make something of us which we have not attained yet, and is dealing with us accordingly.

Perhaps He means to strengthen us in patience, good humour, compassion, humility, or meekness, by giving us some extra practice in exercising these graces under specially difficult conditions. Perhaps He has new lessons in self-denial and self-distrust to teach us. Perhaps He wishes to break us of complacency, or unreality, or undetected forms of pride and conceit. Perhaps His purpose is simply to draw us closer to Himself in conscious communion with Him; for it is often the case, as all the saints know, that fellowship with the Father and the Son is most vivid and sweet, and Christian joy is greatest, when the cross is heaviest. (Remember Samuel Rutherford!) Or perhaps God is preparing us for forms of service of which at present we have no inkling.

Paul saw part of the reason for his own afflictions in the fact that God 'comforteth us in all our tribulation, that we may be able to comfort them which are in any trouble, by the comfort wherewith we ourselves are comforted of God' (2 Cor. 1:4). Even the Lord Jesus 'learned . . . obedience by the things which he suffered', and so was 'made perfect' for his High-Priestly ministry of sympathy and help to His hard-pressed disciples (Heb. 5:8 f.): which means that, as on the one hand He is able to uphold us and make us more than conquerors in all our troubles and distresses, so on the other hand we must not be surprised if He calls us to follow in His steps, and to let ourselves be prepared for the service of others by painful experiences which are quite undeserved. 'He knows the way He taketh,' even if for the moment we do not. We may be frankly bewildered at things that happen to us, but God knows exactly what He is doing, and what He is after, in His handling of our affairs. Always, and in everything, He is wise: we shall see that hereafter, even where we never saw it here. (Job in heaven knows the full reason why he was afflicted, though he never knew it in this life.) Meanwhile, we ought not to hesitate to trust His wisdom, even when He leaves us in the dark.

But how are we to meet these baffling and trying situations, if we cannot for the moment see God's purpose in them? First, by taking them as from God, and asking ourselves what reactions to them, and in them, the gospel of God requires of us; second, by seeking God's face specifically about them. If we do these two things, we shall never find ourselves wholly in the dark as to God's purpose in our troubles. We shall always be able to see at least as much purpose in them as Paul was enabled to see in his thorn in the flesh (whatever it was). It came to him, he tells us, as a 'messenger of Satan', tempting him to hard thoughts of God. He resisted this temptation, and sought Christ's face three times, asking that it might be removed. The only answer he had was this, 'My grace is sufficient for thee: for my strength is made perfect in weakness.' On reflection, he perceived a reason why he should have been thus afflicted: it was to keep him humble, 'lest I should be exalted above measure through the abundance of the revelations.' This thought, and Christ's word, were enough for him. He looked no further. Here is his final attitude: 'Most gladly therefore will I rather glory in my infirmities, that the power of Christ may rest upon me' (2 Cor. 12:7-9).

This attitude of Paul is a model for us. Whatever further purpose a Christian's troubles may or may not have in equipping him for future service, they will always have at least that purpose which Paul's thorn in the flesh had: they will have been sent us to make and keep us humble, and to give us a new opportunity of showing forth the power of Christ in our mortal lives. And do we ever need to know any more about them than that? Is not this enough of itself to convince us of the wisdom of God in them? Once Paul saw that his trouble was sent him to enable him to glorify Christ, he accepted it as wisely appointed, and rejoiced in it. God give us grace, in all our own troubles, to go and do likewise.

CHAPTER 10

God's Wisdom and Ours

I

When the old Reformed theologians dealt with the attributes of God, they used to classify them in two groups: *incommunicable* and *communicable*.

In the first group, they put those qualities which highlight God's transcendence and show how vastly different a being He is from us, His creatures. The usual list was — God's *independence* (self-existence and self-sufficiency); His *immutability* (entire freedom from change, leading to entire consistency in action); His *infinity* (freedom from all limits of time and space: i.e., His eternity and omnipresence); and His *simplicity* (the fact that there are in Him no elements that can conflict, so that, unlike man, He cannot be torn different ways by divergent thoughts and desires). The theologians called these qualities *incommunicable* because they are characteristic of God alone; man, just because he is man and not God, does not and cannot share any of them.

In the second group, the theologians lumped together qualities like God's spirituality, freedom, and omnipotence, along with all His moral attributes — goodness, truth, holiness, righteousness, etc. What was the principle of classification here? It was this — that when God made man, he *communicated* to him qualities corresponding to all these. This is what the Bible means when it tells us that God made man in His own image (Gen. 1:26 f.) — namely, that God made man a free spiritual being, a responsible moral agent with powers of choice and action, able to commune with Him and respond to Him, and by nature good, truthful, holy, upright (cf. Eccles. 7:29): in a word, *godly*.

The moral qualities which belonged to the divine image were

lost at the Fall; God's image in man has been universally defaced, for all mankind has in one way or another lapsed into ungodliness. But the Bible tells us that now, in fulfilment of His plan of redemption, God is at work in Christian believers to repair His ruined image by communicating these qualities to them afresh. This is what Scripture means when it says that Christians are being renewed in the image of Christ (2 Cor. 3:18) and of God (Col 3:10).

Among these communicable attributes, the theologians put wisdom. As God is wise in Himself, so He imparts wisdom to men.

The Bible has a great deal to say about the divine gift of wisdom. The first nine chapters of the book of Proverbs are a single sustained exhortation to seek this gift. 'Wisdom is the principal thing; therefore get wisdom: and with all thy getting get understanding . . . Take fast hold of instruction; let her not go; keep her; for she is thy life' (Prov. 3:7,13). Wisdom is personified and made to speak in her own cause, 'Blessed is the man that heareth me, watching daily at my gates, waiting at the posts of my doors. For whoso findeth me findeth life, and shall obtain favour of the LORD. But he that sinneth against me wrongeth his own soul: all they that hate me love death' (Prov. 8: 34 ff.).

As a hostess, wisdom summons the needy to her banquet, 'Whoso is simple, let him turn in hither' (Prov. 9:4). The emphasis throughout is upon God's readiness to give wisdom (pictured as wisdom's readiness to give herself) to all who desire the gift, and will take the steps necessary to obtain it. Similar emphases appear in the New Testament. Wisdom is required of Christians ('walk . . . not as fools, but as wise . . . be ye not unwise, but understanding what the will of the Lord is', Eph. 5:15ff.; 'walk in wisdom toward them that are without . . .', Col. 4:5). Prayer is made that wisdom may be supplied to them ('that ye might be filled with the knowledge of his will in all wisdom . . .', Col. 1:9). And James in God's name makes a promise, 'If any of you lack wisdom, let him ask of God . . . and it shall be given him' (Jas. 1:5).

Whence comes wisdom? What steps must a man take to lay hold of this gift? There are two prerequisites, according to Scripture. First, one must learn to *reverence God*. 'The fear of the Lord is the beginning of wisdom' (Ps. 111:10; Prov. 9:10; cf. Job 28:28; Prov. 1:7; 15:33). Not till we have become humble and teachable, standing in awe of God's holiness and sovereignty ('the great and terrible God', Neh. 1:5; cf. 4:14; 9:32; Deut. 7:21; 10:17; Ps. 99:3; Jer. 20:11), acknowledging our own littleness, distrusting our own thoughts, and willing to have our minds turned upside down, can divine wisdom become ours. It is to be feared that many Christians spend all their lives in too unhumbled and conceited a frame of mind ever to gain wisdom from God at all. Not for nothing does Scripture say, *'with the lowly* is wisdom' (Prov. 11:2).

Then, second, one must learn to *receive God's word*. Wisdom is divinely wrought in those, and those only, who apply themselves to God's revelation. 'Thou *through thy commandments* hast made me wiser than mine enemies,' declares the psalmist, 'I have more understanding than all my teachers:' why?—'for *thy testimonies are my meditation*' (Ps. 119:99 f.). So Paul admonishes the Colossians: 'Let *the word of Christ* dwell in you richly in all wisdom' (Col 3:16). How are we men of the twentieth century to do this? By soaking ourselves in the Scriptures, which, as Paul told Timothy (and he had in mind the Old Testament alone!), 'are able to make thee *wise* unto salvation' through faith in Christ, and to perfect the man of God for 'all good works' (2 Tim. 3:15–17).

Again, it is to be feared that many today who profess to be Christ's never learn wisdom, through failure to attend sufficiently to God's written word. Cranmer's Prayer Book lectionary (which all Anglicans are meant to follow) will take one through the Old Testament once, and the New Testament twice, every year. William Gouge, the Puritan, read fifteen chapters regularly each day. The late Archdeacon T. C. Hammond used to read right through the Bible once a quarter. How long is it since you read right through the Bible? Do you spend as much time with the Bible each day as you do even with the newspaper? What fools some of us are!—and we remain fools all our lives, simply because we will not take the trouble to do what has to be done to receive the wisdom which is God's free gift.

II

But what sort of thing is God's gift of wisdom? What effect does it have on a man?

Here many go wrong. We can make clear the nature of their mistake by an illustration.

If you stand at the end of a platform on York station, you can watch a constant succession of engine and train movements which, if you are a railway enthusiast, will greatly fascinate you. But you will only be able to form a very rough and general idea of the overall plan in terms of which all these movements are being determined (the operational pattern set out in the working time-table, modified if need be on a minute-to-minute basis according to the actual running of the trains). If, however, you are privileged enough to be taken by one of the high-ups into the magnificent electrical signal-box that lies athwart platforms 7 and 8, you will see on the longest wall a diagram of the entire track layout for five miles on either side of the station, with little glow-worm lights moving or stationary on the different tracks to show the signalmen at a glance exactly where every engine and train is. At once you will be able to look at the whole situation through the eyes of the men who control it: you will see from the diagram why it was that this train had to be signalled to a halt, and that one diverted from its normal running line, and that one parked temporarily in a siding. The why and the wherefore of all these movements becomes plain, once you can see the overall position.

Now, the mistake that is commonly made is to suppose that this is an illustration of what God does when He bestows wisdom: to suppose, in other words, that the gift of wisdom consists in a deepened insight into the providential meaning and purpose of events going on around us, an ability to see why God has done what He has done in a particular case, and what He is going to do next. People feel that if they were really walking close to God, so that He could impart wisdom to them freely, then they would, so to speak, find themselves in the signal-box; they would discern the real purpose of everything that happened to them, and it would be clear to them every moment how God was making all things work together for good. Such people spend much time poring over the book of providence, wondering why God should have allowed this or that to take place, whether they should take it as a sign to stop doing one thing and start doing another, or what they should deduce from it. If they end up baffled, they put it down to their own lack of spirituality.

Christians suffering from depression, physical, mental, or spiritual (note, these are three different things!) may drive themselves almost crazy with this kind of futile enquiry. For it *is* futile: make no mistake about that. It is true that when God has given us guidance by application of principles He will on occasion confirm it to us by unusual providences, which we recognise at once as corroborative signs. But this is quite a different thing from trying to read a message about God's secret purposes out of every unusual thing that happens to us. So far from the gift of wisdom consisting in the power to do this, the gift actually presupposes our conscious inability to do it; as we shall see in a moment.

III

We ask again: what does it mean for God to give us wisdom?
What kind of a gift is it?

If another transport illustration may be permitted, it is like
being taught to drive. What matters in driving is the speed and
appropriateness of your reactions to things, and the soundness of
your judgment as to what scope a situation gives you. You do not
ask yourself why the road should narrow or screw itself into a dog-
leg wiggle just where it does, nor why that van should be parked
where it is, nor why the lady (or gentleman) in front should hug
the crown of the road so lovingly; you simply try to see and do
the right thing in the actual situation that presents itself. The
effect of divine wisdom is to enable you and me to do just that in
the actual situations of everyday life.

To drive well, you have to keep your eyes skinned to notice
exactly what is in front of you. To live wisely, you have to be clear-
sighted and realistic—ruthlessly so—in looking at life as it is.
Wisdom will not go with comforting illusions, false sentiment, or
the use of rose-coloured spectacles. Most of us live in a dream
world, with our heads in the clouds and our feet off the ground;
we never see the world, and our lives in it, as they really are. This
deep-seated, sin-bred unrealism is one reason why there is so
little wisdom among us — even the soundest and most orthodox of
us. It takes more than sound doctrine to cure us of unrealism.
There is, however, one book in Scripture that is expressly designed
to turn us into realists: and that is the book of Ecclesiastes. We
need to pay more heed to its message than we commonly do. Let
us look at that message for a moment now.

IV

'Ecclesiastes' (the Greek equivalent of the Hebrew title, *Qoheleth*)
means simply 'the preacher'; and the book is a sermon, with a
text ('vanity of vanities . . .' 1:2; 12:8), an exposition of its theme
(chaps. 1–10), and an application (chaps. 11–12:7). Much of the
exposition is autobiographical. *Qoheleth* identifies himself as 'the
son of David, king in Jerusalem' (1:1). Whether this means that
Solomon himself was the preacher, or that the preacher put his
sermon into Solomon's mouth as a didactic device, as scholars so
conservative as Hengstenberg and E. J. Young have argued, need
not concern us. The sermon is certainly Solomonic in the sense
that it teaches lessons which Solomon had unique opportunities to
learn.

'Vanity of vanities, saith the preacher, vanity of vanities; all is

93

vanity.' In what spirit, and for what purpose, does the preacher announce this text? Is it the confession of an embittered cynic, 'a selfish and callous old man of the world who found at the end nothing but a dire disillusionment' (W. H. Elliot), now seeking to share with us his sense of the cheapness and nastiness of life? Or is he speaking as an evangelist, trying to bring home to the unbeliever the impossibility of finding happiness 'under the sun' apart from God? The answer is neither, though the second suggestion is not so wide of the mark as the first.

The author speaks as a mature teacher giving a young disciple the fruits of his own long experience and reflection (11:9; 12:1, 12). He wants to lead this young believer into true wisdom, and to keep him from falling into the 'York-signal-box' mistake. Apparently the young man (like many since) was inclined to equate wisdom with wide knowledge, and to suppose that one gains wisdom simply by assiduous bookwork (12:12). Clearly, he took it for granted that wisdom, when he gained it, would tell him the reasons for God's various doings in the ordinary course of providence. What the preacher wants to show him is that the real basis of wisdom is a frank acknowledgment that this world's course is enigmatic, that much of what happens is quite inexplicable to us, and that most occurrences 'under the sun' bear no outward sign of a rational, moral God ordering them at all. As the sermon itself shows, the text is intended as a warning against the misconceived quest for understanding: for it states the despairing conclusion to which this quest, if honestly and realistically pursued, must at length lead. We may formulate the message of the sermon as follows:

Look (says the preacher) at the sort of world we live in. Take off your rose-coloured spectacles, rub your eyes, and look at it long and hard. What do you see? You see life's background set by aimlessly recurring cycles in nature (1:4 ff.). You see its shape fixed by times and circumstances over which we have no control (3: 1 ff.; 9:11 f.). You see death coming to everyone sooner or later, but coming haphazard; its coming bears no relation to good or ill desert (7:15; 8:8). Men die like beasts (3: 19 f.), good men like bad, wise men like fools (2:14, 17; 9:2 f.). You see evil running rampant (3:16; 4:1; 5:8; 8:11; 9:3); rotters get on, good men don't (8:14). Seeing all this, you realise that God's ordering of events is inscrutable; much as you want to make it out, you cannot do so (3:11; 7:13f.; 8:17 RV; 11:5). The harder you try to understand the divine purpose in the ordinary providential course of events, the more obsessed and oppressed you grow with the apparent aimlessness of everything, and the more you are tempted to conclude that life really is as pointless as it looks.

But once you conclude that there really is no rhyme or reason in things, what 'profit' — value, gain, point, purpose — can you find henceforth in any sort of constructive endeavour? (1:3; 2:11, 22; 3:9; 5:16). If life is senseless, then it is valueless; and in that case, what use is it working to create things, to build a business, to make money, even to seek wisdom — for none of this can do you any obvious good (2:15 f., 22 f.; 5:11); it will only make you an object of envy (4:4); you can't take any of it with you (2: 18 ff.; 4:8; 5:15 f.); and what you leave behind will probably be mismanaged after you have gone (2:19). What point is there, then, in sweating and toiling at anything? Must not all man's work be judged 'vanity (emptiness, frustration) and a striving after wind' (1:14 RV)? — activity that we cannot justify as being either significant in itself or worth while to us? It is to this pessimistic conclusion, says the preacher, that optimistic expectations of finding the divine purpose of everything will ultimately lead you (cf. 1:17 f.). And of course he is right. For the world we live in is in fact the sort of place that he has described. The God who rules it hides Himself. Rarely does this world look as if a beneficent Providence were running it. Rarely does it appear that there is a rational power behind it at all. Often and often what is worthless survives, while what is valuable perishes. Be realistic, says the preacher; face these facts; see life as it is. You will have no true wisdom till you do.

Many of us need this admonition. For not only are we caught up with the 'York-signal-box' conception, or misconception, of what wisdom is; we feel that, for the honour of God (and also, though we do not say this, for the sake of our own reputation as spiritual Christians), it is necessary for us to claim that we are, so to speak, already in the signal-box, here and now enjoying inside information as to the why and wherefore of God's doings. This comforting pretence becomes part of us: we feel sure that God has enabled us to understand all His ways with us and our circle thus far, and we take it for granted that we shall be able to see at once the reason for anything that may happen to us in the future. And then something very painful and quite inexplicable comes along, and our cheerful illusion of being in God's secret councils is shattered. Our pride is wounded; we feel that God has slighted us; and unless at this point we repent, and humble ourselves very thoroughly for our former presumption, our whole subsequent spiritual life may be blighted.

Among the seven deadly sins of medieval lore was sloth (accidie)

—a state of hard-bitten, joyless apathy of spirit. There is a lot of it around today in Christian circles; the symptoms are personal spiritual inertia combined with critical cynicism about the churches and supercilious resentment of other Christians' initiative and enterprise. Behind this morbid and deadening condition often lies the wounded pride of one who thought he knew all about the ways of God in providence and then was made to learn by bitter and bewildering experience that he didn't. This is what happens when we do not heed the message of Ecclesiastes. For the truth is that God in His wisdom, to make and keep us humble and to teach us to walk by faith, has hidden from us almost everything that we should like to know about the providential purposes which He is working out in the churches and in our own lives. 'As thou knowest not what is the way of the wind, nor how the bones do grow in the womb of her that is with child; even so thou knowest not the work of God who doeth all' (11: 5 RV).

But what, in that case, is wisdom? The preacher has helped us to see what it is not; does he give us any guidance as to what it is? Indeed he does, in outline at any rate. 'Fear God, and keep his commandments' (12:13); trust and obey Him, reverence Him, worship Him, be humble before Him, and never say more than you mean and will stand to when you pray to Him (5: 1–7); do good (3:12); remember that God will some day take account of you (11:9; 12:14), so eschew, even in secret, things of which you will be ashamed when they come to light at God's assizes (12:14). Live in the present, and enjoy it thoroughly (7:14; 9:7 ff.; 11:9 f.); present pleasures are God's good gifts. Though Ecclesiastes condemns flippancy (cf. 7:4–6), he clearly has no time for the super-spirituality which is too proud, or 'pi', ever to laugh and have fun. Seek grace to work hard at whatever life calls you to do (9:10), and enjoy your work as you do it (2:24; 3:12 f.; 5:18 ff.; 8:15). Leave to God its issues; let Him measure its ultimate worth; your part is to use all the good sense and enterprise at your command in exploiting the opportunities that lie before you (11:1–6).

This is the way of wisdom. Clearly, it is just one facet of the life of faith. For what underlies and sustains it? Why, the conviction that the inscrutable God of providence is the wise and gracious God of creation and redemption. We can be sure that the God who made this marvellously complex world-order, and who compassed the great redemption from Egypt, and who later compassed the even greater redemption from sin and Satan, knows what He is doing, and 'doeth all things well', even if for the moment He hides His hand. We can trust Him and rejoice in Him, even when we cannot discern His path. Thus the preacher's way of wisdom boils down to what was expressed by Richard Baxter:

> *Ye saints, who toil below,*
> *Adore your heavenly King,*
> *And onward as ye go*
> *Some joyful anthem sing.*
> *Take what He gives,*
> *And praise Him still*
> *Through good and ill*
> *Who ever lives.*

V

Such, then, is the wisdom with which God makes us wise. And our analysis of it discloses to us still further the wisdom of the God who gives it. We have said that wisdom consists in choosing the best means to the best end. God's work of giving wisdom is a means to His chosen end of restoring and perfecting the relationship between Himself and men for which He made them. For what is this wisdom that He gives? As we have seen, it is not a sharing in all His knowledge, but a disposition to confess that He is wise, and to cleave to Him and live for Him in the light of His word through thick and thin.

Thus the effect of His gift of wisdom is to make us more humble, more joyful, more godly, more quick-sighted as to His will, more resolute in the doing of it and less troubled (not less sensitive, but less bewildered) than we were at the dark and painful things of which our life in this fallen world is full. The New Testament tells us that the fruit of wisdom is Christlikeness—peace, and humility, and love (Jas. 3:17)—and the root of it is faith in Christ (1 Cor. 3:18; cf. 1 Tim. 3:15) as the manifested wisdom of God (1 Cor. 1:24, 30). Thus, the kind of wisdom that God waits to give to those who ask Him, is a wisdom that will bind us to Himself, a wisdom that will find expression in a spirit of faith and a life of faithfulness.

Let us see to it, then, that our own quest for wisdom takes the form of a quest for these things, and that we do not frustrate the wise purpose of God by neglecting faith and faithfulness in order to pursue a kind of knowledge which in this world it is not given to us to have.

CHAPTER 11

Thy Word is Truth

I

Two facts about the Triune Jehovah are assumed, if not actually stated, in every single biblical passage. The first is that He is *king* — absolute monarch of the universe, ordering all its affairs, working out His will in all that happens within it. The second fact is that He *speaks* — uttering words that express His will in order to cause it to be done. The first theme, that of God's *rule*, has been touched on in earlier chapters. It is the second theme, that of God's *word*, that concerns us now. The study of the second theme will in fact advance our understanding of the first theme, for just as God's relations with His world have to be understood in terms of His sovereignty, so His sovereignty is to be understood in terms of what the Bible tells us about His word.

An absolute ruler, such as all kings were in the ancient world, will in the ordinary course of things speak regularly on two levels, and for two purposes. On the one hand, he will enact regulations and laws which directly determine the environment — judicial, fiscal, cultural — within which his subjects must henceforth live. On the other hand, he will make public speeches, in order to establish, as far as possible, a personal link between himself and his subjects, and to evoke from them the maximum of support and co-operation in the things he is doing. The Bible pictures the word of God as having a similar twofold character. God is the king; we, His creatures, are His subjects. His word relates both to things around us and to us directly: God speaks both to determine our environment and to engage our minds and hearts.

In the former connection, which is the sphere of creation and providence, God's word takes the form of a sovereign fiat—'let there be . . .' In the latter connection, the sphere in which God's word is addressed to us personally, the word takes the form of royal *torah* (the Hebrew word translated 'law' in our Old Testament, which actually denotes 'instruction' in all its manifold forms). *Torah* from God the king has a threefold character: some of it is *law* (in the narrow sense of commands, or prohibitions, with sanctions attached); some of it is *promise* (favourable or unfavourable, conditional or unconditional); some of it is *testimony* (information given by God about Himself, and men, and their respective acts, purposes, natures, and prospects).

The word which God addresses directly to us is (like a royal speech, only more so) an instrument, not only of government, but also of fellowship. For, though God is a great king, it is not His wish to live at a distance from His subjects. Rather the reverse: He made us with the intention that He and we might walk together for ever in a love-relationship. But such a relationship can only exist when the parties involved know something of each other. God, our Maker, knows all about us before we say anything (Ps. 139:1-4); but we can know nothing about Him unless He tells us. Here, therefore, is a further reason why God speaks to us: not only to move us to do what He wants, but to enable us to know Him so that we may love Him. Therefore God sends His word to us in the character of both information and invitation. It comes to woo us as well as to instruct us; it not merely puts us in the picture of what God has done and is doing, but also calls us into personal communion with the loving Lord Himself.

II

We meet the word of God in its various relations in the first three chapters of the Bible. Look first at the story of creation in Genesis 1. Part of the purpose of this chapter is to assure us that every item in our natural environment has been set there by God. The opening verse states the theme which the rest of the chapter is to expound—'In the beginning God created the heaven and the earth.' The second verse pictures the state of affairs in terms of which the detailed analysis of God's work is to be given: it is a state in which the earth was lying waste, empty of life, dark, and completely waterlogged. Then verse 3 tells us how amid this chaos and sterility God spoke. 'And God said, Let there be light.' What happened? Immediately 'there was light'. Seven times more (verses 6, 9, 11, 14, 20, 24, 26) God's creative word, 'let there be . . .', was spoken, and step by step things sprang into being and order. Day and night (verse 5), sky and sea (verse 6), sea and land (verse 9), were separated out; green vegetation (verse 12), heavenly bodies (verse 14), fish and fowl (verse 20), insects and animals (verse 24), and finally man himself (verse 26), made their appearance. All was done by the word of God (cf. Ps. 33: 6, 9; Heb. 11:3; 2 Peter 3: 5).

But now the story carries us on a further stage. God speaks to the man and woman whom He has made. 'God said *unto them . . .*' (verse 28). Here is God addressing man directly; thus fellowship between God and man is inaugurated. Note the categories into which God's utterances to man in the rest of the story fall. God's first word to Adam and Eve is a word of *command*, summoning them to fulfil mankind's vocation of ruling the created order. ('Be fruitful . . . and have dominion . . .', verse 28.) Then follows a word of *testimony* ('Behold . . .', verse 29) in which God explains that greenstuff, crops, and fruit, have been made for man and animals to eat. Next we meet a *prohibition*, with sanction appended: 'of the tree of the knowledge of good and evil, thou shalt not eat of it: for in the day that thou eatest thereof thou shalt surely die' (2:17). Finally, after the Fall, God comes near to Adam and Eve and speaks to them again, and this time His words are words of *promise*, both favourable and unfavourable—for while He undertakes, on the one hand, that the woman's seed shall bruise the serpent's head, on the other hand He ordains for Eve grief in childbirth, for Adam frustrating labour, and for both certain death (verses 15–20).

Here, within the compass of these three short chapters, we see the word of God in all the relations in which it stands to the world, and to man within it—on the one hand, fixing man's circumstances and environment, on the other, commanding man's obedience, inviting his trust, and opening to him the mind of his Maker. The rest of the Bible sets before us many new utterances of God, but no further categories of relationship between God's word and His creatures. Instead, the presentation of the word of God in Genesis 1–3 is reiterated and confirmed.

Thus, on the one hand, the whole Bible insists that all circumstances and events in the world are determined by the word of God, the Creator's omnipotent 'Let there be . . .' Scripture describes all that happens as the fulfilling of God's word, from changes in the weather (Ps. 147: 15–18; 148: 8) to the rise and fall of nations. The fact that the word of God really determines world events was the first lesson that God taught Jeremiah when He called him to be a prophet. 'See,' God told him, 'I have this day set thee over the kingdoms, to root out, and to pull down, and to destroy, and to throw down, to build, and to plant' (Jer. 1:10).

But how could this be? Jeremiah's call was not to be a statesman or a world potentate, but to be a prophet, God's messenger-boy (verse 7). How could a man with no official position, whose only job was to talk, be described as the God-appointed ruler of the nations? Why, simply because he had the word of the Lord in his mouth (verse 9): and any word that God gave him to speak about the destiny of nations would certainly be fulfilled. To fix this in Jeremiah's mind, God gave him his first vision. 'Jeremiah, what do you see?' . . . 'A rod of almond' *(shaqed)* . . . 'You have seen well, for I am watching *(shoqed)* over my word to perform it' (Jer. 1: 11 f., RSV).

God through Isaiah proclaims the same truth in this form: 'As the rain cometh down, and the snow from heaven, and returneth not thither, but watereth the earth, and maketh it bring forth and bud . . . so shall my word be that goeth forth out of my mouth: it shall not return unto me void, but it shall accomplish that which I please . . .' (Isa. 55: 10 f.). The whole Bible maintains this insistence that God's word is His executive instrument in all human affairs. Of Him, as of no one else, it is true that what He says *goes*. It is in truth the word of God that rules the world, and that fixes our fortunes for us.

And then, on the other hand, the Bible consistently presents the word of God as coming directly to us in the threefold character in which it was spoken in the garden of Eden. Sometimes it comes as *law* — as at Sinai, and in many sermons of the prophets, and in much of Christ's teaching, and in the evangelical command to repent (Acts 17:30) and believe on the Lord Jesus Christ (1 John 3:23). Sometimes it comes as *promise* — as in the promise of posterity, and the covenant promise, given to Abraham (Gen. 15:5; 17:1 ff.), the promise of redemption from Egypt (Exod. 3:7 ff.), the promises of the Messiah (cf. Isa. 9:6 f., 11:1 f.) and of the kingdom of God (Dan. 2:44 f., 7:13 f.), and the New Testament promises of justification, resurrection, and glorification, for believers.

Sometimes, again, it comes as *testimony* — divine instruction concerning the facts of faith and the principles of piety, in the form of historical narration, theological argument, psalmody, and wisdom. Always it is stressed that the claim of the word of God upon us is absolute: the word is to be received, trusted, and obeyed, because it is the word of God the king. The essence of impiety is the proud wilfulness of 'this evil people, which refuse to hear my words' (Jer. 13:10). The mark of true humility and godliness, on the other hand, is that a man 'trembleth at my word' Isa. 66: 2).

III

But the claim of the word of God upon us does not depend merely upon our relationship to Him, as creatures and subjects. We are to believe and obey it, not only because He tells us to, but also, and primarily, because it is a true word. Its author is the 'God of truth' (Ps. 31:5; Isa. 65:16), 'abundant in . . . truth' (Exod. 34:6); His 'truth reacheth unto the clouds' (Ps. 108:4; cf. 57:10), i.e. is universal and limitless. Therefore His 'word is truth' (John 17:17). 'Thy word is true from the beginning' (Ps. 119:160). 'Thou art God, and thy words are true' (2 Sam. 7:28, RSV).

Truth in the Bible is a quality of persons primarily, and of propositions only secondarily: it means stability, reliability, firmness, trustworthiness, the quality of a person who is entirely self-consistent, sincere, realistic, and undeceived. God is such a person: truth, in this sense, is His nature, and He has not got it in Him to be anything else. That is why He cannot lie (Titus 1:2; cf. Num. 23:19; 1 Sam. 15:29; Heb. 6:18). That is why His words to us are true, and cannot be other than true. They are the index of reality: they show us things as they really are, and as they will be for us in the future according to whether we heed God's words to us or not.

Let us work this out a little, in two connections.

1 *God's commands are true.*

'All thy commandments are truth' (Ps. 119:151). Why are they so described? First, because they have stability and permanence as setting forth what God wants to see in human lives in every age; second, because they tell us the unchanging truth about our own nature. For this is part of the purpose of God's law: it gives us a working definition of true humanity. It shows us what man was made to be, and teaches us how to be truly human, and warns us against moral self-destruction. This is a matter of great importance, and one which calls for much consideration at the present time.

We are familiar with the thought that our bodies are like machines, needing the right routine of food, rest, and exercise if they are to run efficiently, and liable, if filled up with the wrong fuel—alcohol, drugs, poison—to lose their power of healthy functioning and ultimately to 'seize up' entirely in physical death. What we are, perhaps, slower to grasp is that God wishes us to think of our souls in a similar way. As rational persons, we were made to bear God's moral image — that is, our souls were made to 'run' on the practice of worship, law-keeping, truthfulness, honesty, discipline, self-control, and service to God and our fellows. If we abandon these practices, not only do we incur guilt before God; we also progressively destroy our own souls. Conscience atrophies, the sense of shame dries up, one's capacity for truthfulness, loyalty, and honesty is eaten away, one's character disintegrates. One not only becomes desperately miserable; one is steadily being de-humanised. This is one aspect of spiritual death. Richard Baxter was right to formulate the alternatives as 'A Saint — or a Brute': that, ultimately, is the only choice, and everyone, sooner or later, consciously or unconsciously opts for one or the other. Nowadays, some will maintain, in the name of Humanism, that the 'Puritan' sexual morality of the Bible is inimical to the attainment of true human maturity, and that a little more license makes for richer living. Of this ideology we would only say that the proper name for it is not Humanism, but Brutism. Sexual laxity does not make you more of a man, but less so; it brutalises you, and tears your soul to pieces. The same is true wherever any of God's commandments are disregarded. We are only living truly human lives just so far as we are labouring to keep God's commandments; no further.

2 *God's promises are true:* for God keeps them.

'He is faithful that promised' (Heb. 10: 23). The Bible proclaims God's faithfulness in superlative terms. 'Thy faithfulness reacheth unto the clouds' (Ps. 36:5); 'thy faithfulness is unto all generations' (Ps. 119:90); 'great is thy faithfulness' (Lam. 3: 23). How does God's faithfulness show itself? By His unfailing fulfilment of His promises. He is a covenant-keeping God; He never fails those who trust His word. Abraham proved God's faithfulness, waiting through a quarter of a century of old age for the birth of his promised heir, and millions more have proved it since.

In the days when the Bible was universally acknowledged in the churches as 'God's Word written', it was clearly understood that the promises of God recorded in Scripture were the proper, God-given basis for all our life of faith, and that the way to strengthen one's faith was to focus it upon particular promises that spoke to one's condition. The latter-day Puritan, Samuel Clark, in the Introduction to his *Scripture Promises; or, the Christian's Inheritance, A collection of the Promises of Scripture under their proper Heads,* wrote as follows:

A fixed, constant attention to the promises, and a firm belief of them, would prevent solicitude and anxiety about the concerns of this life. It would keep the mind quiet and composed in every change, and support and keep up our sinking spirits under the several troubles of life . . . Christians deprive themselves of their most solid comforts by their unbelief and forgetfulness of God's promises. For there is no extremity so great, but there are promises suitable to it, and abundantly sufficient for our relief in it.

A thorough acquaintance with the promises would be of the greatest advantage in prayer. With what comfort may the Christian address himself to God in Christ when he considers the repeated assurances that his prayers shall be heard! With how much satisfaction may he offer up the several desires of his heart when he reflects upon the texts wherein those very mercies are promised! And with what fervour of spirit and strength of faith may he enforce his prayers, by pleading the several gracious promises which are expressly to his case!

These things were understood once; but liberal theology, with its refusal to identify the written Scriptures with the word of God, has largely robbed us of the habit of meditating on the promises, and basing our prayers on the promises, and venturing in faith in our ordinary daily life just as far as the promises will take us. People sneer today at the promise-boxes which our grandparents used, but this attitude is not a wise one; the promise-boxes may have been open to abuse, but the approach to Scripture, and to prayer, which they expressed was right. It is something we have lost, and need to recover.

IV

What is a Christian? He can be described from many angles, but from what we have said it is clear that we can cover everything by saying: he is a man who acknowledges and lives under the word of God. He submits without reserve to the word of God written in 'the Scripture of truth' (Dan. 10:21), believing the teaching, trusting the promises, following the commands. His eyes are to the God of the Bible as his Father, and the Christ of the Bible as his Saviour. He will tell you, if you ask him, that the word of God has both convinced him of sin and assured him of forgiveness. His conscience, like Luther's, is captive to the word of God, and he aspires, like the psalmist, to have his whole life brought into line with it. 'O that my ways were directed to keep thy statutes!' 'O let me not wander from thy commandments.' 'Teach me thy statutes. Make me to understand the way of thy precepts.' 'Incline my heart unto thy testimonies.' 'Let my heart be sound in thy statutes.'

(Ps. 119:5, 10, 26 f., 36, 80.) The promises are before him as he prays, and the precepts are before him as he moves among men. He knows that in addition to the word of God spoken directly to him in the Scriptures, God's word has also gone forth to create, and control, and order things around him; but since the Scriptures tell him that all things work together for his good, the thought of God ordering his circumstances brings him only joy. He is an independent fellow, for he uses the word of God as a touchstone by which to test the various views that are put to him, and he will not touch anything which he is not sure that Scripture sanctions.

Why does this description fit so few of us who profess to be Christians in these days? You will find it profitable to ask your conscience, and let it tell you.

CHAPTER 12

The Love of God

I

St. John's twice-repeated statement, 'God is love' (1 John 4:8, 16), is one of the most tremendous utterances in the Bible—and also one of the most misunderstood. False ideas have grown up round it like a hedge of thorns, hiding its real meaning from view, and it is no small task cutting through this tangle of mental undergrowth. Yet the hard thought involved is more than repaid when the true sense of these texts comes home to the Christian soul. Those who climb Ben Nevis do not complain of their labour once they see the view from the top!

Happy indeed are those who can say, as John says in the sentence preceding the second 'God is love', 'we have known and believed the love that God hath to us' (verse 16). To know God's love is indeed heaven on earth. And the New Testament sets forth this knowledge, not as the privilege of a favoured few, but as a normal part of ordinary Christian experience, something to which only the spiritually unhealthy or malformed will be strangers. When Paul says, 'the love of God is shed abroad in our hearts by the Holy Ghost which is given unto us' (Rom. 5:5), he means, not love for God, as Augustine thought, but knowledge of God's love for us. And though he had never met the Roman Christians to whom he was writing, he took it for granted that the statement would be as true of them as it was of him.

Three points in Paul's words deserve comment. First, notice the verb 'shed abroad'. It means literally 'poured (or, tipped) out'. It is the word used of the 'outpouring' of the Spirit Himself in Acts 2:17 f., 33; 10:45; Titus 3:6. It suggests a free flow and a large quantity—in fact, an inundation. Hence the rendering of the

NEB, 'God's love has *flooded* our inmost heart.' Paul is not talking of faint and fitful impressions, but of deep and overwhelming ones.

Then, second, notice the tense of the verb. It is in the perfect, which implies a settled state consequent upon a completed action. The thought is that knowledge of the love of God, having flooded our hearts, *fills them now*, just as a valley once flooded remains full of water. Paul assumes that all his readers, like himself, will be living in the enjoyment of a strong and abiding sense of God's love for them.

Third, notice that the instilling of this knowledge is described as part of the regular ministry of the Spirit to those who receive Him—to all, that is, who are born again, all who are true believers. One could wish that this aspect of His ministry was prized more highly than it is at the present time. With a perversity as pathetic as it is impoverishing, we have become preoccupied today with the extraordinary, sporadic, non-universal ministries of the Spirit to the neglect of the ordinary, general ones. Thus, we show a great deal more interest in the gifts of healing and tongues—gifts of which, as Paul pointed out, not all Christians are meant to partake anyway (1 Cor. 12: 28–30)—than in the Spirit's ordinary work of giving peace, joy, hope, and love, through the shedding abroad in our hearts of knowledge of the love of God. Yet the latter is much more important than the former. To the Corinthians, who had taken it for granted that the more tongues the merrier, and the godlier too, Paul had to insist that without love—sanctification, Christ-likeness—tongues were worth precisely nothing (1 Cor.13:1 ff.).

He would undoubtedly see reason to issue a similar caveat today. It will be tragic if the concern for revival that is stirring at the present time in many places gets diverted into the cul-de-sac of a new Corinthianism. The best thing that Paul could desire for the Ephesians in connection with the Spirit was that He might continue towards them the Romans 5:5 ministry with ever-increasing power, leading them deeper and deeper into knowledge of the love of God in Christ. The NEB rendering of Ephesians 3:14 ff. is somewhat free, but brings the sense out well. 'I kneel in prayer to the Father . . . that . . . he may grant you strength and power through his Spirit in your inner being . . . may you be strong to grasp, with all God's people, what is the breadth and length and height and depth of the love of Christ, and to know it, though it is beyond knowledge . . .' Revival means the work of God restoring to a moribund church, in a manner out of the ordinary, those standards of Christian life and experience which the New Testament sets forth as being entirely ordinary; and a right-minded concern for revival will express itself, not in a hankering after tongues (ultimately it is of no importance whether we speak in tongues or not), but rather in a longing that the Spirit may shed God's love abroad in our hearts with greater power. For it is with this (to which deep exercise of soul about sin is often preliminary) that personal revival begins, and by this that revival in the church, once begun, is sustained.

Our aim in this chapter is to show the nature of the divine love which the Spirit sheds abroad. For this purpose we focus attention on John's great assertion that God *is* love: that, in other words, the love which He shows to men, and which Christians know and rejoice in, is a revelation of His own inner being. Our theme will lead us as deep into the mystery of God's nature as man can go, deeper than any of our previous studies have taken us. When we looked at God's wisdom, we saw something of His mind; when we thought of His power, we saw something of His hand and His arm; when we considered His word, we learned about His mouth; but now, contemplating His love, we are to look into His heart. We shall stand on holy ground; we need the grace of reverence, that we may tread it without sin.

II

Two general comments on John's statement will clear the way ahead.

1 *'God is love' is not the complete truth about God so far as the Bible is concerned*. It is not an abstract definition which stands alone, but a summing up, from the believer's standpoint, of what the whole revelation set forth in Scripture tells us about its Author. This statement presupposes all the rest of the biblical witness to God. The God of whom John is speaking is the God who made the world, who judged it by the Flood, who called Abraham and made of him a nation, who chastened His Old Testament people by conquest, captivity, and exile, who sent His Son to save the world, who cast off unbelieving Israel and shortly before John wrote had destroyed Jerusalem, and who would one day judge the world in righteousness. It is this God, says John, who is love. It is perverse to quote John's statement, as some do, as if it called in question the biblical witness to the severity of God's justice. It is not possible to argue that a God who is love cannot also be a God who condemns and punishes the disobedient; for it is precisely of the God who does these very things that John is speaking.

If we are to avoid misunderstanding John's statement, we must take it in conjunction with two other great statements of exactly similar grammatical form which we find elsewhere in his writings, both of them, interestingly enough, deriving directly from Christ Himself. The first comes from John's gospel. It is our Lord's own word to the Samaritan woman, 'God is spirit' (John 4:24, RSV, NEB; 'God is *a* spirit', the more familiar rendering, is incorrect). The second comes from the opening section of this very epistle. John offers it as a summary of 'the message which we heard of him (Jesus), and declare unto you', and it is this, 'God is light' (1 John 1:5). The assertion that God is love has to be interpreted in the light of what these other two statements teach, and it will help us if we glance at them briefly now.

'God is *spirit*.' When our Lord said this, He was seeking to disabuse the Samaritan woman of the idea that there could be only one right place for worship, as if God were locally confined in some way. 'Spirit' contrasts with 'flesh': Christ's point is that while man, being 'flesh', can only be present in one place at a time, God, being 'spirit', is not so limited. God is non-material, non-corporeal, and therefore non-localised. Thus (Christ continues) the true condition of acceptable worship is not that your feet should be standing in either Jerusalem or Samaria, or anywhere else for that matter, but that your heart should be receptive and responsive to His revelation. 'God is spirit, and those who worship him must worship him in spirit and in truth' (RSV).

The first of the Thirty-nine Articles further brings out the meaning of God's 'spirituality' (as the books call it) by the rather odd-sounding assertion that He is 'without body, parts, or passions'. Something very positive is being expressed by these negations. God has no *body*—therefore, as we have just said, He is free from all limitations of space and distance, and is omnipresent. God has no *parts*—this means that His personality and powers and qualities are perfectly integrated, so that nothing in Him ever alters. With Him 'there is no variation or shadow due to change' (James 1:17, RSV). Thus He is free from all limitations of time and natural processes, and remains eternally the same. God has no *passions*—this does not mean that He is unfeeling (impassive), or that there is nothing in Him that corresponds to emotions and affections in us, but that whereas human passions—specially the painful ones, fear, grief, regret, despair—are in a sense passive and involuntary, being called forth and constrained by circumstances not under our control, the corresponding attitudes in God have the nature of deliberate, voluntary choices, and therefore are not of the same order as human passions at all.

So the love of the God who is spirit is no fitful, fluctuating thing, as the love of man is, nor is it a mere impotent longing for things that may never be; it is, rather, a spontaneous determination of God's whole being in an attitude of benevolence and benefaction, an attitude freely chosen and firmly fixed. There are no inconstancies or vicissitudes in the love of the almighty God who is spirit. His love is 'strong as death . . . many waters cannot quench it' (Song, 8:6 f.). Nothing can separate from it those whom it has once embraced (Rom. 8:35–9).

But, we are told, the God who is spirit is also *'light'*. John made this statement against certain professing Christians who had lost touch with moral realities, and were claiming that nothing they did was sin. The force of John's words is brought out by the next clause, 'and in him is no darkness at all'. 'Light' means holiness and purity, as measured by God's law; 'darkness' means moral perversity and unrighteousness, as measured by the same law (cf. 1 John 2:7–11, 3:10). John's point is that only those who 'walk in the light', seeking to be like God in holiness and righteousness of life, and eschewing everything inconsistent with this, enjoy fellowship with the Father and the Son; those who 'walk in darkness', whatever they may claim for themselves, are strangers to this relationship (verse 6 f.).

So the God who is love is first and foremost light, and sentimental ideas of His love as an indulgent, benevolent softness, divorced from moral standards and concerns, must therefore be ruled out from the start. God's love is holy love. The God whom Jesus made known is not a God who is indifferent to moral distinctions, but a God who loves righteousness and hates iniquity, a God whose ideal for His children is that they should be 'perfect, even as your Father in heaven is perfect' (Matt. 5:48). He will not take into His company any person, however orthodox in mind, who will not follow after holiness of life, and those whom He does accept He exposes to drastic discipline, in order that they may attain what they seek. 'Whom the Lord loveth he chasteneth, and scourgeth every son whom he receiveth . . . for our profit, that we might be partakers of his holiness . . . it (chastening) yieldeth the peaceable fruit of righteousness unto them which are exercised thereby' (Heb. 12: 6–11). God's love is stern, for it expresses holiness in the lover and seeks holiness for the beloved. Scripture does not allow us to suppose that because God is love we may look to Him to confer happiness on people who will not seek holiness, or to shield His loved ones from trouble when He knows that they need trouble to further their sanctification.

The Love of God

But now we must make a second, balancing comment.

2 *'God is love' is the complete truth about God so far as the Christian is concerned.* To say 'God *is* light' is to imply that God's holiness finds expression in everything that He says and does. Similarly, the statement 'God *is* love' means that His love finds expression in everything that He says and does. The knowledge that this is so for him personally is the Christian's supreme comfort. As a believer, he finds in the cross of Christ assurance that he, as an individual, is beloved of God; 'the Son of God . . . loved *me*, and gave himself for *me*' (Gal. 2:20). Knowing this, he is able to apply to himself the promise that all things work together for good to them that love God and are called according to His purpose (Rom. 8:28). Not just *some* things, note, but *all* things! Every single thing that happens to him expresses God's love to him, and comes to him for the furthering of God's purpose for him. Thus, so far as he is concerned, God is love to him—holy, omnipotent love—at every moment and in every event of every day's life. Even when he cannot see the why and the wherefore of God's dealings, he knows that there is love in and behind them, and so he can rejoice always, even when, humanly speaking, things are going wrong. He knows that the true story of his life, when known, will prove to be, as the hymn says, 'mercy from first to last'—and he is content.

III

But so far we have merely circumscribed the love of God, showing in general terms how and when it operates, and this is not enough. What essentially is it? we ask. How should we define and analyse it? In answer to this question, the Bible sets forth a conception of God's love which we may formulate as follows:

God's love is *an exercise of His goodness towards individual sinners whereby, having identified Himself with their welfare, He has given His Son to be their Saviour, and now brings them to know and enjoy Him in a covenant relation.*

Let us explain the constituent parts of this definition.

1 God's love is *an exercise of His goodness*. The Bible means by God's goodness His cosmic generosity. Goodness in God, writes Berkhof, is 'that perfection in God which prompts Him to deal bountifully and kindly with all His creatures. It is the affection which the Creator feels towards His sentient creatures as such' (*Systematic Theology*, p. 70, citing Ps. 145:9, 15, 16; cf. Luke 6:26; Acts 14:17). Of this goodness God's love is the supreme and

most glorious manifestation. 'Love, generally,' wrote James Orr, 'is that principle which leads one moral being to desire and delight in another, and reaches its highest form in that personal fellowship in which each lives in the life of the other, and finds his joy in imparting himself to the other, and in receiving back the outflow of that other's affection unto himself' (*Hastings's Dictionary of the Bible*, III, 153). Such is the love of God.

2 God's love is an exercise of His goodness *towards sinners*. As such, it has the nature of *grace* and *mercy*. It is an outgoing of God in kindness which not merely is undeserved, but is actually contrary to desert; for the objects of God's love are rational creatures who have broken God's law, whose nature is corrupt in God's sight, and who merit only condemnation and final banishment from His presence. It is staggering that God should love sinners; yet it is true. God loves creatures who have become unlovely and (one would have thought) unlovable. There was nothing whatever in the objects of His love to call it forth; nothing in man could attract or prompt it. Love among men is awakened by something in the beloved, but the love of God is free, spontaneous, unevoked, uncaused. God loves men because He has chosen to love them — as Charles Wesley put it, 'He hath loved us, He hath loved us, because he would love' (an echo of Deut. 7:8) — and no reason for His love can be given save His own sovereign good pleasure. The Greek and Roman world of New Testament times had never dreamed of such love; its gods were often credited with lusting after women, but never with loving sinners; and the New Testament writers had to introduce what was virtually a new Greek word *agape* to express the love of God as they knew it.

3 God's love is an exercise of His goodness towards *individual* sinners. It is not a vague, diffused good-will towards everyone in general and nobody in particular; rather, as being a function of omniscient almightiness, its nature is to particularise both its objects and its effects. God's purpose of love, formed before creation (cf. Eph. 1:4), involved, first, the choice and selection of those whom He would bless and, second, the appointment of the benefits to be given them and the means whereby these benefits would be procured and enjoyed. All this was made sure from the start. So Paul writes to the Thessalonian Christians, 'we are bound to give thanks to God always for you, brethren *beloved by the Lord*, because God chose you (selection) from the beginning (before creation) to be saved (the appointed end) through sancti-

fication by the Spirit and belief in the truth (the appointed means)' (2 Thess. 2:13, RSV). The exercise of God's love towards individual sinners in time is the execution of a purpose to bless those same individual sinners which He formed in eternity.

4 God's love to sinners involves His *identifying Himself with their welfare*. Such an identification is involved in all love: it is, indeed, the test of whether love is genuine or not. If a father continues cheerful and carefree while his son is getting into trouble, or if a husband remains unmoved when his wife is in distress, we wonder at once how much love there can be in their relationship, for we know that those who truly love are only happy when those whom they love are truly happy also. So it is with God in His love for man.

We have in previous chapters made the point that God's end in all things is His own glory—that He should be manifested, known, admired, adored. This statement is true, but it is incomplete. It needs to be balanced by a recognition that through setting His love on men God has voluntarily bound up His own final happiness with theirs. It is not for nothing that the Bible habitually speaks of God as the loving Father and Husband of His people. It follows from the very nature of these relationships that God's happiness will not be complete till all His beloved ones are finally out of trouble:

> *Till all the ransomed church of God*
> *Be saved, to sin no more.*

God was happy without man before man was made; He would have continued happy had He simply destroyed man after man had sinned; but as it is He has set His love upon particular sinners, and this means that, by His own free voluntary choice, He will not know perfect and unmixed happiness again till He has brought every one of them to heaven. He has in effect resolved that henceforth for all eternity His happiness shall be conditional upon ours. Thus God saves, not only for His glory, but also for His gladness. This goes far to explain why it is that there is joy (God's own joy) in the presence of the angels when a sinner repents (Luke 15:10), and why there will be 'exceeding joy' when God sets us faultless at the last day in His own holy presence (Jude 24). The thought passes understanding and almost beggars belief, but there is no doubt that, according to Scripture, such is the love of God.

5 God's love to sinners was expressed by *the gift of His Son to be their Saviour*. The measure of love is how much it gives, and the measure of the love of God is the gift of His only Son to be made man, and to die for sins, and so to become the one mediator who can bring us to God. No wonder Paul speaks of God's love as 'great', and passing knowledge! (Eph. 2:4, 3:19.) Was there ever such costly munificence? Paul argues that this supreme gift is itself the guarantee of every other: 'He that spared not his own Son, but delivered him up for us all, how shall he not with him also freely give us all things?' (Rom. 8:32). The New Testament writers constantly point to the Cross of Christ as the crowning proof of the reality and boundlessness of God's love. Thus, John goes straight on from his first 'God is love' to say, 'In this was manifested the love of God towards us, because that God sent his only begotten Son into the world, that we might live through him. Herein is love, not that we loved God, but that he loved us, and sent his Son to be the propitiation for our sins' (1 John 4:9 f.). Similarly, in his gospel, 'God so loved the world, that he gave his only begotten Son, that whosoever believeth on him should . . . have everlasting life' (John 3:16). So too Paul writes, 'God commendeth his love towards us, in that, while we were yet sinners, Christ died for us' (Rom. 5:8). And he finds the proof that 'the Son of God . . . loved me' in the fact that He 'gave himself for me' (Gal. 2: 20).

6 God's love to sinners reaches its objective as it *brings them to know and enjoy Him is a covenant relation*. A covenant relation is one in which two parties are permanently pledged to each other in mutual service and dependence (example: marriage). A covenant promise is one by which a covenant relation is set up (example: marriage vows). Biblical religion has the form of a covenant relation with God. The first occasion on which the terms of the relation were made plain was when God showed Himself to Abraham as El Shaddai (God Almighty, God All-sufficient) and formally gave him the covenant promise, 'to be a God unto thee' (Gen. 17:1 ff., 7). All Christians inherit this promise through faith in Christ, as Paul argues in Galatians 3:15 ff. (note verse 29). What does it mean? It is in truth a pantechnicon promise: it contains everything. 'This is the first and fundamental promise,' declared Sibbes, the Puritan, 'indeed, it is the life and soul of all the promises' (*Works*, VI, 8). Brooks, another Puritan, opens it up as follows,

'. . . that is as if he said, You shall have as true an interest in all

my attributes for your good, as they are mine for my own glory
. . . My grace, saith God, shall be yours to pardon you, and my
power shall be yours to protect you, and my wisdom shall be yours
to direct you, and my goodness shall be yours to relieve you, and
my mercy shall be yours to supply you, and my glory shall be
yours to crown you. This is a comprehensive promise, for God
to be our God: it includes all. *Deus meus et omnia* [God is mine,
and everything is mine], said Luther' (*Works*, V, 308).

'This is true love to any one,' said Tillotson, 'to do the best for
him we can.' This is what God does for those He loves—*the best
He can;* and the measure of the best that God can do is omnipotence! Thus faith in Christ introduces us into a relation big with
incalculable blessing, both now and for eternity.

IV

Is it true that God is love to me as a Christian? And does the love
of God mean all that has been said? If so, certain questions arise.

Why do I ever grumble and show discontent and resentment at
the circumstances in which God has placed me?

Why am I ever distrustful, fearful, or depressed?

Why do I ever allow myself to grow cool, formal, and half-
hearted in the service of the God who loves me so?

Why do I ever allow my loyalties to be divided, so that God has
not all my heart?

John wrote that 'God is love' in order to make an ethical point,
'if God so loved us, we also ought to love one another' (1 John
4:11). Could an observer learn from the quality and degree of
love that I show to others—my wife? my husband? my family?
my neighbours? people at church? people at work?—anything at
all about the greatness of God's love to me?

Meditate upon these things. Examine yourself.

CHAPTER 13

The Grace of God

I

It is a commonplace in all the churches to call Christianity a religion of grace. It is a truism of Christian scholarship that grace, far from being an impersonal force, a sort of celestial electricity received like a battery charge by 'plugging in' to the sacraments, is a personal activity, God operating in love manwards. It is repeatedly pointed out in books and sermons that the Greek New Testament word for grace *(charis)*, like that for love *(agape)*, is a wholly Christian usage, expressing a notion of spontaneous self-determined kindness which was previously quite unknown to Graeco-Roman ethics and theology. It is staple diet in the Sunday School that grace is God's Riches At Christ's Expense. And yet, despite these facts, there do not seem to be many in our churches who actually believe in grace.

To be sure, there have always been some who have found the thought of grace so overwhelmingly wonderful that they could never get over it. Grace has become the constant theme of their talk and prayers. They have written hymns about it, some of the finest in the language—and it takes deep feeling to produce a good hymn. They have fought for it, accepting ridicule and loss of privilege if need be as the price of their stand; as Paul fought the Judaizers, so Augustine fought the Pelagians, and the Reformers fought scholasticism, and the spiritual descendants of Paul and Augustine and the Reformers have been fighting Romanising and Pelagianising doctrines ever since. With Paul, their testimony is, 'By the grace of God I am what I am' (1 Cor. 15:10), and their rule of life is, 'I do not frustrate the grace of God' (Gal. 2:21).

But many church people are not like this. They may pay lip-service to the idea of grace, but there they stop. Their conception of grace is not so much debased as non-existent. The thought means nothing to them; it does not touch their experience at all. Talk to them about the church's heating, or last year's accounts, and they are with you at once; but speak to them about the realities to which the word 'grace' points, and their attitude is one of deferential blankness. They do not accuse you of talking nonsense; they do not doubt that your words have meaning; but they feel that, whatever it is that you are talking about, it is beyond them, and the longer they have lived without it the surer they are that at their stage of life they do not really need it.

What is it that hinders so many who profess to believe in grace from really doing so? Why does the theme mean so little even to some who talk about it a great deal? The root of the trouble seems to be misbelief about the basic relations between man and God— misbelief rooted, not just in the mind, but in the heart, at the deeper level of things that we never question, because we always take them for granted. There are four crucial truths in this realm which the doctrine of grace presupposes, and if they are not acknowledged and felt in one's heart, clear faith in God's grace becomes impossible. Unhappily, the spirit of our age is as directly opposed to them as it well could be. It is not to be wondered at, therefore, that faith in grace is a rarity today. The four truths are these:

1 *The moral ill-desert of man.*
Modern man, conscious of his tremendous scientific achievements in recent years, naturally inclines to a high opinion of himself. His views material wealth as in any case more important than moral character, and in the moral realm he is resolutely kind to himself, treating small virtues as compensating for great vices and refusing to take seriously the idea that, morally speaking, there is anything much wrong with him. He tends to dismiss a bad conscience, in himself as in others, as an unhealthy psychological freak, a sign of disease and mental aberration rather than an index of moral reality. For modern man is convinced that, despite all his little peccadilloes—drinking, gambling, reckless driving, 'fiddling', black and white lies, sharp practice in trading, dirty reading, and what have you—he is at heart a thoroughly good fellow. Then, as pagans do (and modern man's heart is pagan—make no mistake about that), he imagines God as a magnified image of himself, and assumes that God shares his own complacency about himself. The thought of himself as a creature fallen from God's image, a rebel

against God's rule, guilty and unclean in God's sight, fit only for God's condemnation, never enters his head.

2 *The retributive justice of God.*

Modern man's way is to turn a blind eye to all wrongdoing as long as he safely can. He tolerates it in others, feeling that there, but for the accident of circumstances, goes he. Parents hesitate to correct their children, and teachers to punish their pupils, and the public puts up with vandalism and anti-social behaviour of all sorts with scarcely a murmur. The accepted maxim seems to be that as long as evil can be ignored, it should be; one should only punish as a last resort, and then only so far as is necessary to prevent the evil having too grievous social consequences. Willingness to tolerate and indulge evil up to the limit is seen as a virtue, while living by fixed principles of right and wrong is censured by some as doubtfully moral. In our pagan way, we take it for granted that God feels as we do. The idea that retribution might be the moral law of God's world, and an expression of His holy character, seems to modern man quite fantastic: those who uphold it find themselves accused of projecting on to God their own pathological impulses of rage and vindictiveness. Yet the Bible insists throughout that this world which God in His goodness has made is a moral world, in which retribution is as basic a fact as breathing. God is the Judge of all the earth, and He will do right, vindicating the innocent, if such there be, but punishing (in the Bible phrase, 'visiting their sins upon') law-breakers (cf. Gen. 18:25). God is not true to Himself unless He punishes sin. And unless one knows and feels the truth of this fact, that wrongdoers have no natural hope of anything from God but retributive judgment, one can never share the biblical faith in divine grace.

3 *The spiritual impotence of man.*

Dale Carnegie's *How to Win Friends and Influence People* has been almost a modern Bible, and a whole technique of business relations has been built up in recent years on the principle of putting the other man in a position where he cannot decently say 'no'. This has confirmed modern man in the faith which has animated pagan religion ever since there was such a thing—namely, the belief that we can repair our own relationship with God, by putting God in a position where He cannot say 'no' any more. Ancient pagans thought to do this by multiplying gifts and sacrifices; modern pagans seek to do it by churchmanship and morality. Conceding that they are not perfect, they still have no doubt that respectability henceforth will guarantee God's acceptance of them in the end, whatever they may have done in the past. But the Bible position is as stated by Toplady:

> *Not the labours of my hands*
> *Can fulfil Thy law's demands.*
> *Could my zeal no respite know,*
> *Could my tears for ever flow,*
> *All for sin could not atone*

—leading to the admission of one's own helplessness, and the conclusion:

> *Thou must save, and Thou alone.*

'By the deeds of the law (i.e., morality and churchmanship) shall no flesh be justified in his sight,' declares Paul (Romans 3:20). To mend our own relationship with God, regaining God's favour after having once lost it, is beyond the power of any one of us. And one must see and bow to this before one can share the biblical faith in God's grace.

4 *The sovereign freedom of God.*

Ancient paganism thought of each god as bound to his worshippers by bonds of self-interest, because he depended on their service and gifts for his welfare. Modern paganism has at the back of its mind a similar feeling that God is somehow obliged to love and help us, little though we deserve it. This was the feeling voiced by the French freethinker who died muttering 'God will forgive—that's his *job (c'est son métier)*'. But this feeling is not well founded. The God of the Bible does not depend on His human creatures for His well-being (see Psalm 50:8–13; Acts 17:25), nor, now that we have sinned, is He bound to show us favour. We can only claim from Him justice—and justice, for us, means certain condemnation. God does not owe it to anyone to stop justice taking its course. He is not obliged to pity and pardon; if He does so it is an act done, as we say, 'of His own free will', and nobody forces His hand. 'It does not depend on man's will or effort, but on God's mercy' (Romans 9:16, NEB). Grace is free, in the sense of being self-originated, and of proceeding from One who was free not to be gracious. Only when it is seen that what decides each man's destiny is whether or not God resolves to save him from his sins, and that this is a decision which God need not make in any single case, can one begin to grasp the biblical view of grace.

II

The grace of God is love freely shown towards guilty sinners, contrary to their merit and indeed in defiance of their demerit. It is God showing goodness to persons who deserve only severity, and had no reason to expect anything but severity. We have seen why the thought of grace means so little to some churchpeople — namely, because they do not share the beliefs about God and man which it presupposes. Now we have to ask: why should this thought mean so much to others? The answer is not far to seek; indeed, it is evident from what has already been said. It is surely clear that, once a man is convinced that his state and need are as described, the New Testament gospel of grace cannot but sweep him off his feet with wonder and joy. For it tells how our Judge has become our Saviour.

'Grace' and 'salvation' belong together as cause and effect. 'By grace ye are saved' (Ephesians 2:5, cf. verse 8). 'The grace of God that bringeth salvation hath appeared' (Titus 2: 11). The gospel declares how 'God so loved the world, that he gave his only begotten Son, that whosoever believeth in him should not perish, but have everlasting life' (John 3:16), how 'God commendeth his love towards us, in that, while we were yet sinners, Christ died for us' (Romans 5:8), how a fountain has been opened, according to prophecy (Zechariah 13:2), for sin and for uncleanness, and how the living Christ now cries to all who hear the gospel, 'Come unto me . . . and I will give you rest' (Matthew 11:28). As Isaac Watts put it, in his most evangelical, if not his most exalted, strain, we are by nature in a state of utter lostness,

> *But there's a voice of princely grace*
> *Sounds from God's holy Word;*
> *Ho! ye poor captive sinners, come,*
> *And trust upon the Lord.*

> *My soul obeys the sovereign call,*
> *And runs to this relief;*
> *I would believe thy promise, Lord,*
> *Oh, help my unbelief.*

> *To the blest fountain of thy blood,*
> *Incarnate God, I fly,*
> *To wash my soul from scarlet stains,*
> *And sins of deepest dye.*

The Grace of God

A guilty, weak, and helpless worm,
Into thy hands I fall;
Thou art the Lord, my righteousness,
My Saviour, and my all.

The man who can sincerely take Watts's words on his lips will not soon tire of singing the praises of grace.

The New Testament sets forth the grace of God in three particular connections, each of them a perpetual marvel to the Christian believer.

1 *Grace as the source of the pardon of sin.*
The gospel centres upon justification; that is, upon the remission of sins and the acceptance of our persons that goes with it. Justification is the truly dramatic transition from the status of a condemned criminal awaiting a terrible sentence to that of an heir awaiting a fabulous inheritance. Justification is by faith; it takes place the moment a man puts vital trust in the Lord Jesus Christ as his Saviour. Justification is free to us, but it was costly to God, for its price was the atoning death of God's Son. Why was it that God 'spared not his own Son, but delivered him up for us all' (Romans 8: 32)? Because of His grace. It was His own free decision to save which brought about the atonement. Paul makes this explicit. We are justified, he says, 'freely (i.e. with nothing to pay) by his grace (i.e. in consequence of God's merciful resolve) through the redemption that is in Christ Jesus: whom God set forth to be a propitiation (i.e. one who averts divine wrath by expiating sins), through (i.e. becoming effective for individuals by means of) faith, by his blood' (Romans 3:24 f., RV; cf. Titus 3:7). Again, Paul tells us that in Christ we have 'our redemption through his blood, the forgiveness of our trespasses, according to the riches of his grace' (Ephesians 1: 7, RV). The reaction of the Christian heart contemplating all this, comparing how things were with how they are in consequence of the appearing of grace in the world, was given supreme expression by the one-time President of Princeton, Samuel Davies:

> *Great God of wonders! all thy ways*
> *Display the attributes divine;*
> *But countless acts of pardoning grace*
> *Beyond thine other wonders shine:*
> *Who is a pardoning God like Thee?*
> *Or who has grace so rich and free?*

In wonder lost, with trembling joy,
  We take the pardon of our God;
Pardon for crimes of deepest dye,
  A pardon bought with Jesu's blood:
Who is a pardoning God like Thee?
Or who has grace so rich and free?

O may this strange, this matchless grace,
  This God-like miracle of love,
Fill the wide earth with grateful praise,
  As now it fills the choirs above!
Who is a pardoning God like Thee?
Or who has grace so rich and free?

2 *Grace as the motive of the plan of salvation.*
Pardon is the heart of the gospel, but it is not the whole doctrine of grace. For the New Testament sets God's gift of pardon in the context of a plan of salvation which began with election before the world was and will only be completed when the Church is perfect in glory. Paul refers briefly to this plan in several places (see, for instance, Romans 8:29 f.; 2 Thessalonians 2:12 f.), but his fullest account of it is in the massive paragraph—for, despite subdivisions, the flow of thought constitutes it essentially one paragraph—running from Ephesians 1:3 to 2:10. As often, Paul starts with a summary statement and spends the rest of the paragraph analysing and explaining it. The statement is, 'God . . . hath blessed us with all spiritual blessings in heavenly places (i.e. the realm of spiritual realities) in Christ' (verse 3). The analysis begins with eternal election and predestination to sonship in Christ (verses 4 f.), proceeds to redemption and remission of sins in Christ (verse 7), and moves on to the hope of glorification in Christ (verse 11 f.) and the gift of the Spirit in Christ to seal us as God's possession for ever (verse 13 f.). From there, Paul concentrates attention on the act of power whereby God regenerates sinners in Christ (1:19;2:7), bringing them to faith in the process (cf. 2:8). Paul depicts all these items as elements in a single great saving purpose (1:5, 9, 11), and tells us that grace (mercy, love, kindness: 2:4, 7) is its motivating force(see 2:4–8), that 'the riches of his grace' appear throughout its administration (1:7, 2:7), and that the praise of grace is its ultimate goal (1:6, cf. 12, 14, 2:7). So the believer may rejoice to know that his conversion was no accident, but an act of God which had its place in an eternal plan to bless him with the free gift of salvation from sin (2:8–10); God promises and purposes to carry

His plan through to completion, and since it is executed by sovereign power (1:19 ff.) nothing can thwart it. Well might Isaac Watts cry, in words as magnificent as they are true:

> *Tell of his wondrous faithfulness,*
> *And sound His power abroad;*
> *Sing the sweet promise of His grace,*
> *And our performing God.*

> *Engraved as in eternal brass*
> *The mighty promise shines;*
> *Nor can the powers of darkness rase*
> *Those everlasting lines.*

> *His very word of grace is strong*
> *As that which built the skies:*
> *The voice that rolls the stars along*
> *Speaks all the promises.*

The stars, indeed, may fall, but God's promises will stand and be fulfilled. The plan of salvation will be brought to a triumphant completion; thus grace will be shown to be sovereign.

3 *Grace as the guarantee of the preservation of the saints.*
If the plan of salvation is certain of accomplishment, then the Christian's future is assured. He is, and will be, 'kept by the power of God through faith unto salvation' (1 Peter 1:5). He need not torment himself with the fear that his faith may fail; as grace led him to faith in the first place, so grace will keep him believing to the end. Faith, both in its origin and continuance, is a gift of grace (cf. Philippians 1:29). So the Christian may say with Doddridge:

> *Grace first inscribed my name,*
> *In God's eternal book:*
> *'Twas grace that gave me to the Lamb*
> *Who all my sorrows took.*

> *Grace taught my soul to pray,*
> *And pardoning love to know;*
> *'Twas grace that kept me to this day,*
> *And will not let me go.*

III

No apology is needed for drawing so freely on our rich heritage of 'free grace hymns' (poorly represented, alas, in most standard hymn books of the twentieth century); for they make our points more piercingly than prose could ever do. Nor need we apologise for quoting yet another of them as we turn, by way of conclusion, to think for a moment of the response which the knowledge of God's grace should draw forth from us. It has been said that in the New Testament doctrine is grace, and ethics is gratitude; and something is wrong with any form of Christianity in which, experimentally and practically, this saying is not being verified. Those who suppose that the doctrine of God's grace tends to encourage moral laxity ('final salvation is certain anyway, no matter what we do; therefore our conduct doesn't matter') are simply showing that, in the most literal sense, they do not know what they are talking about. For love awakens love in return; and love, once awakened, desires to give pleasure; and the revealed will of God is that those who have received grace should henceforth give themselves to 'good works' (Ephesians 2:10, Titus 2:11 f.); and gratitude will move any man who has truly received grace to do as God requires, and daily to cry out thus —

> *Oh! to grace how great a debtor*
> *Daily I'm constrained to be;*
> *Let that grace now, like a fetter,*
> *Bind my wandering heart to Thee!*
> *Prone to wander, Lord, I feel it;*
> *Prone to leave the God I love —*
> *Take my heart, oh, take and seal it,*
> *Seal it from Thy courts above!*

Do you claim to know the love and grace of God in your own life? Prove your claim, then, by going and praying likewise.

CHAPTER 14

God the Judge

I

Do you believe in divine judgment? By which I mean, do you believe in a God who acts as our Judge?

Many, it seems, do not. Speak to them of God as a Father, a friend, a helper, one who loves us despite all our weakness and folly and sin, and their faces light up; you are on their wavelength at once. But speak to them of God as Judge, and they frown and shake their heads. Their minds recoil from such an idea. They find it repellent and unworthy.

But there are few things stressed more strongly in the Bible than the reality of God's work as Judge. 'Judge' is a word often applied to Him. Abraham, interceding for Sodom, the London-like city that God was about to destroy, cried, 'Shall not *the Judge of all the earth* do right?' (Genesis 18:25). Jephthah, concluding his ultimatum to the Ammonite invaders, declared, 'I have not sinned against thee, but thou doest me wrong to war against me: *the Lord the Judge be judge* this day between the children of Israel and the children of Ammon' (Judges 11:27). 'God is *the Judge*' declared the psalmist (Psalm 75:7); 'arise, O God, *judge the earth*' (Psalm 82:8). In the New Testament, the writer to the Hebrews speaks of 'God *the Judge of all*' (Hebrews 12:23).

Nor is this a matter of a word merely; the reality of divine judgment, as a fact, is set forth on page after page of Bible history. God judged Adam and Eve, expelling them from the Garden and pronouncing curses on their future earthly life (Genesis 3). God judged the corrupt world of Noah's day, sending a flood to destroy mankind (Genesis 6–8). God judged Sodom and Gomorrah, engulfing them in a volcanic catastrophe (Genesis 18–19). God judged Israel's Egyptian taskmasters, just as He foretold He would (see Genesis 15:14), unleashing against them the terrors of the ten plagues (Exodus 7–12). God judged those who worshipped the golden calf, using the Levites as His executioners (Exodus 32:26–35). God judged Nadab and Abihu for offering Him strange fire (Leviticus 10:1 ff.), as later He judged Korah, Dathan, and Abiram, who were swallowed up in an earth tremor. God judged Achan for sacrilegious thieving; he and his were wiped out (Joshua 7). God judged Israel for unfaithfulness to Him after their entry into Canaan, causing them to fall under the dominion of other nations (Judges 2:11 ff., 3:5 ff., 4:1 ff.). Before ever they entered the promised land, God threatened His people with deportation as the ultimate penalty for impiety, and eventually, after repeated warnings from the prophets, He judged them by fulfilling this threat; the northern kingdom (Israel) fell victim to the Assyrian captivity, and the southern kingdom (Judah) to the Babylonian captivity (2 Kings 17; 22:15 ff., 23:26 f.). In Babylon, God judged both Nebuchadnezzar and Belshazzar for their impiety. The former was given time for amendment of life, the latter was not (Daniel 4:5). Nor are the narratives of divine judgment confined to the Old Testament. In the New Testament story, judgment falls on the Jews for rejecting Christ (Matthew 21:43 f., 1 Thessalonians 2:14 ff.), on Ananias and Sapphira, for lying to God (Acts 5), on Herod, for his pride (Acts 12:21 ff.), on Elymas, for his opposition to the gospel (Acts 13:8 ff.), and on Christians at Corinth, who were afflicted with illness (which in some cases proved fatal) by reason of their gross irreverence in connection, particularly, with the Lord's Supper (1 Corinthians 11:29–32). And this is only a selection from the abundant accounts of divine acts of judgment which the Bible contains.

When we turn from Bible history to Bible teaching—the law, the prophets, the wisdom writers, the words of Christ and His apostles—we find the thought of God's action in judgment overshadowing everything. The Mosaic legislation is given as from a God who is Himself a just judge, and will not hesitate to inflict penalties by direct providential action if His people break His law. The prophets take up this theme; indeed, the greater part of their recorded teaching consists of exposition and application of the law, and threats of judgment against the lawless and impenitent. They spend a good deal more space preaching judgment than they do predicting the Messiah and His kingdom! In the wisdom literature, the same viewpoint appears: the one basic certainty underlying all discussion of life's problems in Job and Ecclesiastes, and all the practical maxims of Proverbs, is that 'God will bring thee into judgment', 'God shall bring every work into judgment, with every secret thing, whether it be good, or whether it be evil' (Ecclesiastes 11:9, 12:14).

People who do not actually read the Bible confidently assure us that when we move from the Old Testament to the New, the theme of divine judgment fades into the background; but if we examine the New Testament, even in the most cursory way, we find at once that the Old Testament emphasis on God's action as Judge, far from being reduced, is actually intensified. The entire New Testament is overshadowed by the certainty of a coming day of universal judgment, and by the problem thence arising: how may we sinners get right with God while there is yet time? The New Testament looks on to 'the day of judgment', 'the day of wrath', 'the wrath to come', and proclaims Jesus, the divine Saviour, as the divinely appointed Judge. 'The judge' who stands before the door (James 5:9), 'ready to judge the quick and the dead' (1 Peter 4: 5), 'the righteous judge' who will give Paul his crown (2 Timothy 4:8), is the Lord Jesus Christ. 'He is the one who has been designated by God as judge of the living and the dead' (Acts 10:42, NEB). 'God . . . hath appointed a day, in the which he will judge the world by that man whom he has ordained,' Paul told the Athenians (Acts 17:31); and to the Romans he wrote, 'God shall judge the secrets of men by Jesus Christ according to my gospel' (Romans 2:16). Jesus Himself says the same. 'The Father . . . hath committed all judgment unto the Son . . . the Father . . . hath given him authority to execute judgment . . . the hour is coming, in the which all that are in the graves shall hear his voice, and shall come forth; they that have done good, unto the resurrection of life; and they that have done evil unto the resurrection of damnation' (NEB has 'will rise to hear their doom') (John 5:22, 26 f., 28 f.). The Jesus of the New Testament, who is the world's Saviour, is its Judge too.

II

But what does this mean? What is involved in the idea of the Father, or Jesus, being a *judge*? Four thoughts at least are involved.

1 *The judge is a person with authority.*

In the Bible world, the king was always the supreme judge, because his was the supreme ruling authority. It is on that basis, according to the Bible, that God is judge of His world. As our Maker, He owns us, and as our Owner, He has a right to dispose of us; He has, therefore, a right to make laws for us, and to reward us according to whether or not we keep them. In most modern states, the legislature and the judiciary are divided, so that the judge does not make the laws he administers; but in the ancient world this was not so, and it is not so with God. He is both the Lawgiver and the Judge.

2 *The judge is a person identified with what is good and right.*
The modern idea that a judge should be cold and dispassionate has no place in the Bible. The biblical judge is expected to love justice and fair play and to loathe all ill-treatment of man by his fellow-man. An unjust judge, one who has no interest in seeing right triumph over wrong, is by biblical standards a monstrosity. The Bible leaves us in no doubt that God loves righteousness and hates iniquity, and that the ideal of a judge wholly identified with what is good and right is perfectly fulfilled in Him.

3 *The judge is a person of wisdom, to discern truth.*
In the biblical world, the judge's first task is to ascertain the facts in the case that is before him. There is no jury; it is his responsibility, and his alone, to question, and cross-examine, and detect lies and pierce through evasions and establish how matters really stand. When the Bible pictures God judging, it emphasises His omniscience and wisdom as the searcher of hearts and the finder of facts. Nothing can escape Him; we may fool men, but we cannot fool God. He knows us, and judges us, as we really are. When Abraham met the Lord in human form at the oaks of Mamre, He gave Abraham to understand that He was on the way to Sodom, to establish the truth about the moral situation there. 'The Lord said, Because the cry of Sodom and Gomorrah is great, and because their sin is very grievous; I will go down now, and see whether they have done altogether according to the cry of it, which is come unto me; and if not, I will know' (Genesis 18:20 f.). So it is always. *God will know.* His judgment is according to truth — factual truth, as well as moral truth. He judges 'the secrets of men', not just their public façade. Not for nothing does Paul say, 'we must all be *made manifest* before the judgment-seat of Christ' (2 Corinthians 5:10, RV).

4 *The judge is a person of power, to execute sentence.*
The modern judge does no more than pronounce the sentence; another department of the judicial executive then carries it out.

The same was true in the ancient world. But God is His own executioner. As He legislates, and sentences, so He punishes. All judicial functions coalesce in Him.

III

From what has been said, it becomes clear that the Bible's proclamation of God's work as Judge is part of its witness to His character. It confirms what is said elsewhere of His moral perfection, His righteousness and justice, His wisdom, omniscience, and omnipotence. It shows us also that the heart of the justice which expresses God's nature is *retribution*, the rendering to men what they have deserved; for this is the essence of the judge's task. To reward good with good, and evil with evil, is natural to God. So, when the New Testament speaks of the final judgment, it always represents it in terms of retribution. God will judge all men, it says, 'according to their works' (Matthew 16: 27; Revelation 20: 12 f.). Paul amplifies. 'God . . . will render to every man according to his deeds: to them who by patient continuance in well doing seek for glory and honour and immortality, eternal life; but unto them that are contentious, and do not obey the truth, but obey unrighteousness, indignation and wrath, tribulation and anguish, upon every soul of man that doeth evil . . . but glory, honour, and peace, to every man that worketh good . . . for there is no respect of persons with God . . .' (Romans 2:6–11). The retributive principle applies throughout: Christians, as well as non-Christians, will receive 'according to their works'. Christians are explicitly included in the reference when Paul says 'we must all be made manifest before the judgment seat of Christ; that each one may receive the things done in the body, according to what he hath done, whether it be good or bad' (2 Corinthians 5:10, RV).

Thus retribution appears as a natural and predetermined expression of the divine character. God has resolved to be every man's Judge, rewarding every man according to his works. Retribution is the inescapable moral law of creation; God will see that each man sooner or later receives what he deserves—if not here, then hereafter. This is one of the basic facts of life. And, being made in God's image, we all know in our hearts that this is *right*. This is how it ought to be. Often we complain that, as the gangster put it (not, in his case, with very good warrant), 'there ain't no justice'. The problem of the psalmist who saw inoffensive men being victimised, and the ungodly 'not in trouble as other men', but prospering and at peace (Psalm 73), is echoed again and again in human experience. But the character of God is the guarantee that all wrongs will be righted some day; when 'the day of wrath and revelation of the righteous judgment of God' (Romans 2:5) arrives, retribution will be exact, and no problems of cosmic unfairness will remain to haunt us. God is the Judge, so justice will be done.

Why, then, do men fight shy of the thought of God as a Judge? Why do they feel the thought to be unworthy of Him? The truth is that part of God's moral perfection is His perfection in judgment. Would a God who did not care about the difference between right and wrong be a good and admirable Being? Would a God who put no distinction between the beasts of history, the Hitlers and Stalins (if we dare use names), and His own saints, be morally praiseworthy and perfect? Moral indifference would be an imperfection in God, not a perfection. But not to judge the world would be to show moral indifference. The final proof that God is a perfect moral Being, not indifferent to questions of right and wrong, is the fact that He has committed Himself to judge the world.

It is clear that the reality of divine judgment must have a direct effect on our view of life. If we know that retributive judgment faces us at the end of the road, we shall not live as otherwise we would. But it must be emphasised that the doctrine of divine judgment, and particularly of the final judgment, is not to be thought of primarily as a bogey, with which to frighten men into an outward form of conventional 'righteousness'. It has its frightening implications for godless men, it is true; but its main thrust is as a revelation of the moral character of God, and an imparting of moral significance to human life. As Leon Morris has written:

> The doctrine of final judgment . . . stresses man's accountability and the certainty that justice will finally triumph over all the wrongs which are part and parcel of life here and now. The former gives a dignity to the humblest action, the latter brings calmness and assurance to those in the thick of the battle. This doctrine gives meaning to life . . . The Christian view of judgment means that history moves to a goal . . . Judgment protects the idea of the triumph of God and of good. It is unthinkable that the present conflict between good and evil should last throughout eternity. Judgment means that evil will be disposed of authoritatively, decisively, finally. Judgment means that in the end God's will will be perfectly done (*The Biblical Doctrine of Judgment*, p. 72).

IV

It is not always realised that the main New Testament authority on final judgment, just as on heaven and hell, is the Lord Jesus Christ himself. Rightly does the Anglican burial service address Jesus in a single breath as 'holy and merciful Saviour, thou most worthy Judge eternal'. For Jesus constantly affirmed that in the day when all appear before God's throne to receive the abiding and eternal consequences of the life they have lived, he himself will be the Father's agent in judgment, and his word of acceptance or rejection will be decisive. Passages to note in this connection are, among others, Matthew 7:13–27, 10:26–33, 12:36 f., 13:24–49, 22:1–14, 24:36–25:46; Luke 13:23–30, 16:19–31; John 5:22–29.

The clearest prefiguration of Jesus as judge is in Matthew 25:31 ff.: 'The Son of man shall . . . sit upon the throne of his glory: and before him shall be gathered all nations (i.e., everybody): and he shall separate them . . . Then shall the King say unto them on his right hand, Come, ye blessed of my Father, inherit . . . Then shall he say also unto them on the left hand, depart from me, ye cursed, into everlasting fire . . .' The clearest account of Jesus's prerogative as judge is in John 5:22 ff.: 'The Father judges no one, but has given all judgment to the Son, that all may honour the Son, even as they honour the Father . . . the Father . . . has given him authority to execute judgment, because he is the Son of man (to whom dominion, including judicial functions, was promised: Daniel 7:13 f.) . . . the hour is coming when all who are in the tombs will hear his voice and come forth, those who have done good, to the resurrection of life, and those who have done evil, to the resurrection of judgment' (RSV). God's own appointment has made Jesus Christ inescapable. He stands at the end of life's road for everyone without exception. 'Prepare to meet thy God' was Amos's message to Israel (Amos 4:12); 'prepare to meet the risen Jesus' is God's message to the world today (see Acts 17:31). And we can be sure that he who is true God and perfect man will make a perfectly just judge.

V

Final judgment, as we saw, will be according to our *works* — that is, our *doings*, our whole course of life. The relevance of our 'doings' is not that they ever merit an award from the court — they are too far short of perfection to do that — but that they provide an index of what is in the heart — what, in other words, is the real nature of each agent. Jesus once said, 'on the day of judgment men will render account for every careless word they utter; for by your words you will be justified, and by your words you will be condemned' (Matthew 12:36 f., RSV). What is the significance of the words we utter (which utterance is, of course, a 'work' in the relevant sense)? Just this: the words show what you are inside. Jesus had just made this very point. 'The tree is known by its fruit . . . how can you speak good, when you are evil? For out of the abundance of the heart the mouth speaks' (verse 33 ff.). Similarly, in the sheep-and-goats passage appeal is made to whether men had or had not relieved Christians' needs. What is the significance of that? It is not that one way of acting was meritorious while the other was not, but that from these actions one can tell whether there was love to Christ, the love that springs from faith, in the heart. (See Matthew 25:34 ff.).

Once we see that the significance of works in the last judgment is that of a spiritual character-index, it becomes possible to answer a question which puzzles many. It may be put in this way. Jesus said, 'he that heareth my word, and believeth on him that sent me, hath everlasting life, and shall not come into condemnation; but is passed from death unto life' (John 5:24). Paul said, 'we must all appear before the judgment seat of Christ; that every one may receive the things done in his body' (2 Corinthians 5:10). How can these two statements be fitted together? How does free forgiveness and justification by faith square with judgment according to works? The answer seems to be as follows. First, the gift of justification certainly shields believers from being condemned and banished from God's presence as sinners. This appears from the vision of judgment in Revelation 20:11–15, where alongside 'the books' recording each man's works 'the book of life' is opened, and those whose names are written there are not 'cast into the lake of fire' as the rest of men are. But, second, the gift of justification does not at all shield believers from being assessed as Christians, and from forfeiting good which others will enjoy if it turns out that as Christians they have been slack, mischievous and destructive. This appears from Paul's warning to the Corinthians to be careful what life-style they build on Christ, the one foundation. 'If any man builds upon this foundation gold, silver, precious stones, wood, hay, stubble; every man's work shall be made manifest: for the day shall declare it, because it shall be revealed by fire . . . If any man's work abide . . . he shall receive a reward. If any man's work shall be burned, he shall suffer loss: but he himself shall be saved; yet so as by fire' (1 Corinthians 3:12–15). 'Reward' and 'loss' signify an enriched or impoverished relationship with God, though in what ways it is beyond our present power to know.

Final judgment will also be according to our *knowledge*. Everyone knows something of God's will through general revelation, even if they have not been instructed in the law or the gospel, and everyone is guilty before God for falling short of the best they knew. But ill-desert is graded according to what that best was; see Rom. 2:12, and compare Luke 12:47 f. The principle operating here is that 'where a man has been given much, much will be expected of him' (verse 48, NEB). The justice of this is obvious. In every case the judge of all the earth will do right.

VI

Paul refers to the fact that we must all appear before Christ's judgment-seat as 'the terror of the Lord' (2 Corinthians 5:11), and well he might. Jesus the Lord, like His Father, is holy and pure; we are neither. We live under His eye, He knows our secrets, and on judgment day the whole of our past life will be played back, as it were, before Him, and brought under review. If we know ourselves at all, we know we are not fit to face Him. What then are we to do? The New Testament answer is: *call on the coming Judge to be your present Saviour.* As Judge, He is the law, but as Saviour He is the gospel. Run from Him now, and you will meet Him as Judge then—and without hope. Seek Him now, and you will find Him (for 'he that seeketh findeth'), and you will then discover that you are looking forward to that future meeting with joy, knowing that there is now 'no condemnation to them that are in Christ Jesus' (Romans 8:1). So

> *Whilst I draw this fleeting breath;*
> *When my eyelids close in death;*
> *When I soar through tracts unknown,*
> *See thee on thy judgment-throne;*
> *Rock of Ages, cleft for me,*
> *Let me hide myself in thee.*

CHAPTER 15

The Wrath of God

II

'Wrath' is an old English word defined in my dictionary as 'deep, intense anger and indignation'. 'Anger' is defined as 'stirring of resentful displeasure and strong antagonism, by a sense of injury or insult'; 'indignation' as 'righteous anger aroused by injustice and baseness'. Such is wrath. And wrath, the Bible tells us, is an attribute of God.

The modern habit throughout the Christian church is to play this subject down. Those who still believe in the wrath of God (not all do) say little about it; perhaps they do not think much about it. To an age which has unashamedly sold itself to the gods of greed, pride, sex, and self-will, the Church mumbles on about God's kindness, but says virtually nothing about His judgment. How often during the past year did you hear, or, if you are a minister, did you preach, a sermon on the wrath of God? How long is it, I wonder, since a Christian spoke straight on this subject on radio or television, or in one of those half-column sermonettes that appear in some national dailies and magazines? (And if a man did so, how long would it be before he would be asked to speak or write again?) The fact is that the subject of divine wrath has become taboo in modern society, and Christians by and large have accepted the taboo and conditioned themselves never to raise the matter.

We may well ask whether this is as it should be; for the Bible behaves very differently. One cannot imagine that talk of divine judgment was ever very popular, yet the biblical writers engage in it constantly. One of the most striking things about the Bible is the vigour with which both Testaments emphasise the reality and terror of God's wrath. 'A study of the concordance will show that there are *more* references in Scripture to the anger, fury, and wrath of God, than there are to His love and tenderness' (A. W. Pink, *The Attributes of God*, p. 75).

The Bible labours the point that just as God is good to those who trust Him, so He is terrible to those who do not. 'The Lord is a jealous God and avengeth; the Lord avengeth and is full of wrath; the Lord taketh vengeance on His adversaries, and He reserveth wrath for His enemies. The Lord is slow to anger, and great in power, and will by no means clear the guilty. . . . Who can stand before His indignation? and who can abide the fierceness of His anger? His fury is poured out like fire, and the rocks are broken asunder by Him. The Lord is good, a strong hold in the day of trouble; and He knoweth them that put their trust in Him. But . . . He . . . will pursue His enemies into darkness' (Nahum 1:2–8, RV).

Paul's expectation that the Lord Jesus will one day appear 'in flaming fire taking vengeance on them that know not God, and that obey not the gospel of our Lord Jesus Christ: who shall be punished with everlasting destruction from the presence of the Lord, and from the glory of His power; when He shall come to be glorified in His saints' (2 Thessalonians 1:8 ff.) is sufficient reminder that Nahum's emphasis is not peculiar to the Old Testament. In fact, throughout the New Testament 'the wrath of God', 'the wrath', or simply 'wrath', are virtually technical terms for the outgoing of God in retributive action, by whatever means, against those who have defied Him (see Romans 1:18, 2:5, 5:9, 12:19, 13; 4 f.; 1 Thessalonians 1:10, 2:16, 5:9; Revelation 6:16 f., 16:19; Luke 21:22–24; etc.).

Nor does the Bible make known to us the wrath of God merely by general statements like those quoted. Bible history, as we saw in our last chapter, loudly proclaims the severity, as well as the goodness, of God. In the same sense that *Pilgrim's Progress* might be called a book about roads to hell, the Bible could be called the book of God's wrath, for it is full of portrayals of divine retribution, from the cursing and banishment of Adam and Eve in Genesis 3 to the overthrow of 'Babylon' and the great assizes of Revelation 17–18 and 20.

Clearly, the theme of God's wrath is one about which the biblical writers feel no inhibitions whatever. Why, then, should we? Why, when the Bible is vocal about it, should we feel obliged to be silent? What is it that makes us awkward and embarrassed when the subject comes up, and prompts us to soft-pedal it and hedge when we are asked about it? What lies at the bottom of our hesitations and difficulties? We are not thinking now of those whose dismissal of the idea of divine wrath means only that they are not prepared to take any part of the biblical faith seriously. We are thinking, rather, of the many who count themselves 'insiders', who have firm beliefs about God's love and pity, and the redeeming work of the Lord Jesus Christ, and who follow Scripture robustly on other things, yet who boggle at robustly echoing it on this point. What really is the trouble here?

II

The root cause of our unhappiness seems to be a disquieting suspicion that ideas of wrath are in one way or another *unworthy of God*.

To some, for instance, 'wrath' suggests a loss of self-control, an outburst of 'seeing red' which is partly, if not wholly, irrational. To others, it suggests the rage of conscious impotence, or wounded pride, or plain bad temper. Surely, it is said, it would be wrong to ascribe to God such attitudes as these?

The reply is: indeed it would, but the Bible does not ask us to do this. There seems to be here a misunderstanding of the 'anthropomorphic' language of Scripture—that is, the biblical habit of describing God's attitudes and affections in terms ordinarily used for talking about man. The basis of this habit is the fact that God made man in His own image, so that human personality and character are more like the being of God than anything else we know. But when Scripture speaks of God anthropomorphically, it does not imply that the limitations and imperfections which belong to the personal characteristics of us sinful creatures belong also to the corresponding qualities in our holy Creator; rather, it takes for granted that they do not. Thus, God's love, as the Bible views it, never leads Him to foolish, impulsive, immoral actions in the way that its human counterpart too often leads us. And in the same way, God's wrath in the Bible is never the capricious, self-indulgent, irritable, morally ignoble thing that human anger so often is. It is, instead, a right and necessary reaction to objective moral evil. God is only angry where anger is called for. Even among men, there is such a thing as *righteous* indignation, though it is, perhaps, rarely found. But all God's indignation is righteous. Would a God who took as much pleasure in evil as He did in good be a good God? Would a God who did not react adversely to evil in His world be morally perfect? Surely not. But it is precisely this adverse reaction to evil, which is a necessary part of moral perfection, that the Bible has in view when it speaks of God's wrath. Then to others the thought of God's 'wrath' suggests cruelty. They think, perhaps, of what they have been told about Jonathan Edwards's famous gospel sermon, *Sinners in the Hands of an Angry God*, which God used to bring awakening to the town of Enfield, in New England, in 1741. In this sermon Edwards, enlarging on his theme that 'natural men are held in the hand of God over the pit of hell', used some most vivid furnace imagery to make his congregation feel the horror of their position, and so give force to his conclusion — 'Therefore, let every one that is out of Christ, now awake and fly from the wrath to come.' Anyone who has read the sermon will know that A. H. Strong, the great Baptist theologian, was right to stress that Edwards's imagery, however sharply focused, was no more than imagery — that, in other words, Edwards 'did not regard hell as consisting in fire and brimstone, but rather in the unholiness and separation from God of a guilty and accusing conscience, of which the fire and brimstone are symbols' (*Systematic Theology*, p. 1035). But this does not wholly meet the point of Edwards's critics, which is that a God who could inflict punishment that required such language as this to describe it must be a fierce and cruel monster.

Does this follow? Two biblical considerations show that it does not.

In the first place, God's wrath in the Bible is always *judicial* — that is, it is the wrath of the Judge, administering justice. Cruelty is always immoral, but the explicit presupposition of all that we find in the Bible — and in Edwards's sermon, for that matter — on the torments of those who experience the fulness of God's wrath is that each receives precisely what he deserves. 'The day of wrath', Paul tells us, is also the day of 'revelation of the righteous judgment of God: who will render to every man according to his deeds' (Romans 2:5 f.). Jesus himself — who actually had more to say on this subject than any other New Testament figure — made the point that retribution would be proportioned to individual desert. 'That servant, which knew his lord's will, and prepared not himself, neither did according to his will, shall be beaten with many stripes. But he that knew not, and did commit things worthy of stripes, shall be beaten with few stripes. For unto whomsoever much is given, of him shall much be required; and to whom men have committed much, of him they will ask the more' (Luke 12:47 f.). God will see, says Edwards in the sermon already referred to, 'that you shall not suffer beyond what strict justice requires' — but it is precisely 'what strict justice requires', he insists, that will be so grievous for those who die in unbelief. If it is asked: can disobedience to our Creator really deserve great and grievous punishment? anyone who has ever been convicted of sin knows beyond any shadow of doubt that the answer is yes, and knows too that those whose consciences have not yet been awakened to consider, as Anselm put it, 'how weighty is sin' are not yet qualified to give an opinion.

In the second place, God's wrath in the Bible is something which men *choose* for themselves. Before hell is an experience inflicted by God, it is a state for which man himself opts, by retreating from the light which God shines in his heart to lead him to Himself. When John writes, 'he who does not believe (in Jesus) is condemned (judged) already, because he has not believed in the name of the only Son of God', he goes on to explain himself as follows, 'And *this is the judgment*, that the light has come into the world, and men loved darkness rather than light, because their deeds were evil' (John 3:18 f. RSV). He means just what he says: the decisive act of judgment upon the lost in the judgment which they pass upon themselves, be rejecting the light that comes to them in and through Jesus Christ. In the last analysis, all that God does subsequently in judicial action towards the unbeliever, whether in this life or beyond it, is to show him, and lead him into, the full implications of the choice he has made.

The basic choice was and is simple—either to respond to the summons 'come unto me . . . take my yoke upon you, and learn of me' (Matthew 11: 28 f.), or not; either to 'save' one's life by keeping it from Jesus's censure, and resisting His demand to take it over, or to 'lose' it by denying oneself, shouldering one's cross, becoming a disciple, and letting Jesus have His own disruptive way with one. In the former case, Jesus tells us, we may gain the world, but it will do us no good, for we shall lose our souls; though in the latter case, by losing our life for His sake, we shall find it (Matthew 16: 24 ff.).

But what does it mean to lose our souls? To answer this question, Jesus uses His own solemn imagery—'Gehenna' ('hell' in Mark 9:47 and ten other gospel texts), the valley outside Jerusalem where rubbish was burned; the 'worm' that 'dieth not' (Mark 9:47), an image, it seems, for the endless dissolution of the personality by a condemning conscience; 'fire' for the agonising awareness of God's displeasure; 'outer darkness' for knowledge of the loss, mot merely of God, but of all good, and everything that made life seem worth living; 'gnashing of teeth' for self-condemnation and self-loathing. These things are, no doubt, unimaginably dreadful, though those who have been convicted of sin know a little of their nature. But they are not arbitrary inflictions; they represent, rather, a conscious growing into the state in which one has chosen to be. The unbeliever has preferred to be by himself, without God, defying God, having God against him, and he shall have his preference. Nobody stands under the wrath of God save those who have chosen to do so. The essence of God's action in wrath is to *give men what they choose*, in all its implications: nothing more, and equally nothing less. God's readiness to respect human choice to this extent may appear disconcerting and even terrifying, but it is plain that His attitude here is supremely just, and poles apart from the wanton and irresponsible inflicting of pain which is what we mean by cruelty.

We need, therefore, to remember that the key to interpreting the many biblical passages, often highly figurative, which picture the divine King and Judge as active against men in wrath and vengeance, is to realise that what God is hereby doing is no more than to ratify and confirm judgments which those whom He 'visits' have already passed on themselves by the course they have chosen to follow. This appears in the story of God's first act of wrath towards man, in Genesis 3, where we learn that Adam had already chosen to hide from God, and keep clear of His presence, before ever God drove him from the garden; and the same principle applies throughout the Bible.

III

The classical New Testament treatment of the wrath of God is found in the epistle to the Romans, which Luther and Calvin regarded as the gateway to the Bible, and which actually contains more explicit references to God's wrath than all the rest of Paul's letters put together. We shall end this chapter by analysing what Romans tells us about it: a study which will serve to clarify some points already made.

1 *The meaning of God's wrath.*

The wrath of God in Romans denotes God's resolute action in punishing sin. It is as much the expression of a personal, emotional attitude of the Triune Jehovah as is His love to sinners: it is the active manifesting of His hatred of irreligion and moral evil. The phrase 'the wrath' may refer specifically to the future crowning manifestation of this hatred on 'the day of wrath' (5:9, 2:5), but it may also refer to present providential events and processes in which divine retribution for sin may be discerned. Thus, the magistrate sentencing criminals is 'the servant of God to execute his wrath on the wrongdoer' (13:4, cf. 5, RSV). God's wrath is His reaction to our sin, and 'the law worketh wrath' (4:15) because the law stirs up sin latent within us and causes transgression—the behaviour that evokes wrath—to abound (5:20, 7:7-13). As a reaction to sin, God's wrath is an expression of His justice, and Paul indignantly rejects the suggestion 'that God is unjust to inflict wrath upon us' (4:5, RSV). Persons 'fitted for destruction' he describes as 'vessels of wrath'—that is, objects of wrath—in a similar sense to that in which he elsewhere calls servants of the world, the flesh, and the devil, 'children of wrath' (Ephesians 2:3). Such persons, simply by being what they are, call down God's wrath upon themselves.

2 *The revelation of God's wrath.*

'The wrath of God is revealed from heaven against all ungodliness and unrighteousness of men, who hold down the truth in unrighteousness' (1:18, RV). The present tense, 'is revealed', implies a *constant* disclosure, going on all the time; 'from heaven', which stands in contrast to 'in the gospel' in the previous verse, implies a *universal* disclosure, reaching those whom the gospel has not yet reached.

How is this disclosure made? It imprints itself directly on every man's conscience: those whom God has given up to a 'reprobate mind' (1:28), to do uninhibited evil, still know 'the ordinance of God, that they which practise such things are worthy of death' (1:32). No man is entirely without inklings of judgment to come. And this immediate disclosure is confirmed by the revealed word of the gospel, which prepares us for its good news by telling us the bad news of a coming 'day of wrath, and revelation of the righteous judgment of God' (2:5).

Nor is this all. To those who have eyes to see, tokens of the active wrath of God appear here and now in the actual state of mankind. Everywhere the Christian observes a pattern of degeneration, constantly working itself out—from knowledge of God to worship of that which is not God, and from idolatry to immorality of an ever grosser sort, so that each generation grows a fresh crop of 'ungodliness and unrighteousness of men'. In this decline we are to recognise the present action of divine wrath, in a process of judicial hardening and withdrawal of restraints, whereby men are given up to their own corrupt preferences and so come to put into practice more and more uninhibitedly the lusts of their sinful hearts. Paul describes the process, as he knew it from his

Bible and the world of his day, in Romans 1:19–31, where the key-phrases are, 'God . . . gave them up to uncleanness', 'God gave them up unto vile affections', 'God gave them over to a reprobate mind' (verses 24, 26, 28). If you want proof that the wrath of God, revealed as a fact in your conscience, is already working as a force in the world, Paul would say, you need only look at life around you, and see what God has given men up to. And who today, nineteen centuries after he wrote, could challenge his thesis?

3 *The deliverance from God's wrath.*

In the first three chapters of Romans, Paul is concerned to force on us the question, if 'the wrath of God is revealed from heaven against all ungodliness and unrighteousness of men', and a 'day of wrath' is coming when God will 'render to every man according to his deeds', how can any of us escape disaster? The question presses because we are 'all under sin', 'there is none righteous, no, not one'; 'all the world' is 'guilty before God' (3:9, 10, 19). The law cannot save us, for its only effect is to stimulate sin and show us how far short we fall of righteousness. The outward trappings of religion cannot save us either, any more than mere circumcision can save the Jew. Is there any way of deliverance, then, from the wrath to come? There is, and Paul knows it. 'Being now justified by his blood,' Paul proclaims, 'we shall be saved from (God's) wrath through him' (5:9). By whose blood? The blood of Jesus Christ, the incarnate Son of God. And what does it mean to be 'justified'? It means to be forgiven, and accepted as righteous. And how do we come to be justified? Through faith — that is, self-abandoning trust in the person and work of Jesus. And how does Jesus's blood — that is, His sacrificial death — form a basis for our justification? Paul explains this in Romans 3:24 f., where he speaks of 'the redemption that is in Christ Jesus: whom God set forth to be a propitiation, through faith, by his blood'. What is a 'propitiation'? It is a sacrifice that averts wrath through expiating sin, and cancelling guilt.

This as we shall see more fully later, is the real heart of the gospel: that Jesus Christ, by virtue of His death on the cross as our substitute and sin-bearer, 'is the propitiation for our sins' (1 John 2:2). Between us sinners and the thunder-clouds of divine wrath stands the cross of the Lord Jesus. If we are Christ's, through faith, then we are justified through His cross, and the wrath will never touch us, neither here nor hereafter. Jesus 'delivers us from the wrath to come' (1 Thessalonians 1:10, RSV).

IV

No doubt it is true that the subject of divine wrath has in the past been handled speculatively, irreverently, even malevolently. No doubt there have been some who have preached of wrath and damnation with tearless eyes and no pain in their hearts. No doubt the sight of small sects cheerfully consigning the whole world, apart from themselves, to hell has disgusted many. Yet if we would know God, it is vital that we face the truth concerning His wrath, however unfashionable it may be, and however strong out initial prejudices against it. Otherwise, we shall not understand the gospel of salvation from wrath, nor the propitiatory achievement of the cross, nor the wonder of the redeeming love of God. Nor shall we understand the hand of God in history, and God's present dealings with our own people; nor shall we be able to make head or tail of the book of Revelation; nor will our evangelism have the urgency enjoined by Jude—'save some, by snatching them out of the fire' (Jude 23). Neither our knowledge of God, nor our service Him, will be in accord with His Word.

The wrath of God [wrote A. W. Pink] is a perfection of the Divine character on which we need to meditate frequently. First, that our hearts may be duly impressed by God's detestation of sin. We are ever prone to regard sin lightly, to gloss over its hideousness, to make excuses for it. But the more we study and ponder God's abhorrence of sin and His frightful vengeance upon it, the more likely are we to realise its heinousness. Second, to beget a true fear in our souls for God. 'Let us have grace whereby we may serve God acceptably with reverence and godly fear: for our God is a consuming fire' (Heb. 12:28,29). We cannot serve Him 'acceptably' unless there is due 'reverence' for His awful Majesty and 'godly fear' of His righteous anger, and these are best promoted by frequently calling to mind that 'our God is a consuming fire'. Third, to draw out our soul in fervent praise [to Jesus Christ] for having delivered us from 'the wrath to come' (1 Thess. 1:10). Our readiness or our reluctancy to meditate upon the wrath of God becomes a sure test of how our hearts really stand affected towards Him (*op. cit.*, p. 77).

Pink is right. If we would truly know God, and be known of Him, we should ask Him to teach us here and now to reckon with the solemn reality of His wrath.

CHAPTER 16

Goodness and Severity

I

'Behold therefore the goodness and severity of God,' writes Paul in Romans 11:22. The crucial word here is 'and'. The apostle is explaining the relation between Jew and Gentile in the plan of God. He has just reminded his Gentile readers that God rejected the great mass of their Jewish contemporaries for unbelief, while at the same time bringing many pagans like themselves to saving faith. Now he invites them to take note of the two sides of God's character which appeared in this transaction. 'Behold therefore the goodness and severity of God: on them which fell, severity; but toward thee, goodness.' The Christians at Rome are not to dwell on God's goodness alone, nor on His severity alone, but to contemplate both together. Both are attributes of God—aspects, that is, of His revealed character. Both appear alongside each other in the economy of grace. Both must be acknowledged together if God is to be truly known.

Never, perhaps, since Paul wrote has there been more need to labour this point than there is today. Modern muddle-headedness and confusion as to the meaning of faith in God is almost beyond description. Men say they believe in God, but have no idea who it is that they believe in, or what difference believing in Him may make. The Christian who wants to help his floundering fellows into what a famous old tract used to call 'safety, certainty, and enjoyment' is constantly bewildered as to where to begin: the fantastic hotch-potch of fancies about God that confronts him quite takes his breath away. How on earth have people got into such a muddle? he asks. What lies at the root of their confusion? And where is the starting-point for setting them straight? To these questions there are several complementary sets of answers. One is that people have got into the way of following private religious hunches rather than learning of God from His own Word; and we have to try and help them to unlearn the pride and, in some cases, misconceptions about Scripture which gave rise to this attitude, and to base their convictions henceforth, not on what they feel, but on what the Bible says. A second answer is that modern man thinks of all religions as equal and equivalent, and draws his stock of ideas about God from pagan as well as Christian sources; and we have to try and show people the uniqueness and finality of the Lord Jesus Christ, God's last word to man. A third answer is that men have ceased to recognise the reality of their own sinfulness, which imparts a degree of perversity and enmity against God to all that they think and do; and it is our task to try and introduce people to this fact about themselves, and so make them self-distrustful and open to correction by the word of Christ. A fourth answer, no less basic than the three already given, is that people today are in the habit of dissociating the thought of God's goodness from that of His severity; and we must seek to wean them from this habit, since nothing but misbelief is possible as long as it persists.

The habit in question, first learned from some gifted German theologians of the last century, has infected modern Western Protestantism as a whole. To reject all ideas of divine wrath and judgment, and to assume that God's character, misrepresented (forsooth!) in many parts of the Bible, is really one of indulgent benevolence without any severity, is the rule rather than the exception among ordinary folk today. It is true that some recent theologians, in reaction, have tried to reaffirm the truth of God's holiness, but their efforts have seemed half-hearted and their words have fallen for the most part on deaf ears. Modern Protestants are not going to give up their 'enlightened' adherence to the doctrine of a celestial Santa Claus merely because a Brunner or a Niebuhr suspect this is not the whole story. The certainty that there is no more to be said of God (if God there be) than that He is infinitely forbearing and kind, is as hard to eradicate as bindweed. And when once it has put down roots, Christianity, in the true sense of the word, simply dies off. For the substance of Christianity is faith in the forgiveness of sins through the redeeming work of Christ on the cross. But on the basis of the Santa Claus theology, sins create no problem, and atonement becomes needless; God's active favour extends no less to those who disregard His commands than to those who keep them. The idea that God's attitude to me is affected by whether or not I do what He says has no place in the thought of the man in the street, and any attempt to show the need for fear in God's presence, and trembling at His word, gets written off as impossibly old-fashioned—'Victorian', and 'Puritan', and 'sub-Christian'.

Yet the Santa Claus theology carries within itself the seeds of its own collapse, for it cannot cope with the fact of evil. It is no accident that when belief in the 'good God' of liberalism became widespread, about the turn of this century, the so-called 'problem of evil' (which was not regarded as a problem before) suddenly leaped into prominence as the number-one concern of Christian apologetics. This was inevitable, for it is not possible to see the good-will of a heavenly Santa Claus in heartbreaking and destructive things like cruelty, or marital infidelity, or death on the road, or lung cancer. The only way to save the liberal view of God is to dissociate Him from these things, and to deny that He has any direct relation to them or control over them; in other words, to deny His omnipotence and lordship over His world. Liberal theologians took this course fifty years ago, and the man in the street takes it today. Thus he is left with a kind God who means well, but cannot always insulate His children from trouble and grief. When trouble comes, therefore, there is nothing to do but grin and bear it. In this way, by an ironic paradox, faith in a God who is all goodness and no severity tends to confirm men in a fatalistic and pessimistic attitude to life.

Here, then, is one of the religious By-Path Meadows of our day, leading (as in one way or another they all do) into the land of Doubting Castle and Giant Despair. How can those who have strayed this way get back on the true road? Only by learning to relate God's goodness to His severity, according to the Scriptures. The purpose of the present article is to sketch out the substance of biblical teaching on this point.

II

Goodness, in God as in man, means something admirable, attractive, and praiseworthy. When the biblical writers call God 'good', they are thinking in general of all those moral qualities which prompt His people to call him 'perfect', and in particular of the generosity which moves them to call Him 'merciful' and 'gracious', and to speak of His 'love'. Let us elaborate a little.

The Bible is constantly ringing the changes on the theme of the moral perfection of God, as declared in His own words and verified in the experience of His people. When God stood with Moses on Sinai and 'proclaimed the name (that is, the revealed character) of the LORD (that is, God as His people's Jehovah, the sovereign saviour who says of Himself "I am what I am" in the covenant of grace)', what He said was this, 'The LORD, the LORD God, merciful and gracious, longsuffering, and abundant in goodness and truth, keeping mercy for thousands, forgiving iniquity and transgression and sin, and that will by no means clear the guilty . . .' (Exodus 34:5–7). And this proclaiming of God's moral perfection was carried out as the fulfilment of His promise to make all His *goodness* pass before Moses (Exodus 33:19). All the particular perfections that are mentioned here, and all that go with them – God's truthfulness and trustworthiness, His unfailing justice and wisdom, His tenderness, forbearance, and entire adequacy to all who penitently seek His help, His noble kindness in offering men the exalted destiny of fellowship with Him in holiness and love – these things together make up God's goodness, in the overall sense of the sum total of His revealed excellences. And when David declared, 'As for God, his way is perfect' (2 Samuel 22:31 = Psalm 18:30), what he meant was that God's people find in experience, as he himself had found, that God never comes short of the goodness to which He has laid claim. 'His way is perfect; the promise of the LORD proves true; he is a shield for all who take refuge in him' (RSV). The psalm as a whole is David's retrospective declaration of how he had himself proved that God is faithful to His promises and all-sufficient as a shield and defender; and every child of God who has not forfeited his birthright by backsliding enjoys a parallel experience.

(Incidentally, if you have never read carefully through this psalm, asking yourself at each point how far your testimony matches up to that of David, I would urge you to do so at once – and then to do it again at frequent intervals. You will find it a salutary, if shattering, discipline.)

However, there is more to be said. Within the cluster of God's moral perfections there is one in particular to which the term 'goodness' points – the quality which God specially singled out from the whole when, proclaiming 'all his goodness' to Moses, He spoke of Himself as 'abundant in *goodness* and truth' (Exodus 34:6). This is the quality of *generosity*. Generosity means a disposition to give to others in a way which has no mercenary motive and is not limited by what the recipients deserve, but consistently goes beyond it. Generosity expresses the simple wish that others should have what they need to make them happy. Generosity is, so to speak, the focal point of God's moral perfection; it is the

146

quality which determines how all God's other excellences are to be displayed. God is 'abundant in goodness'—*ultro bonus*, as Latin-speaking theologians long ago used to put it, spontaneously good, overflowing with generosity. Theologians of the Reformed school use the New Testament word 'grace' (free favour) to cover every act of divine generosity, of whatever kind, and hence distinguish between the 'common grace' of 'creation, preservation, and all the blessings of this life', and the 'special grace' manifested in the economy of salvation—the point of the contrast between 'common' and 'special' being that all benefit from the former, but not all are touched by the latter. The biblical way of putting this distinction would be to say that God is good to all in some ways and to some in all ways.

God's generosity in bestowing natural blessings is acclaimed in Psalm 145. 'The LORD is good to all: and his tender mercies are over all his works. . . . The eyes of all wait upon thee; and thou givest them their meat in due season. Thou openest thine hand, and satisfiest the desire of every living thing' (verses 9, 15, 16; cf. Acts 14:17). The psalmist's point is that, since God controls all that happens in His world, every meal, every pleasure, every possession, every bit of sun, every night's sleep, every moment of health and safety, everything else that sustains and enriches life, is a divine gift. And how abundant these gifts are! 'Count your blessings, name them one by one', urges the children's chorus, and anyone who seriously begins to list his natural blessings alone will soon feel the force of the next line—'and it will surprise you what the Lord has done.' But the mercies of God on the natural level, however abundant, are overshadowed by the greater mercies of spiritual redemption. When the singers of Israel summoned the people to give thanks to God because 'he is good: for his mercy endureth for ever' (Psalms 106:1, 107:1, 118:1, 136:1; cf. 100:4 f.; 2 Chronicles 5:13, 7:13; Jeremiah 33:11), it was usually of re-demptive mercies that they were thinking: mercies such as God's 'mighty acts' in saving Israel from Egypt (Psalm 106:2 ff., 136), His willingness to forbear and forgive when His servants fall into sin (Psalm 86:5), and His readiness to teach men His way (Psalm 119:68). And the goodness to which Paul was referring in Romans 11:22 was God's mercy in grafting 'wild' Gentiles into His olive tree—that is, the fellowship of His covenant people, the commu-nity of saved believers.

The classical exposition of God's goodness is Psalm 107. Here, to enforce his summons to 'give thanks unto the LORD, for he is good', the psalmist generalises from past experiences of Israel in captivity and Israelites in personal need to give four examples of how men 'cried unto the LORD in their trouble, and he delivered them out of their distresses' (verses 6, 13, 19, 28). The first example is of God redeeming the helpless from their enemies and leading them out of barrenness to find a home; the second is of God delivering from 'darkness and the shadow of death' those whom He had himself brought into this condition because of their rebellion against Him; the third is of God healing the diseases with which He had chastened 'fools' who disregarded Him; the fourth is of God protecting voyagers by stilling the storm which they thought would sink their ship. Each episode ends with the refrain, 'O that men would praise the LORD for his goodness, and for his wonderful works to the children of men!' (verses 8, 15, 21, 31). The whole psalm is a majestic panorama of the operations of divine goodness, transforming human lives.

III

What, now, of God's severity? The word Paul uses in Romans 11:22 means literally 'cutting off'; it denotes God's decisive withdrawal of His goodness from those who have spurned it. It reminds us of a fact about God which He Himself declared when He proclaimed His name to Moses; namely, that though He is 'abundant in goodness and truth', He 'will by no means clear the guilty'—that is, the obstinate and impenitent guilty (Exodus 34:6 f.). The act of severity to which Paul referred was God's rejection of Israel as a body—breaking them off from His olive tree, of which they were the natural branches—because they did not believe the gospel of Jesus Christ. Israel had presumed on God's goodness, while disregarding the concrete manifestation of His goodness in His Son; and God's reaction had been swift—He had cut Israel off. Paul takes occasion from this to warn his Gentile Christian readers that if they should lapse as Israel had lapsed, God would cut them off too. 'You stand fast only through faith. So do not become proud, but stand in awe. For if God did not spare the natural branches, neither will he spare you' (Romans 11: 20 f.).

The principle which Paul is applying here is that behind every display of divine goodness stands a threat of severity in judgment if that goodness is scorned. If we do not let it draw us to God in gratitude and responsive love, we have only ourselves to blame when God turns against us. Earlier in Romans, Paul addressed the self-satisfied non-Christian critic of human nature as follows, 'the goodness of God leadeth thee to repentance'—that is, as J. B.

Phillips correctly paraphrases, 'is meant to lead you to repentance'. 'Thou that judgest doest the same things'—yet God has borne with your faults, the very faults which you regard as meriting His judgment when you see them in others, and you ought to be very humble and very thankful. But if, while tearing strips off others, you omit to turn to God yourself, then 'thou ... despisest ... the riches of his goodness and forbearance and longsuffering', and thereby 'after thy hardness and impenitent heart treasurest up unto thyself wrath' (Romans 2:1–5). Similarly, Paul tells the Roman Christians that God's goodness is their portion only on a certain condition—'if thou continue in his goodness: otherwise thou also shalt be cut off' (Romans 11:22). It is the same principle in each case. Those who decline to respond to God's goodness by repentance, and faith, and trust, and submission to His will, cannot wonder or complain if sooner or later the tokens of His goodness are withdrawn, the opportunity of benefiting from them ends, and retribution supervenes.

But God is not impatient in His severity; just the reverse. He is 'slow to anger' (Nehemiah 9:17; Psalms 103:8, 145:8; Joel 2:13; Jonah 4:2) and 'longsuffering' (Exodus 34:6; Numbers 14:18; Psalm 86:15). The Bible makes much of the patience and forbearance of God in postponing merited judgments in order to extend the day of grace and give more opportunity for repentance. Peter reminds us how, when the earth was corrupt and crying out for judgment, nevertheless 'the longsuffering of God *waited* in the days of Noah' (1 Peter 3:20)—a reference, probably, to the hundred and twenty years' respite (as it seems to have been) that is mentioned in Genesis 6:3. Again, in Romans 9:22 Paul tells us that down the course of history God has '*endured* with much longsuffering the vessels of wrath fitted to destruction'. Again, Peter explains to his first-century readers that the reason why the promised return of Christ to judgment has not happened yet is that God 'is longsuffering to us-ward, not willing that any should perish, but that all should come to repentance' (2 Peter 3:9); and the same explanation presumably applies today. The patience of God in giving 'space to repent' (Revelation 2:4) before judgment finally falls is one of the marvels of the Bible story. It is no wonder that the New Testament stresses that longsuffering is a Christian virtue and duty; it is in truth a part of the image of God (Galatians 5:22; Ephesians 4:2; Colossians 3:12).

IV

From the above line of thought we can learn at least three lessons.

1 Appreciate the *goodness* of God. Count your blessings. Learn not to take natural benefits, endowments, and pleasures for granted; learn to thank God for them all. Do not slight the Bible, or the gospel of Jesus Christ, by an attitude of casualness towards either. The Bible shows you a Saviour who suffered and died in order that we sinners might be reconciled to God; Calvary is the measure of the goodness of God; lay it to heart. Ask yourself the psalmist's question – 'What shall I render unto the LORD for all his benefits toward me?' Seek grace to give his answer – 'I will take the cup of salvation, and call upon the name of the LORD . . . O LORD, truly I am thy servant . . . I will pay my vows unto the LORD now . . .' (Psalm 116:12 ff.).

2 Appreciate the *patience* of God. Think how He has borne with you, and still bears with you, when so much in your life is unworthy of Him, and you have so richly deserved His rejection. Learn to marvel at His patience, and seek grace to imitate it in your dealings with other men; and try not to try His patience any more.

3 Appreciate the *discipline* of God. He is both your upholder and, in the last analysis, your environment; all things come of Him, and you have tasted His goodness every day of your life. Has this experience led you to repentance and faith in Christ? If not, you are trifling with God, and stand under the threat of His severity. But if, now, He, in Whitefield's phrase, puts thorns in your bed, it is only to awaken you from the sleep of spiritual death, and to make you rise up to seek His mercy. Or if you are a true believer, and He still puts thorns in your bed, it is only to keep you from falling into the somnolence of complacency, and to ensure that you 'continue in his goodness' by letting your sense of need bring you back constantly in self-abasement and faith to seek His face. This kindly discipline, in which God's severity touches us for a moment in the context of His goodness, is meant to keep us from having to bear the full brunt of that severity apart from that context. It is a discipline of love, and must be received accordingly. 'My son, despise not thou the chastening of the Lord' (Hebrews 12: 5). 'It is good for me that I have been afflicted; that I might learn thy statutes' (Psalm 119: 71).

CHAPTER 17

The Jealous God

I

'The jealous God' — doesn't it sound offensive? For we know jealousy, 'the green-ey'd monster', as a vice, one of the most cancerous and soul-destroying vices that there is; whereas God, we are sure, is perfectly good. How, then, could anyone ever imagine that jealousy is found in Him?

The first step in answering this question is to make it clear that this is not a case of *imagining* anything. Were we imagining a God, then naturally we should ascribe to Him only characteristics which we admired, and jealousy would not enter the picture. Nobody would *imagine* a jealous God. But we are not making up an idea of God by drawing on our imagination; we are seeking instead to listen to the words of Holy Scripture, in which God Himself tells us the truth about Himself. For God our Creator, whom we could never have discovered by any exercise of imagination, has revealed Himself. He has talked. He has spoken through many human agents and messengers, and supremely through His Son, our Lord Jesus Christ. Nor has He left His messages, and the memory of His mighty acts, to be twisted and lost by the distorting processes of oral transmission. Instead, He has had them put on record in permanent written form. And there in the Bible, God's 'public record', as Calvin called it, we find God speaking repeatedly of His jealousy.

When God brought Israel out of Egypt to Sinai, to give them His law and covenant, His jealousy was one of the first facts about Himself which He taught them. The sanction of the second commandment, spoken audibly to Moses and 'written with the finger of God' on tables of stone (Exodus 31:18), was this, 'I the LORD thy God am a jealous God' (20:5). A little later, God told Moses, even more strikingly, 'the LORD, whose name is Jealous, is a jealous God' (34:14). Coming where it does, this latter is a most significant text. The making known of God's name—that is, as always in Scripture, His nature and character—is a basic theme in Exodus. In chapter 3, God had declared His name as 'I am that I am', or 'I AM' simply, and in chapter 6 as 'Jehovah' ('the LORD'). These names spoke of Him as self-existing, self-determining, and sovereign. Then, in chapter 34:5 ff., God had proclaimed His name to Moses by telling him that 'the LORD' is 'merciful and gracious, longsuffering, and abundant in goodness and truth, keeping mercy . . . forgiving iniquity . . . visiting the iniquity . . .' Here was a 'name' that set forth His moral glory. Finally, seven verses further on, as part of the same conversation with Moses, God summed up and rounded off the revelation of His name by declaring it to be 'Jealous'. Clearly, this unexpected word stood for a quality in God which, so far from being inconsistent with the exposition of His name that had gone before, was in some sense an epitome of it. And since this quality was in a true sense His 'name', it was clearly important that His people should understand it.

In fact, the Bible says a good deal about God's jealousy. There are references to it elsewhere in the Pentateuch (Numbers 25:11; Deuteronomy 4:24, 6:15, 29:20, 32:16, 21), in the history books (Joshua 24:19; 1 Kings 14:22), in the prophets (Ezekiel 8:3–5, 16:38, 42, 23:25, 36:5 ff., 38:19, 39:25; Joel 2:18; Nahum 1:2; Zephaniah 1:18, 3:8; Zechariah 1:14, 8:2), and in the Psalms (78:58, 79:5). It is constantly presented as a motive to action, whether in wrath or mercy. 'I will be jealous for my holy name' (Ezekiel 39:25); 'I am jealous for Jerusalem and for Zion with a great jealousy' (Zechariah 1: 14); 'The LORD is a jealous God and avengeth' (Nahum 1:2, RV). In the New Testament, Paul asks the presumptuous Corinthians, 'Shall we provoke the Lord to jealousy?' (1 Corinthians 10:22, RSV); and RSV is probably right to render the difficult sentence in James 4:5 as 'He yearns jealously (literally "unto jealousy") over the spirit which he has made to dwell in us.'

II

But, we ask, what is the nature of this divine jealousy? How can jealousy be a virtue in God when it is a vice in men? God's perfections are matter for praise; but how can we praise God for being jealous?

The answer to these questions will be found if we bear in mind two facts.

First: biblical statements about God's jealousy are *anthropomorphisms*—that is, descriptions of God in language drawn from the life of man. The Bible is full of anthropomorphisms—God's arm, hand, and finger, His hearing, seeing, and smelling, His tenderness, anger, repentance, laughter, joy, and so forth. The reason why God uses these terms to speak to us about Himself is that language drawn from our own personal life is the most accurate medium for communicating thoughts about Him that we have. He is personal, and so are we, in a way that nothing else in the physical creation is. Only man, of all physical creatures, was made in God's image. Since we are more like God than is any other being known to us, it is more illuminating, and less misleading, for God to picture Himself to us in human terms than it would be if He used any other. We made this point two chapters back (p. 136).

When faced with God's anthropomorphisms, however, it is easy to get hold of the wrong end of the stick. We have to remember that man is not the measure of his Maker, and that when the language of human personal life is used of God none of the limitations of human creaturehood are thereby being implied—limited knowledge, or power, or foresight, or strength, or consistency, or anything of that kind. And we must remember that those elements in human qualities which show the corrupting effect of sin have no counterpart in God. Thus, for instance, His wrath is not the ignoble outburst that human anger so often is, a sign of pride and weakness, but it is holiness reacting to evil in a way that is morally right and glorious. 'The wrath of man worketh not the righteousness of God' (James 1:20)—but the wrath of God is precisely His righteousness in judicial action. And in the same way, God's jealousy is not a compound of frustration, envy, and spite, as human jealousy so often is, but appears instead as a (literally) praiseworthy zeal to preserve something supremely precious. This leads us to our next point.

Second: there are two sorts of jealousy among men, and only one of them is a vice. Vicious jealousy is an expression of the attitude, 'I want what you've got, and I hate you because I haven't got it.' It is an infantile resentment springing from unmortified covetousness, which expresses itself in envy, malice, and meanness of action. It is terribly potent, for it feeds and is fed by pride, the taproot of our fallen nature. There is a mad obsessiveness about jealousy which, if indulged, can tear an otherwise firm character to shreds. 'Wrath is cruel, anger is overwhelming; but who can stand

153

before jealousy?' asks the wise man (Proverbs 27:4, RSV). What is often called sexual jealousy, the lunatic fury of a rejected or supplanted suitor, is of this kind.

But there is another sort of jealousy—zeal to protect a love-relationship, or to avenge it when broken. This jealousy also operates in the sphere of sex; there, however, it appears, not as the blind reaction of wounded pride, but as the fruit of marital affection. As Professor Tasker has written, married persons 'who felt no jealousy at the intrusion of a lover or an adulterer into their home would surely be lacking in moral perception; for the exclusiveness of marriage is the essence of marriage' (*The Epistle of James*, p. 106). This sort of jealousy is a positive virtue, for it shows a grasp of the true meaning of the husband-wife relationship, together with a proper zeal to keep it intact. Old Testament law recognised the propriety of such jealousy, and prescribed a 'jealousy offering' and a cursing ordeal whereby a husband who feared that his wife had been unfaithful, and was possessed of a 'spirit of jealousy' in consequence, might have his mind set at rest, one way or the other (Numbers 5:11–31). Neither here nor in the further reference to the wronged husband's 'jealousy' in Proverbs 6:34 does Scripture hint that his attitude is morally questionable; rather, it treats his resolve to guard his marriage against attack, and to take action against anyone who violates it, as natural, normal, and right, and a proof that he values marriage as he should.

Now, Scripture consistently views God's jealousy as being of this latter kind: that is, as an aspect of His covenant love for His own people. The Old Testament regards God's covenant as His marriage with Israel, carrying with it a demand for unqualified love and loyalty. The worship of idols, and all compromising relations with non-Israelite idolators, constituted disobedience and unfaithfulness, which God saw as spiritual adultery, provoking Him to jealousy and vengeance. All the Mosaic references to God's jealousy have to do with idol-worship in one form or another; they all hark back to the sanction of the second commandment, which we quoted earlier. The same is true of Joshua 24:19; 1 Kings 14:22; Psalm 78:58, and in the New Testament 1 Corinthians 10:22. In Ezekiel 8:3, an idol worshipped in Jerusalem is called 'the image of jealousy, which provoketh to jealousy'. In Ezekiel 16, God depicts Israel as His adulterous wife, embroiled in unholy liaisons with idols and idolators of Canaan, Egypt, and Assyria, and pronounces sentence as follows, 'I will judge you as women who break wedlock and shed blood are judged, and bring upon you the blood of wrath and jealousy' (verse 38, RSV; cf. verse 42; 23:25).

From these passages we see plainly what God meant by telling Moses that His name was 'Jealous'. He meant that He demands from those whom He has loved and redeemed utter and absolute loyalty, and will vindicate His claim by stern action against them if they betray His love by unfaithfulness. Calvin hit the nail on the head when he explained the sanction of the second commandment as follows:

The Lord very frequently addresses us in the character of a husband . . . As He performs all the offices of a true and faithful husband, so He requires love and chastity from us; that is, that we do not prostitute our souls to Satan . . . As the purer and chaster a husband is, the more grievously he is offended when he sees his wife inclining to a rival; so the Lord, who has betrothed us to Himself in truth, declares that He burns with the hottest jealousy whenever, neglecting the purity of His holy marriage, we defile ourselves with abominable lusts, and especially when the worship of His deity, which ought to have been most carefully kept unimpaired, is transferred to another, or adulterated with some superstition; since in this way we not only violate our plighted troth, but defile the nuptial couch, by giving access to adulterers (*Institutes*, II, viii, 18).

One further point, however, must be made, if we are to view this matter in its true light. God's jealousy over His people, as we have seen, presupposes His covenant love; and this love is no transitory affection, accidental and aimless, but is the expression of a sovereign purpose. The goal of the covenant love of God is that He should have a people on earth as long as history lasts, and after that should have all His faithful ones of every age with Him in glory. Covenant love is the heart of God's plan for His world. And it is in the light of God's overall plan for His world that His jealousy must, in the last analysis, be understood. For God's ultimate objective, as the Bible declares it, is threefold—to vindicate His rule and righteousness by showing His sovereignty in judgment upon sin; to ransom and redeem His chosen people; and to be loved and praised by them for His glorious acts of love and self-vindication. God seeks what we should seek—His glory, in and through men—and it is for the securing of this end, ultimately, that He is jealous. His jealousy, in all its manifestations, is precisely 'the zeal of the LORD of hosts' (Isaiah 9:7, 37:32;

cf. Ezekiel 5:13) for fulfilling His own purpose of justice and mercy.

So God's jealousy leads Him, on the one hand, to judge and destroy the faithless among His people, who fall into idolatry and sin (Deuteronomy 6:14 f.; Joshua 24:19; Zephaniah 1:18), and indeed to judge the enemies of righteousness and mercy everywhere (Nahum 1:2; Ezekiel 36:5 f.; Zephaniah 3:8); it also leads Him, on the other hand, to restore His people after national judgment has chastened and humbled them (the judgment of captivity, Zechariah 1:14, 8:2; the judgment of the locust plague, Joel 2:18). And what is it that motivates these actions? Simply the fact that He is 'jealous for (His) holy name' (Ezekiel 39:25). His 'name' is His nature and character as Jehovah, 'the LORD', ruler of history, guardian of righteousness and saviour of sinners, and God means His 'name' to be known, honoured, and praised. 'I am the LORD: that is my name: and my glory will I not give to another, neither my praise to graven images.' 'For mine own sake, even for mine own sake, will I do it: for how should my name be polluted? and I will not give my glory unto another' (Isaiah 42:8, 48:11). Here in these texts is the quintessence of the jealousy of God.

III

What practical bearing has all this on those who profess to be the Lord's people? The answer may be given under two headings.

1 *The jealousy of God requires us to be zealous for God.*

As our right response to God's love for us is love for Him, so our right response to His jealousy over us is zeal for Him. His concern for us is great; ours for Him must be great too. What the prohibition of idolatry in the second commandment implies is that God's people should be positively and passionately devoted to His person, His cause, and His honour. The Bible word for such devotion is *zeal*, sometimes actually called *jealousy for God*. God Himself, as we saw, manifests this zeal, and the godly must manifest it too.

The classic description of zeal for God was given by Bishop J. C. Ryle. We quote it at length.

> Zeal in religion is a burning desire to please God, to do His will, and to advance His glory in the world in every possible way. It is a desire which no man feels by nature—which the Spirit puts in the heart of every believer when he is converted— but which some believers feel so much more strongly than others that they alone deserve to be called 'zealous' men . . .

A zealous man in religion is pre-eminently *a man of one thing*. It is not enough to say that he is earnest, hearty, uncompromising, thorough-going, whole-hearted, fervent in spirit. He only sees one thing, he cares for one thing, he lives for one thing, he is swallowed up in one thing; and that one thing is to please God. Whether he lives, or whether he dies—whether he has health, or whether he has sickness—whether he is rich, or whether he is poor—whether he pleases man, or whether he gives offence—whether he is thought wise, or whether he is thought foolish—whether he gets blame, or whether he gets praise—whether he get honour, or whether he gets shame—for all this the zealous man cares nothing at all. He burns for one thing; and that one thing is to please God, and to advance God's glory. If he is consumed in the very burning, he cares not for it —he is content. He feels that, like a lamp, he is made to burn; and if consumed in burning, he has but done the work for which God appointed him. Such a one will always find a sphere for his zeal. If he cannot preach, work, and give money, he will cry, and sigh, and pray. . . . If he cannot fight in the valley with Joshua, he will do the work of Moses, Aaron, and Hur, on the hill (Exodus 17:9–13). If he is cut off from working himself, he will give the Lord no rest till help is raised up from another quarter, and the work is done. This is what I mean when I speak of 'zeal' in religion (*Practical Religion*, 1959 ed., p. 130).

Zeal, we note, is commanded and commended in the Scriptures. Christians are to be 'zealous of good works' (Titus 2:14). For 'zeal' after rebuke the Corinthians are applauded (2 Corinthians 7:11). Elijah was 'very jealous for the LORD God of hosts' (1 Kings 19:10, 14), and God honoured his zeal by sending a chariot of fire to take him up to heaven, and by choosing him as the representative of 'the goodly fellowship of the prophets' to stand with Moses on the mount of transfiguration and talk with the Lord Jesus. When Israel had provoked God to anger by idolatry and prostitution, and Moses had sentenced the offenders to death, and the people were in tears, and a man chose that moment to swagger up with a Midianite party-girl on his arm, and Phinehas, almost beside himself with despair, speared them both, God commended Phinehas as having been 'jealous for his God', 'jealous with my jealousy . . . so that I consumed not the children of Israel in my jealousy' (Numbers 25:11, 13, RV). Paul was a zealous man, single-minded and at full stretch for his Lord. Facing prison and pain, he declared, 'None of these things move me, neither count I my life dear unto myself, so that I might finish my course with joy, and the ministry which I have received of the Lord Jesus, to testify the gospel of the grace of God' (Acts 20:24). And the Lord Jesus himself was a supreme example of zeal. Watching Him cleanse the temple, 'his disciples remembered that it was written, The zeal of thine house hath eaten me up' (John 2:17).

What now, of us? Does zeal for the house of God, and the cause of God, eat us up?—possess us?—consume us? Can we say, with the Master, 'My meat is to do the will of him that sent me, and to finish his work' (John 4:34)? What sort of discipleship is ours? Have we not need to pray, with that flaming evangelist, George Whitefield—a man as humble as he was zealous—'Lord help me to begin to begin'?

2 *The jealousy of God threatens churches which are not zealous for God.*

We love our churches; they have hallowed associations; we cannot imagine them displeasing God, at any rate not seriously. But the Lord Jesus once sent a message to a church very much like some of ours—the complacent church of Laodicea—in which He told the Laodicean congregation that their lack of zeal was a source of supreme offence to Him. 'I know thy works, that thou art neither cold nor hot; I would thou wert cold or hot.' Anything would be better than self-satisfied apathy! 'So then because thou art luke-warm, and neither cold nor hot, *I will spue thee out of my mouth.* . . . Be zealous* therefore, and repent' (Revelation 3:15 f., 19). How many of our churches today are sound, respectable—and luke-warm? What, then, must Christ's word be to them? What have we to hope for?—unless, by the mercy of the God who in wrath remembers mercy, we find zeal to repent? Revive us, Lord, before judgment falls!

III

IF GOD
BE
FOR US...

CHAPTER 18

The Heart of the Gospel

I

Prince Paris had carried off Princess Helen to Troy. The Greek expeditionary force had taken ship to recover her, but was held up half-way by persistent contrary winds. Agamemnon, the Greek general, sent home for his daughter and ceremonially slaughtered her as a sacrifice, to mollify the evidently hostile gods. The move paid off; west winds blew again, and the fleet reached Troy without further difficulty.

This bit of the Trojan war legend, which dates from about 1000 B.C., mirrors an idea of propitiation on which pagan religion all over the world, and in every age, has been built. The idea is as follows. There are various gods, none enjoying absolute dominion, but each with some power to make life easier or harder for you. Their temper is uniformly uncertain; they take offence at the smallest things, or get jealous because they feel you are paying too much attention to other gods and other people, and not enough to themselves, and then they take it out of you by manipulating circumstances to your hurt. The only course at that point is to humour and mollify them by an offering. The rule with offerings is the bigger the better, for the gods are inclined to hold out for something sizeable. In this they are cruel and heartless, but they have the advantage, and what can you do? The wise man bows to the inevitable, and makes sure that he offers something impressive enough to produce the desired result. Human sacrifice, in particular, is expensive but effective. Thus pagan religion appears as a callous commercialism, a matter of managing and manipulating your gods by cunning bribery; and within paganism propitiation, the appeasing of celestial bad tempers, takes its place as a regular part of life, one of the many irksome necessities that one cannot get on without.

Now, the Bible takes us right away from the world of pagan religion. It condemns paganism out of hand, as a monstrous distortion of truth. In place of a cluster of gods who are all too obviously made in the image of man, and who behave like a crowd of Hollywood film stars, the Bible sets the one almighty Creator, the only real God, in Whom all goodness and truth find their source, and to Whom all moral evil is abhorrent. With Him there is no bad temper, no capriciousness, no vanity, no ill-will. One might expect, therefore, that there would be no place for the idea of propitiation in biblical religion.

But we do not find this at all: just the opposite. The idea of propitiation—that is, of averting God's anger by an offering—runs right through the Bible.

In the Old Testament, it underlies the prescribed rituals of the sin-offering, the guilt-offering ('trespass-offering' in the AV), and the day of atonement (Leviticus 4:1–6:7; 16); also, it finds clear expression in such narratives as that of Numbers 16:41 ff., where God threatens to destroy the people for maligning His judgment on Korah, Dathan, and Abiram, 'and Moses said unto Aaron, Take a censer, and put fire therein from off the altar, and put on incense, and go quickly unto the congregation, and make atonement for them: for there is wrath gone out from the Lord; the plague is begun. And Aaron . . . made an atonement for the people. And . . . the plague was stayed' (verses 46 ff.).

In the New Testament, the 'propitiation' word-group appears in four passages of such transcendent importance that we may well pause to set them out in full.

The first is Paul's classic statement of *the rationale of God's justification of sinners.*

'But now apart from the law a righteousness of God hath been manifested . . . even the righteousness of God through faith in Jesus Christ unto all them that believe; for there is no distinction; for all have sinned, and fall short of the glory of God; being justified freely by his grace through the redemption that is in Christ Jesus: whom God set forth to be a *propitiation*, through faith, by his blood, to show his righteousness, because of the passing over of the sins done aforetime, in the forbearance of God; for the shewing, I say, of his righteousness at this present season: that he might himself be just, and the justifier of him that hath faith in Jesus' (Romans 3:21–26, RV).

The second is part of the exposition in Hebrews of *the rationale of the incarnation of God the Son.*

'It behoved him in all things to be made like unto his brethren, that he might be a merciful and faithful high priest, in things pertaining to God, to make *propitiation* for the sins of the people' (Hebrews 2:17, RV).

The third is John's testimony to *the heavenly ministry of our Lord.*

'If any man sin, we have an advocate with the Father, Jesus Christ the righteous: and he is the *propitiation* for our sins' (1 John 2:1 f.).

The fourth is John's *definition of the love of God.*

'God is love. In this was manifested the love of God toward us, because that God sent his only begotten Son into the world, that we might live through him. Herein is love, not that we loved God, but that he loved us, and sent his Son to be the *propitiation* for our sins' (1 John 4:8–10).

Has the word 'propitiation' any place in your Christianity? In the faith of the New Testament it is central. The love of God, the taking of manhood by the Son, the meaning of the cross, Christ's heavenly intercession, and the way of salvation, are all to be explained in terms of it, as the passages quoted show, and any explanation from which the thought of propitiation is missing will be incomplete, and indeed actually misleading, by New Testament standards. In saying this, we swim against the stream of much modern teaching and condemn at a stroke the views of a great number of distinguished Church leaders today, but we cannot help that. Paul wrote, 'though we, or an angel from heaven' — let alone a minister, bishop, college lecturer, university professor, or noted author — 'should preach unto you any gospel other than that which we preached unto you, let him be anathema' (accursed, AV; outcast, NEB; damned, Phillips) (Galatians 1:8). And a gospel without propitiation at its heart is another gospel than that which Paul preached. The implications of this must not be evaded.

II

If, however, you look at the RSV or NEB versions of the four texts quoted above, you will find that the word 'propitiation' does not appear. In both the 1 John passages, NEB has 'remedy for the defilement' of our sins; elsewhere, these versions replace the thought of *propitiation* by that of *expiation*. What is the difference? The difference is that expiation only means half of what propitiation means. Expiation is an action that has sin as its object; it denotes the covering, putting away, or rubbing out of sin so that it no longer constitutes a barrier to friendly fellowship between man and God. Propitiation, however, in the Bible, denotes all that expiation means, *and the pacifying of the wrath of God thereby*. So, at any rate, Christian scholars have maintained since the Reformation, when these things first began to be studied with precision, and the case can still be made compellingly today (see Leon Morris, *The Apostolic Preaching of the Cross*, pp. 125–185, for one example). But in this century a number of scholars, notably Dr. C. H. Dodd, have revived the view of the sixteenth-century Unitarian Socinus, a view which had already been picked up in the late nineteen-hundreds by Albrecht Ritschl, a founder of German liberalism, to the effect that there is in God no such thing as anger occasioned by human sin, and consequently no need or possibility of propitiation. Dr. Dodd has laboured to prove that the 'propitiation' word-group in the New Testament does not carry the sense of appeasing God's anger, but only denotes the putting away of sin, and that therefore 'expiation' is a better rendering; and the RSV and NEB at this point reflect his view.

Does he make out his case? We cannot here go into the technicalities of what is very much a scholars' discussion; but, for what it is worth, we give our own verdict. Dodd, it appears, has shown that this word-group need not mean more than 'expiation', if the context does not require a wider meaning, *but* he has not shown that the word-group cannot mean 'propitiation' in contexts where this meaning is called for. This, however, is the crucial point: in the epistle to the Romans (to take the clearest and most obvious of the four passages) the context *does* call for the meaning 'propitiation' in 3:25.

For in Romans 1:18 Paul sets the stage for his declaration of the gospel by affirming that 'the wrath of God is revealed from heaven against all ungodliness and unrighteousness of men'. 'The wrath of God is dynamically, effectively operative in the world of men and it is as proceeding from heaven, the throne of God, that it is thus active' (John Murray, *The Epistle to the Romans*, vol. I, p. 34). In the rest of Romans 1 Paul traces out the present activity of God's wrath in the judicial hardening of apostate man, expressed in the thrice-repeated phrase 'God gave them up (verses 24, 26, 28). Then in Romans 2:1–16 Paul confronts us with the certainty of the 'day of wrath and revelation of the righteous judgment of God; who will render to every man according to his works: . . . unto them that . . . obey not the truth, but obey unrighteousness, shall be wrath and indignation . . . in the day when God shall judge the secrets of men, according to my gospel, by Jesus Christ' (verses 5 f., 8, 16, RV). In the first part of Romans 3, Paul carries on his argument to prove that every man, Jew and Gentile alike, being 'under sin' (verse 9), stands exposed to the wrath of God in both its present and future manifestation. Here, then, is every man in his natural state, without the gospel; the finally controlling reality in his life, whether he is aware of it or not, is the active anger of God. But now, says Paul, acceptance, pardon, and peace, are freely given to those who hitherto were 'ungodly' (4:5) and 'enemies' of God (5:10), but who now put faith in Christ Jesus, 'whom God set forth to be a propitiation . . . by his blood'. And believers know that 'much more then, being now justified by his blood, shall we be saved from the wrath of God through him' (5:9, RV).

What has happened? The wrath of God against us, both present and to come, has been quenched. How was this effected? Through the death of Christ. 'While we were enemies, we were reconciled to God through the death of his Son' (5:10). The 'blood'—that is, the sacrificial death—of Jesus Christ abolished God's anger against us, and ensured that His treatment of us for ever after would be propitious and favourable. Henceforth, instead of showing Himself to be against us, He would show Himself in our life and experience to be for us. What, then, does the phrase 'a propitiation . . . by His blood' express? It expresses, in the context of Paul's argument, precisely this thought: that *by His sacrificial death for our sins Christ pacified the wrath of God.*

It is true that a generation ago Dr. Dodd tried to evade this conclusion by arguing that the wrath of God in Romans is an impersonal cosmic principle of retribution in which the mind and heart of God towards men do not find true expression—that, in other words, God's wrath is a process external to the will of God Himself. But it is now increasingly admitted that this attempt was a gallant failure. 'It is inadequate', writes R. V. G. Tasker, 'to regard this term (wrath) merely as a description of "the inevitable process of cause and effect in a moral universe" or as another way of speaking of the results of sin. It is rather a personal quality, without which God would cease to be fully righteous and His love would degenerate into sentimentality' (*New Bible Dictionary*, s.v. 'Wrath'). The wrath of God is as personal, and as potent, as His Love; and, just as the blood-shedding of the Lord Jesus was the direct manifesting of His Father's love towards us, so it was the direct averting of His Father's wrath against us.

III

What manner of thing is the wrath of God which was propitiated at Calvary? It is not the capricious, arbitrary, bad-tempered and conceited anger which pagans attribute to their gods. It is not the sinful, resentful, malicious, infantile anger which we find among men. It is a function of that holiness which is expressed in the demands of God's moral law ('be ye holy, for I am holy' [1 Peter 1:16]), and of that righteousness which is expressed in God's acts of judgment and reward. 'We know who it is that has said, "Justice is mine: I will repay"' (Hebrews 10:30, NEB). God's wrath is 'the holy revulsion of God's being against that which is the contradiction of His holiness'; it issues in 'a positive outgoing of the divine displeasure' (John Murray, *loc. cit.*). And this is *righteous* anger—the *right* reaction of moral perfection in the Creator towards moral perversity in the creature. So far from the manifestation of God's wrath in punishing sin being morally doubtful, the thing that would be morally doubtful would be for Him *not* to show His wrath in this way. God is not *just*—that is, He does not act in the way that is *right*, He does not do what is proper to a *judge*—unless He inflicts upon all sin and wrongdoing the penalty it deserves. We shall see Paul himself arguing on this basis in a moment.

IV

Note, now, three facts about the propitiation, as Paul describes it.

1 *Propitiation is the work of God Himself.*
In paganism, man propitiates his gods, and religion becomes a form of commercialism and, indeed, of bribery. In Christianity, however, God propitiates His wrath by His own action. *He set forth Jesus Christ,* says Paul, to be a propitiation; *He sent His Son,* says John, to be the propitiation for our sins. It was not man, to whom God was hostile, who took the initiative to make God friendly, nor was it Jesus Christ, the eternal Son, who took the initiative to turn His Father's wrath against us into love. The idea that the kind Son changed the mind of His unkind Father by offering Himself in place of sinful man is no part of the gospel message—it is a sub-Christian, indeed an anti-Christian idea, for it denies the unity of will in the Father and the Son and so in reality falls back into polytheism, asking us to believe in two different gods. But the Bible rules this out absolutely by insisting that it was God Himself who took the initiative in quenching His

own wrath against those whom, despite their ill-desert, He loved and had chosen to save.

The doctrine of the propitiation is precisely this that God loved the objects of His wrath so much that He gave His own Son to the end that He by His blood should make provision for the removal of this wrath. It was Christ's so to deal with the wrath that the loved would no longer by the objects of wrath, and love would achieve its aim of making the children of wrath the children of God's good pleasure (John Murray, *The Atonement*, p. 15).

Paul and John both state this explicitly and emphatically. God reveals His righteousness, says Paul, not only in retribution and judgment according to His law, but also 'apart from the law', in bestowing righteousness on those who put faith in Jesus Christ. They have all sinned, yet they are all justified (acquitted, accepted, reinstated, set right with God) freely and for nothing (Romans 3:21-24). How does this take place? 'By grace' (that is, mercy contrary to merit; love for the unlovely and, one would have said, unlovable.) By what means does grace operate? 'Through the redemption' (rescue by ransom) 'that is in Christ Jesus'. How is it that, to those who put faith in Him, Christ Jesus is the source, means, and substance of redemption? Because, says Paul, God set Him forth to be a propitiation. From this divine initiative the reality and availability of redemption flow.

Love to one another, says John, is the family likeness of God's children; he who does not love Christians is evidently not in the family, for 'God is love' and imparts a loving nature to all who know Him (1 John 4:7 f.). But 'God is love' is a vague formula; how can we form a clear idea of the love that God would reproduce in us? 'In this was the love of God manifested towards us, because that God sent his only-begotten Son . . . that we might live through him.' Nor was this done as God's acknowledgment of some real devotion on our part; not at all. 'Herein is love, not that we loved God, but that' — in a situation where we did *not* love Him, and there was nothing about us to move Him to do anything other than blast and blight us for our ingrained irreligion — 'he loved us, and sent his Son to be the propitiation for our sins.' By this divine initiative, says John, the meaning and measure of the love that we must imitate are made known.

The witness of both apostles to God's initiative in propitiation could scarcely be clearer.

2 *Propitiation was made by the death of Jesus Christ.*
'Blood', as we hinted earlier, is a word pointing to the violent death inflicted in the animal sacrifices of the Old Covenant. God Himself instituted these sacrifices by His own command, and in Leviticus 17:11 He says why. 'The life of the flesh is in the blood: and I have given it to you upon the altar to make an atonement for your souls: for it is the blood that maketh an atonement. . . .' When Paul tells us that God set forth Jesus to be a propitiation 'by His blood', his point is that what quenched God's wrath and so redeemed us from death was not Jesus's life or teaching, not His moral perfection nor His fidelity to the Father, as such, but the shedding of His blood in death. With the other New Testament writers, Paul always points to the death of Jesus as the atoning event, and explains the atonement in terms of *representative substitution*—the innocent taking the place of the guilty, in the name and for the sake of the guilty, under the axe of God's judicial retribution. Two passages may be quoted to illustrate this.

'Christ hath redeemed us from the curse of the law.' How? 'Being made a curse for us' (Galatians 3:13). Christ bore the curse of the law which was directed against us, so that we might not have to bear it. This is representative substitution.

'One died for all,' and through Jesus's death God was 'reconciling the world unto himself'. What does this reconciliation involve? 'Not imputing their trespasses unto them', but causing them in Christ to become 'the righteousness of God'—that is, accepted as righteous by God. How is this non-imputation brought about? Through the imputing of our trespasses to another, who bore their due. 'He hath made him to be sin for us, who knew no sin.' It thus appears that it was as a sacrifice for sinners, enduring the death penalty in their stead, that 'one died for all' (2 Corinthians 5:14, 18–21). This is representative substitution.

Representative substitution, as the way and means of atonement, was taught in typical form by the God-given Old Testament sacrificial system. There, the perfect animal that was to be offered for sin was first symbolically constituted a *representative*, by the sinner laying his hand on its head and so identifying it with him and him with it (Leviticus 4:4, 24, 29, 33), and then it was killed as a *substitute* for the offerer, the blood being sprinkled 'before the Lord' and applied to one or both of the altars in the sanctuary (verses 6 f., 17 f., 25, 30) as a sign that expiation had been made, averting wrath and restoring fellowship. On the annual Day of Atonement, two goats were used: one was killed as a sin-offering in the ordinary way, and the other, after the priest had laid hands on its head and put Israel's sins 'on the head' of the animal by confessing them there, was sent away to 'bear upon him all their iniquities unto a land not inhabited' (Leviticus 16:21 f.). This double ritual taught a single lesson: that through the sacrifice of a representative substitute God's wrath is averted and sins are borne away out of sight, never to trouble our relationship with God again. The second goat (the scapegoat) illustrates what, in terms of the type, was accomplished by the death of the first goat. These rituals are the immediate background of Paul's teaching on propitiation: it is the fulfilment of the Old Testament sacrificial pattern that he proclaims.

3 *Propitiation manifests God's righteousness.*

So far from calling in question the morality of God's way of dealing with sin, says Paul, the truth of propitiation establishes it, and was explicitly intended to establish it. God set forth His Son to propitiate His own wrath 'to shew His *righteousness* (justice) . . . that He might be *just, and* the justifier of him that hath faith in Jesus'. The word 'set forth' implies a public display. Paul's point is that the public spectacle of propitiation, at the cross, was a public manifestation, not merely of justifying mercy on God's part, but of righteousness and justice as the basis of justifying mercy.

Such a manifestation was needed, says Paul, 'because of the passing over of the sins done aforetime, in the forbearance of God'. The point here is that though men were, and had been from time immemorial, every bit as bad as Romans 1 depicts them, God had not at any time since the flood made it His principle to deal publicly with the race as it deserved. Though men since the flood have been no better than their fathers were before the flood, God had not reacted to their impenitence and irreligion and lawlessness by public acts of adverse providence. Instead, He 'did good, and gave us rain . . . and fruitful seasons, filling our hearts with food and gladness' (Acts 14:17). This 'passing over' of sins in 'forbearance' was not, indeed, forgiveness, but postponement of judgment only; nevertheless, it prompts a question. If, as happens, men do evil, and the Judge of all the earth continues to do them good, can He be as concerned about morality and godliness, the distinction between right and wrong in the lives of His creatures, as He formerly appeared to be, and as perfect justice would seem to require? Indeed, if He allows sinners to continue unpunished, does He not Himself come short of perfection in His office as Judge of the world?

Paul has already answered the second part of this question by his doctrine of 'the day of wrath and . . . righteous judgment' in Romans 2:1–16. Here he answers the first part, by saying in effect that, so far from God being unconcerned about moral issues, and the just requirement of retribution for wrongdoing, God is so concerned about these things that He does not—indeed, Paul would, we think, boldly say, cannot—pardon sinners, and justify the ungodly, save on the basis of justice shown forth in retribution. Our sins *have been* punished; the wheel of retribution *has* turned; judgment *has* been inflicted for our ungodliness—but on Jesus, the lamb of God, standing in our place. In this way God is *just*— *and* the justifier of those who put faith in Jesus, 'who was delivered for our offences, and was raised again for our justification' (4:24).

Thus the righteousness of God the Judge, which is set forth so vividly in the doctrine of divine wrath in the first part of Paul's letter is set forth again in Paul's doctrine of how divine wrath was quenched. It is vital to his argument to show that the truths of salvation and damnation alike manifest the essential, inherent retributive justice which belongs to the divine character. In each case—the salvation of those who are saved, and the damnation of those who are lost—retribution falls; punishment is inflicted; God is righteous, and justice is done.

V

What we have said so far may be summed up as follows. The gospel tells us that our Creator has become our Redeemer. It announces that the Son of God has become man 'for us men and for our salvation', and has died on the cross to save us from eternal judgment. The basic description of the saving death of Christ in the Bible is as a *propitiation*, that is, as that which quenched God's wrath against us by obliterating our sins from His sight. God's wrath is His righteousness reacting against unrighteousness; it shows itself in retributive justice. But Jesus Christ has shielded us from the nightmare prospect of retributive justice by becoming our representative substitute, in obedience to His Father's will, and receiving the wages of our sin in our place. By this means justice has been done, for the sins of all that will ever be pardoned were judged and punished in the person of God the Son, and it is on this basis that pardon is now offered to us offenders. Redeeming love and retributive justice joined hands, so to speak, at Calvary, for there God showed Himself to be 'just, and the justifier of him that hath faith in Jesus'.

Do you understand this? If you do, you are now seeing to the very heart of the Christian gospel. No version of that message goes deeper than that which declares man's root problem before God to be his sin, which evokes wrath, and God's basic provision for man to be propitiation, which out of wrath brings peace. Some versions of the gospel, indeed, are open to blame because they never get down to this level.

We have all heard the gospel presented as God's triumphant answer to human problems—problems of man's relation with himself and his fellows and his environment. Well, there is no doubt that the gospel does bring us solutions to these problems, but it does so by first solving a deeper problem—the deepest of all human problems, the problem of man's relation with his Maker; and unless we make it plain that the solution of these former problems depends on the settling of this latter one, we are misrepresenting the message and becoming false witnesses of God— for a half-truth presented as if it were the whole truth becomes something of a falsehood by that very fact. No reader of the New Testament can miss the fact that it knows all about our human problems—fear, moral cowardice, illness of body and mind, loneliness, insecurity, hopelessness, despair, cruelty, abuse of power, and the rest—but equally no reader of the New Testament can miss the fact that it resolves all these problems, one way or another, into the fundamental problem of sin against God. By sin the New Testament means, not social error or failure in the first instance, but rebellion against, defiance of, retreat from, and consequent guilt before, God the Creator; and sin, says the New Testament, is the basic evil from which we need deliverance, and from which Christ died to save us. All that has gone wrong in human life between man and man is ultimately due to sin, and our present state of being in the wrong with our selves and our fellows cannot be cured as long as we remain in the wrong with God.

Space forbids us to embark here on a demonstration that the themes of sin, propitiation, and pardon, are the basic structural features of the New Testament gospel, but if our readers will thoughtfully go over Romans 1–5, Galatians 3, Ephesians 1–2, Hebrews 8–10, 1 John 1–3, and the sermons in Acts, we think they will find that there is really no room for doubt on this point. If a query is raised on the grounds that the *word* 'propitiation' only appears in the New Testament four times, the reply must be that the *thought* of propitiation appears constantly.

Sometimes the death of Christ is depicted as *reconciliation*, or peace-making after hatred and war (Romans 5:10 f.; 2 Corinthians 5:18 ff.; Colossians 1:20 ff.); sometimes it is depicted as *redemption*, or rescue by ransom from danger and captivity

(Romans 3:24; Galatians 3:13, 4:5; 1 Peter 1:18; Revelation 5:9); sometimes it is pictured as a *sacrifice* (Ephesians 5:2; Hebrews 9–10:18), an act of *self-giving* (Galatians 1:4, 2:20; 1 Timothy 2:6), *sin-bearing* (John 1:29; 1 Peter 2:24; Hebrews 9:28), and *blood-shedding* (Mark 14:24; Hebrews 9:14; Revelation 1:5). All these thoughts have to do with the putting away of sin and the restoring of unclouded fellowship between man and God, as a glance at the texts mentioned will show; and all of them have as their background the threat of divine judgment which Jesus's death averted. In other words, they are so many pictures and illustrations of the reality of propitiation, viewed from different standpoints. It is a shallow fallacy to imagine, as many scholars unhappily do, that this variety of language must necessarily imply variation of thought.

A further point must now be made. Not only does the truth of propitiation lead us to the heart of the New Testament gospel; it also leads us to a vantage-point from which we can see to the heart of many other things too. When you stand on top of Snowdon, you see the whole of Snowdonia spread out round you, and you have a wider view than you can get from any other point in the area. Similarly, when you are on top of the truth of propitiation, you can see the entire Bible in perspective, and you are in a position to take the measure of vital matters which cannot be properly grasped on any other terms. In what follows, five of these will be touched on: the driving force in the life of Jesus; the destiny of those who reject God; God's gift of peace; the dimensions of God's love; and the meaning of God's glory. That these matters are vital to Christianity will not be disputed. That they can only be understood in the light of the truth of propitiation cannot, we think, be denied.

VI

Think first, then, of *the driving force in the life of Jesus.*

If you sit down for an hour and read straight through the gospel according to Mark (a very fruitful exercise: may we urge you here and now to do it), you will receive an impression of Jesus which includes at least four features.

Your basic impression will be of a man of action: a man always on the move, always altering situations and precipitating things — working miracles; calling and training disciples; upsetting error that passed as truth, and irreligion that passed as godliness; and finally walking straight and open-eyed into betrayal, condemnation, and crucifixion, a freakish sequence of anomalies which in the oddest way one is made to feel that He Himself controlled all along the line.

Your further impression will be of a man who knew Himself to be a divine person (Son of God) fulfilling a messianic role (Son of Man). Mark makes it clear that the more Jesus gave Himself to His disciples, the more of an awesome enigma they found Him — the closer they came to Him, the less they understood Him. This sounds paradoxical, but it was strictly true, for as their acquaintance with Him deepened they were brought closer to His own understanding of Himself as God and Saviour, and this was something of which they could make neither head nor tail. But Jesus's unique twofold self-consciousness, confirmed by His Father's voice from heaven at His baptism and transfiguration (Mark 1:11; 9:7) came out constantly. One has only to think here of, on the one hand, the breathtaking naturalness with which He assumed absolute authority in everything He said and did (see 1:22, 27; 14:27–33), and on the other hand His answer to the high priest's double question at His trial, 'art thou the Christ (Messiah, God's saviour-king), the Son of the Blessed (a supernatural and divine person)?' — to which Jesus categorically replied, 'I am' (14:61 f.).

Going on from this, your impression will be of One whose messianic mission centred on His being put to death — One who was consciously and single-mindedly preparing to die in this way long before the idea of a suffering Messiah took hold of anyone else. Four times at least after Peter had hailed Him as the Christ at Caesarea Philippi Jesus predicted that He would be killed and rise, though without the disciples being able to make sense of what he said (8:31, cf. verse 34 f.; 9:9; 9:31; 10:33 f.). At other times He spoke of His being put to death as something certain (12:8, 14:18 ff.), something predicted in Scripture (14:21, 49), and something that would win for many a momentously new relationship with God. 'The Son of Man came . . . to give His life a ransom for many' (10:45). 'This is my blood of the covenant, which is shed for many' (14:24, RV).

Your final impression will be of One for whom this experience of death was the most fearful ordeal. In Gethsemane, 'horror and dismay came over Him, and He said . . . "My heart is ready to break with grief"' (14:24, NEB). The earnestness of His prayer (for which 'He threw Himself on the ground', rather than kneel or stand) was an index of the inward revulsion and desolation that He felt as He contemplated what was to come. How strong was His temptation to say 'amen' after 'take away this cup from me', rather than go on to 'nevertheless not what I will, but what thou wilt' (14:26), we shall never know. Then, on the cross, Jesus bore witness to inward darkness matching outward darkness with His cry of dereliction—'My God, my God, why hast thou forsaken me?' (verse 35).

How should we explain Jesus's belief in the necessity of His death? How should we account for the fact that what drove Him on throughout His public ministry, as all four gospels testify, was the conviction that He had to be killed? And how should we explain the fact that, whereas martyrs like Stephen faced death with joy, and even Socrates, the pagan philosopher, drank his hemlock and died without a tremor, Jesus, the perfect servant of God, who had never before showed the least fear of man or pain or loss, manifested in Gethsemane what looked like blue funk, and on the cross declared himself God-forsaken? 'Never man feared death like this man,' commented Luther. Why? What did it mean?

Those who see the death of Jesus as no more than a tragic accident, no different essentially from the death of any other falsely condemned good man, can make nothing of these facts at all. The only course open to them, on their principles, is to suppose that Jesus had in Him a morbid, timid streak which from time to time let Him down—first, inducing in Him a sort of death-wish, and then overwhelming Him with panic and despair when death came close. But since Jesus was raised from the dead, and in the power of His risen life still taught His disciples that His death had been a necessity (Luke 24:26 f.), this so-called explanation appears to be as nonsensical as it is painful. However, those why deny the truth of the atonement have nothing better that they can say.

But if we relate the facts in question to the apostolic teaching about propitiation, all becomes plain at once. 'May we not urge', asked James Denney, 'that these experiences of deadly fear and of desertion are of one piece with the fact that in His death and in the agony of the garden through which He accepted that death as the cup which His Father gave Him to drink, Jesus was taking upon Him the burden of the world's sin, consenting to be, and actually being, numbered with the transgressors?' (*The Death of Christ*, 1911 ed., p. 46). Had Paul or John been asked this question, there is no doubt what they would have answered. It was because Jesus was to be made sin, and bear God's judgment on sin, that He trembled in the garden, and because He was actually bearing that judgment that He declared Himself forsaken of God on the cross. The driving force in Jesus's life was His resolve to be 'obedient unto death, even the death of the cross' (Philippians 2:8), and the unique dreadfulness of His death lies in the fact that He tasted on Calvary the wrath of God which was our due, so making propitiation for our sins. Centuries before, Isaiah had spelt it out. 'We did esteem Him . . . smitten of God . . .; the chastisement of our sins was upon Him . . .; the Lord hath laid on Him the iniquity of us all . . .; for the transgression of my people was He stricken . . .; it pleased the Lord to bruise Him . . .; thou shalt make His soul an offering for sin . . .' (Isaiah 53:4–10).

> *O Christ, what burdens bowed Thy head!*
> *Our load was laid on Thee;*
> *Thou stoodest in the sinner's stead,*
> *Didst bear all ill for me.*
> *A victim led, Thy blood was shed;*
> *Now there's no load for me.*

> *The Holy One did hide His face;*
> *O Christ, 'twas hid from Thee:*
> *Dumb darkness wrapped Thy soul a space,*
> *The darkness due to me.*
> *But now that face of radiant grace*
> *Shines forth in light on me.*

We have been full on this, because of its importance for understanding the basic Christian facts; the next sections can be shorter.

VII

Think, second, of *the destiny of those who reject God.*

Universalists suppose that the class of people mentioned in this heading will ultimately have no members, but the Bible indicates otherwise. Decisions made in this life will have eternal consequences. 'Be not deceived' (as you would be if you listened to the universalists), 'God is not mocked; for whatsoever a man soweth, that shall he also reap' (Galatians 6:7). Those who in this life reject God will for ever be rejected by God. Universalism is the doctrine that, among others, Judas will be saved, but Jesus did not think he would. 'The Son of Man indeed goeth, as it is written of him; but woe to that man by whom the Son of Man is betrayed! good were it for that man if he had never been born' (Mark 14:21). How could Jesus have spoken those last words if He had expected Judas finally to be saved?

Some, then, face an eternity of rejectedness. How can we understand what they will bring on themselves? We cannot, of course, form any adequate notion of hell, any more than we can of heaven, and no doubt it is good for us that this is so; but perhaps the clearest notion we can form is that derived from contemplating the cross.

On the cross, God judged our sins in the person of His Son, and Jesus endured the retributive come-back of our wrongdoing. Look at the cross, therefore, and you see what form God's judicial reaction to human sin will finally take. What form is that? In a word, withdrawal and deprivation of good. On the cross Jesus lost all the good that He had before: all sense of his Father's presence and love, all sense of physical, mental, and spiritual well-being, all enjoyment of God and of created things, all ease and solace of friendship, were taken from Him, and in their place was nothing but loneliness, pain, a killing sense of human malice and callousness, and a horror of great spiritual darkness. The physical pain, though great (for crucifixion remains the cruellest form of judicial execution that the world has ever known), was yet only a small part of the story; Jesus's chief sufferings were mental and spiritual, and what was packed into less than four hundred minutes was an eternity of agony—agony such that each minute was an eternity in itself, as mental sufferers know that individual minutes can be.

So, too, those who reject God face the prospect of losing all good, and the best way to form an idea of eternal death is to dwell on this thought. In ordinary life, we never notice how much good we enjoy through God's common grace till it is taken from us. We never value health, or steady circumstances, or friendship and respect from others, as we should till we have lost them. Calvary shows that under the final judgment of God nothing that one has valued, or could value, nothing that one can call good, remains to one. It is a terrible thought, but the reality, we may be sure, is more terrible yet. 'Good it were for that man if he had never been born . . .' God help us to learn this lesson, which the spectacle of propitiation through penal substitution on the cross teaches so clearly; and may each of us be found in Christ, our sins covered by His blood, at the last.

VIII

Think, third, of *God's gift of peace.*

What does the gospel of God offer us? If we say 'the peace of God', none will demur—but will everyone understand? The use of right words does not guarantee right thoughts! Too often the peace of God is thought of as if it were essentially a feeling of inner tranquillity, happy and carefree, springing from knowledge that

God will shield one from life's hardest knocks. But this is a misrepresentation, for, on the one hand, God does not feather-bed His children in this way, and anyone who thinks He does is in for a shock, and, on the other hand, that which is basic and essential to the real peace of God does not come into this concept at all. The truths after which this account of God's peace is feeling (though it misrepresents them, as we said) are that God's peace brings both power to face, and live with, one's own badness and failings, and also contentment under 'the slings and arrows of outrageous fortune' (for which the Christian name is God's wise providence). The truth which this account ignores is that the basic ingredient in God's peace, without which the rest cannot be, is pardon and acceptance into covenant — that is, adoption into God's family. But where this change of relationship with God — out of hostility into friendship, out of wrath into the fulness of love, out of condemnation into justification — is not set forth, the gospel of peace is not truly set forth either. The peace *of* God is first and foremost peace *with* God; it is the state of affairs in which God, instead of being *against* us, is *for* us. No account of God's peace which does not start here can do other than mislead. One of the miserable ironies of our time is that whereas liberal and 'radical' theologians believe themselves to be re-stating the gospel for to-day, they have for the most part rejected the categories of wrath, guilt, condemnation, and the enmity of God, and so have made it impossible for themselves ever to present the gospel at all, for they cannot now state the basic problem which the gospel of peace solves.

The peace of God, then, primarily and fundamentally, is a new relationship of forgiveness and acceptance — and the source from which it flows is propitiation. When Jesus came to His disciples in the upper room at evening on His resurrection day, He said, 'Peace be unto you'; 'and when He had so said, He showed unto them His hands and His side' (John 20:19 f.). Why did He do that? Not just to establish His identity, but to remind them of the propitiatory death on the cross whereby He had made peace with His Father for them. Having suffered in their place, as their substitute, to make peace for them, He now came in His risen power to bring that peace to them. 'Behold the Lamb of God, which taketh away the sin of the world.' It is here, in the recognition that, whereas we are by nature at odds with God, and God with us, Jesus has 'made peace through the blood of His cross' (Colossians 1:20), that true knowledge of the peace of God begins.

IX

Think, fourth, of *the dimensions of the love of God.*

Paul prays that the readers of his Ephesian letter 'may be able to comprehend with all saints what is the breadth, and length, and depth, and height, and to know the love of Christ, which passeth knowledge' (Ephesians 3:18 f.). The touch of incoherence and paradox in his language reflects Paul's sense that the reality of divine love is inexpressibly great; nevertheless, he believes that some comprehension of it can be reached. How? The answer of Ephesians is, by considering propitiation in its context—that is, be reviewing the whole plan of grace set forth in the first two chapters of the letter (election; redemption; regeneration; preservation; glorification), of which plan the atoning sacrifice of Christ is the centre-piece. See the key references to redemption and remission of sins, and the bringing near to God of those who were far off, through the *blood* (sacrificial death) of Christ (1:7, 2:13). See also the teaching of chapter 5, which twice points to Christ's propitiatory sacrifice of Himself on our behalf as the demonstration and measure of His love for us, the love that we are to imitate in our dealings with each other. 'Walk in love, as Christ also hath loved us, and hath given Himself for us an offering and a sacrifice to God' (verse 2). 'Husbands, love your wives, even as Christ also loved the church, and gave Himself for it' (verse 25). Christ's love was *free*, not elicited by any goodness in us (cf. 2:1 ff.); it was *eternal*, being one with the choice of sinners to save which the Father made 'before the foundation of the world' (1:4); it was *unreserved*, for it led Him down to the depths of humiliation and, indeed, of hell itself on Calvary; and it was *sovereign*, for it has achieved its object—the final glory of the redeemed, their perfect holiness and happiness in the fruition of His love (cf. 5:25–27), is now guaranteed and assured (cf. 1:14; 2:7 ff.; 4:30; 4:11–16). Dwell on these things, Paul urges, if you would catch a sight, however dim, of the greatness and the glory of divine love. It is these things that make up 'the glory of His grace' (1:6); only those who know them can praise the name of the Triune Jehovah as they should. Which brings us to our last point.

X

Think, lastly, of *the meaning of God's glory.*

In the upper room, after Judas had gone out into the night to betray Him, Jesus said, 'Now is the Son of man glorified, and God if glorified in Him' (John 13:31). What did He mean? 'Son of man' was His name for Himself as the Saviour-King who before being enthroned must fulfil Isaiah 53; and when He spoke of the present glorifying of the Son of man, and of God in Him, He was thinking specifically of the atoning death, the 'lifting up' on the cross, which Judas had gone to precipitate. Do you see the glory of God in His wisdom, power, righteousness, truth, and love, supremely disclosed at Calvary, in the making of propitiation for our sins? The Bible does; and we venture to add, if you felt the burden and pressure of your own sins at its true weight, so would you. In heaven, where these things are better understood, angels and men unite to praise 'the Lamb that was slain' (Revelation 5:11 ff.; 7:9 ff.). Here on earth those who by grace have been made spiritual realists do the same.

Bearing shame and scoffing rude
In my place condemned He stood;
Sealed my pardon with His blood:
Hallelujah! What a Saviour! . . .

* * *

He left His Father's throne above,
So free, so infinite His grace;
Emptied Himself of all but love
And bled for Adam's helpless race.
Amazing love! How can it be?
For O, my God, it found out me! . . .

* * *

If Thou hast my discharge procured,
And freely in my room endured
The whole of wrath divine,
Payment God cannot twice demand,
First at my bleeding Surety's hand,
And then again at mine.

Turn then, my soul, unto thy rest;
The merits of thy great High Priest
Have bought thy liberty.
Trust in His efficacious blood,
Nor fear thy banishment from God,
Since Jesus died for thee!

These are the songs of the heirs of heaven, those who have seen 'the light of the knowledge of the glory of God in the face (that is, the person, office, and achievement) of Jesus Christ' (2 Corinthians 4:6). The joyful news of redeeming love and propitiating mercy, which is the heart of the gospel, spurs them to never-ending praise. Are you among their number?

CHAPTER 19

Sons of God

I

What is a Christian? The question can be answered in many ways, but the richest answer I know is that a Christian is one who has God for his Father.

But cannot this be said of every man, Christian or not? Emphatically no! The idea that all men are children of God is not found in the Bible anywhere. The Old Testament shows God as the Father, not of all men, but of His own people, the seed of Abraham. 'Israel is my son, even my firstborn: and I say unto thee, Let my son go . . .' (Exodus 4:22 f.). The New Testament has a world vision, but it too shows God as the Father, not of all men, but of those who, knowing themselves to be sinners, put their trust in the Lord Jesus Christ as their divine sin-bearer and master, and so become Abraham's spiritual seed. 'Ye are all sons of God, through faith, in Christ Jesus . . . ye all are one man in Christ Jesus. And if ye are Christ's, then are ye Abraham's seed' (Galatians 3:26 ff.). Sonship to God is not, therefore, a universal status upon which everyone enters by natural birth, but a supernatural gift which one receives through receiving Jesus. 'No man cometh unto the Father' — in others words, is acknowledged by God as a son — 'but by me' (John 14:6). The gift of sonship to God becomes ours, not through being born, but through being born again. '*As many as received Him,* to *them* gave He power to become the sons of God, even to them that believe on His name: which were born, not of blood, nor of the will of the flesh, nor of the will of man, but of God' (John 1:12 f.).

Sonship to God, then, is a gift of grace. It is not a natural, but an *adoptive* sonship: and so the New Testament explicitly pictures it. In Roman law, it was a recognised practice for an adult who wanted an heir, and someone to carry on the family name, to adopt a male as his son—usually at age, rather than in infancy, as is the common way today. The apostles proclaim that God has so loved those whom He redeemed on the cross that He has adopted them all as His heirs, to see and share the glory into which His only-begotten Son has already come. 'God sent forth His son . . . to redeem them that were under the law, that we might receive the adoption of sons' (Galatians 4:4 f.): we, that is, who were 'fore-ordained unto adoption as sons by Jesus Christ unto Himself' (Ephesians 1:5, RV). 'Behold, what manner of love the Father hath bestowed upon us, that we should be called the sons of God . . . when He shall appear, we shall be like Him; for we shall see Him as He is' (1 John 3:1 f.).

Some years ago, I wrote:

> You sum up the whole of New Testament teaching in a single phrase, if you speak of it as a revelation of the Fatherhood of the holy Creator. In the same way, you sum up the whole of New Testament religion if you describe it as the knowledge of God as one's holy Father. If you want to judge how well a person understands Christianity, find out how much he makes of the thought of being God's child, and having God as his Father. If this is not the thought that prompts and controls his worship and prayers and his whole outlook on life, it means that he does not understand Christianity very well at all. For everything that Christ taught, everything that makes the New Testament new, and better than the Old, everything that is distinctively Christian as opposed to merely Jewish, is summed up in the knowledge of the Fatherhood of God. 'Father' is the Christian name for God (*Evangelical Magazine*, 7, p. 19 f.).

This still seems to me wholly true, and very important. Our understanding of Christianity cannot be better than our grasp of adoption. It is to help us grasp it better that this chapter is being written.

The revelation to the believer that God is his Father is in a sense the climax of the Bible, just as it was a final step in the revelatory process which the Bible records. In Old Testament times, as we have seen, God gave His people a covenant name by which to speak of Him and call upon Him: the name Yahweh ('Jehovah', 'the LORD'). By this name, God announced Himself as the 'great

I AM'—the One who is completely and consistently Himself. He *is*: and it is because He is what He is that everything else is as it is. He is the reality behind all reality, the underlying cause of all causes and all events. The name proclaimed Him as self-existent, sovereign, and wholly free from constraint by, or dependence on, anything outside Himself. Though Yahweh was His covenant name, it spoke to Israel of what their God was in Himself rather than of what He would be in relation to them. It was the official name of Israel's King, and there was something of regal reserve about it. It was an enigmatic name, a name calculated to awaken humility and awe before the mystery of the Divine being rather than anything else.

In full accord with this, the aspect of His character on which God laid most stress in the Old Testament was His holiness. The angels' song which Isaiah heard in the temple, with its emphatic repetitions—'Holy, holy, holy, is the LORD of hosts' (Isaiah 6:3)— could be used as a motto-text to sum up the theme of the whole Old Testament. The basic idea which the word 'holy' expresses is that of separation, or separateness. When God is declared to be 'holy', the thought is of all that separates Him and sets Him apart and makes Him different from His creatures: His *greatness* ('the *majesty* on high', Hebrews 1:3; 8:1), and His *purity* ('Thou art of purer eyes than to behold evil, and canst not look on iniquity', Habakkuk 1:13). The whole spirit of Old Testament religion was determined by the thought of God's holiness. The constant emphasis was that man, because of his weakness as a creature and His defilement as a sinful creature, must learn to humble himself and be reverent before God. Religion was 'the fear of the Lord'—a matter of knowing your own littleness, of confessing your faults and abasing yourself in God's presence, of sheltering thankfully under His promises of mercy, and of taking care above all things to avoid presumptuous sins. Again and again it was stressed that man must keep his place, and his distance, in the presence of a holy God. This emphasis overshadowed everything else.

But in the New Testament we find that things have changed. God and religion are not less than they were; the Old Testament revelation of the holiness of God, and its demand for humility in man, is presupposed throughout. But something has been added. A new factor has come in. New Testament believers deal with God as their Father. 'Father' is the name by which they call Him. 'Father' has now become His covenant name—for the covenant which binds Him to His people now stands revealed as a family covenant. Christians are His children, His own sons and heirs.

And the stress of the New Testament is not on the difficulty and danger of drawing near to the holy God, but on the boldness and confidence with which believers may approach Him: a boldness that springs directly from faith in Christ, and from the knowledge of His saving work. 'We have boldness and access with confidence *by the faith of him*' (Ephesians 3:12). 'Having therefore, brethren, boldness to enter into the holiest *by the blood of Jesus*, by a new and living way, *which he hath consecrated for us* . . . let us draw near with a true heart in full assurance of faith . . .' (Hebrews 10:19 ff.). To those who are Christ's, the holy God is a loving Father; they belong to His family; they may approach Him without fear, and always be sure of His fatherly concern and care. This is the heart of the New Testament message.

Who can grasp this? I have heard it seriously argued that the thought of divine fatherhood can mean nothing to those whose human father was inadequate, lacking wisdom, affection, or both, nor to those many more whose misfortune it was to have a fatherless upbringing. I have heard Bishop Robinson's revealing failure to say anything about divine fatherhood in *Honest to God* defended on these grounds as a brilliant move in commending the faith to a generation in which family life has largely broken down. But this is silly. For, in the first place, it is just not true to suggest that in the realm of personal relations positive concepts cannot be formed by contrast—which is the suggestion implicit here. Many young people get married with a resolve not to make the mess of marriage that they saw their parents make: can this not be a positive ideal? Of course it can. Similarly, the thought of our Maker becoming our perfect parent—faithful in love and care, generous and thoughtful, interested in all we do, respecting our individuality, skilful in training us, wise in guidance, always available, helping us to find ourselves in maturity, integrity, and uprightness—is a thought which can have meaning for everybody, whether we come to it by saying, 'I had a wonderful father, and I see that God is like that, only more so,' or by saying, 'My father disappointed me here, and here, and here, but God, praise His name, will be very different,' or even by saying, 'I have never known what it is to have a father on earth, but thank God I now have one in heaven.' The truth is that all of us have a positive ideal of fatherhood by which we judge our own and others' fathers, and it can safely be said that the person for whom the thought of God's perfect fatherhood is meaningless or repellent does not exist.

But in any case (and this is the second point), God has not left us to guess what His fatherhood amounts to, by drawing analogies from human fatherhood. He revealed the full meaning of this relationship once and for all through our Lord Jesus Christ, His own incarnate Son. As it is from God that 'all fatherhood, earthly or heavenly, derives its name' (Ephesians 3:14, Phillips), so it is from His manifested activity as 'the God and Father of our Lord Jesus Christ' (1:3) that we learn, in this one instance which is also a universal standard, what God's fatherly relation to us who are Christ's really means. For God intends the lives of believers to be a reflection and reproduction of Jesus's own fellowship with Himself.

Where can we learn about this? Chiefly from John's gospel and first epistle. In John's gospel the first evangelical blessing to be named is adoption (1:12), and the climax of the first resurrection appearance is Jesus's statement that He was ascending to 'my Father and your Father, my God and your God' (20:17, NEB). Central in John's first epistle are the thoughts of sonship as the supreme gift of God's love (1 John 3:1); of love to the Father (2:15, cf. 5:1–3) and to one's Christian brothers (2:9–11, 3:10–17, 4:7, 21) as the ethic of sonship; of fellowship with God the Father as the privilege of sonship (2:13, 23f.); of righteousness and avoidance of sin as the evidence of sonship (2:29, 3:9 f.–5:18); and of seeing Jesus, and being like Him, as the hope of sonship (3:3). From these two books together we learn very clearly what God's fatherhood implied for Jesus, and what it now implies for Christians.

According to our Lord's own testimony in John's gospel, God's fatherly relation to Him implied four things.

First, it implied *authority*. The Father commands and disposes; the initiative which He calls His Son to exercise is the initiative of resolute obedience to His Father's will. 'I came down from heaven, not to do mine own will, but the will of him that sent me.' 'I have finished the work which thou gavest me to do.' 'The Son can do nothing of himself.' 'My meat is to do the will of him that sent me' (John 6:38, 17:4, 5:19, 4. 34).

Second, fatherhood implied *affection*. 'The Father loveth the Son.' 'The Father hath loved me . . . I have kept my Father's commandments, and abide in his love' (5:20; 15:9 f.).

Third, fatherhood implied *fellowship*. 'I am not alone, because the Father is with me.' 'He that sent me is with me; he hath not left me alone; for I do always those things that please him' (16:32; 8:29).

Fourth, fatherhood implied *honour*. God wills to exalt His Son. 'Father, glorify thy Son.' 'The Father . . . hath committed all judgment unto the Son; that all men should honour the Son, even as they honour the Father' (17:1; 5:22f.)

All this extends to God's adopted children. In, through, and under Jesus Christ their Lord, they are ruled, loved, companied with, and honoured by their heavenly Father. As Jesus obeyed God, so must they. 'This is the love of God' – the God 'that begat' – 'that we keep His commandments' (1 John 5:1, 3). As God loved His only-begotten Son, so He loves His adopted sons. 'The Father himself loveth you' (John 16:27). As God had fellowship with Jesus, so He does with us. 'Our fellowship is with the Father, and with His Son Jesus Christ' (1 John 1:3). As God exalted Jesus, so He exalts Jesus's followers, as brothers in the one family. If any man serve me, him will my Father honour.' 'Father, I will that they also, whom thou hast given me, be with me where I am', to see and share the glory which Jesus enjoys (John 12:32, 17:24). In these terms the Bible teaches us to understand the shape and substance of the parent-child relationship which binds together the Father of Jesus and the servant of Jesus.

A formal definition and analysis of what adoption means is called for at this point. Here is a fine one, from the Westminster Confession (Chapter XII):

> All those that are justified, God vouchsafeth, in and for His only Son Jesus Christ, to make partakers of the grace of adoption: by which they are taken into the number, and enjoy the liberties and privileges of the children of God; have His name put upon them, receive the Spirit of adoption; have access to the throne of grace with boldness; are enabled to cry, Abba, Father; are pitied, protected, provided for, and chastened by Him, as by a father; yet never cast off, but sealed to the day of redemption, and inherit the promises, as heirs of everlasting salvation.

This is the nature of the divine sonship that is bestowed on believers, which we are now to study.

II

Our first point about adoption is that it is *the highest privilege that the gospel offers:* higher even than justification. This may cause raising of eyebrows, for justification is the gift of God on which since Luther evangelicals have laid the greatest stress, and we are accustomed to say, almost without thinking, that free justification is God's supreme blessing to us sinners. None the less, careful thought will show the truth of the statement we have just made.

That justification – by which we mean God's forgiveness of the past together with His acceptance for the future—is the *primary* and *fundamental* blessing of the gospel is not in question. Justification is the *primary* blessing, because it meets our primary spiritual need. We all stand by nature under God's judgment; His law condemns us; guilt gnaws at us, making us restless, miserable, and in our lucid moments afraid; we have no peace in ourselves, because we have no peace with our Maker. So we need the forgiveness of our sins, and assurance of a restored relationship with God, more than we need anything else in the world; and this the gospel offers us before it offers us anything else. The first gospel sermons to be preached, those recorded in Acts, lead up to the promise of forgiveness of sins to all who repent and receive Jesus as their Saviour and Lord (see Acts 2:38; 3:19; 10:43; 13:38 f.; cf. 5:31; 17:30 f.; 19:21; 22:16; 26:18; Luke 24:47). In Romans, Paul's fullest exposition of his gospel—'the clearest gospel of all', to Luther's mind—justification through the cross of Christ is expounded first (chapters 1–5), and made basic to everything else. Regularly Paul speaks of righteousness, remission of sins, and justification as the first and immediate consequence for us of Jesus's death (Romans 3:22–26; 2 Corinthians 5:18–21; Galatians 3: 13 f.; Ephesians 1:7; etc.). And as justification is the *primary* blessing, so it is the *fundamental* blessing, in the sense that everything else in our salvation assumes it, and rests on it— adoption included.

But this is not to say that justification is the *highest* blessing of the gospel. Adoption is higher, because of the richer relationship with God that it involves. Some textbooks on Christian doctrine— Berkhof's, for instance—treat adoption as a mere sub-section of justification, but this is inadequate. The two ideas are distinct, and adoption is the more exalted. Justification is a *forensic* idea, conceived in terms of *law*, and viewing God as *judge*. In justification, God declares of penitent believers that they are not, and never will be, liable to the death that their sins deserve, because Jesus Christ, their substitute and sacrifice, tasted death in their place on the cross. This free gift of acquittal and peace, won for us at the cost of Calvary, is wonderful enough, in all conscience— but justification does not of itself imply any intimate or deep relationship with God the judge. In idea, at any rate, you could have the reality of justification without any close fellowship with God resulting. But contrast this, now, with adoption. Adoption is a *family* idea, conceived in terms of *love*, and viewing God as *father*. In adoption, God takes us into His family and fellowship, and establishes us as His children and heirs. Closeness, affection and generosity are at the heart of the relationship. To be right with God the judge is a great thing, but to be loved and cared for by God the father is a greater.

This point has never been better put than in the following extract from *The Doctrine of Justification*, by James Buchanan:

> According to the Scriptures, pardon, acceptance, and adoption, are distinct privileges, the one rising above the other in the order in which they have been stated . . . while the first two properly belong to (the sinner's) justification, as being both founded on the same relation—that of a Ruler and Subject—the third is radically distinct from them, as being founded on a nearer, more tender, and more endearing relation—that between a Father and his Son . . . There is a manifest difference between the position of a servant and a friend—and also between that of a servant and a son . . . A closer and dearer intimacy than that of a master and servant is said to subsist between Christ and His people: 'Henceforth I call you not servants: for the servant knoweth not what his lord doeth: but I have called you friends' (John 15: 15); and a still closer and dearer relation is said to exist in consequence of adoption; for 'Thou art no more a servant, but a son, and an heir of God through Christ' (Galatians 4: 7). The privilege of adoption presupposes pardon and acceptance, but is higher than either; for, 'To as many as received Him, to them gave He power'—not inward strength, but authority, right, or privilege—'to become the sons of God, even to them that believe on His name' (John 1:12). This is a higher privilege than of Justification, as being founded on a closer and more endearing relation—'Behold! what manner of love the Father hath bestowed on us, that we should be called the sons of God' (1 John 3:1) (*op. cit.*, p. 276 f.).

We do not fully feel the wonder of the passage from death to life which takes place in the new birth till we see it as a transition, not simply out of condemnation into acceptance, but out of bondage and destitution into the 'safety, certainty, and enjoyment' of the family of God. This is the view of the great change which Paul sets out in Galatians 4:1–7, contrasting his readers' previous life of slavish legalism and superstition in religion (verses 5 and 3, cf. 8) with their present knowledge of their Creator as their Father (verse 6) and their pledged benefactor (verse 7). This, says Paul, is where your faith in Christ has brought you; you have received 'the adoption of sons' (verse 5); 'you are no longer a slave, but a son, and if a son then an heir' (verse 7, RSV).

When Charles Wesley found Christ on Whit Sunday, 1738, his experience overflowed into some marvellous verses ('The Wesleys' Conversion Hymn', Methodist Hymn Book 361) in which the transition from slavery to sonship is the main theme.

> *Where shall my wondering soul begin?*
> *How shall I all to heaven aspire?*
> *A* slave *redeemed from death and sin,*
> *A brand plucked from eternal fire,*
> *How shall I equal triumphs raise,*
> *Or sing my great Deliverer's praise?*
>
> *O how shall I the goodness tell*
> Father, *which thou to me hast showed?*
> *That I, a child of wrath and hell,*
> *I should be called a* child of God,
> *Should know, should feel my sins forgiven,*
> *Blest with this antepast of heaven!*

Three days later, Charles tells us in his diary, brother John burst in with 'a troop of our friends' to announce that he too was now a believer, and 'we sang the hymn with great joy'. Had you been there, could you sincerely have joined in? Can you make Wesley's words your own? If you are truly a child of God and 'the Spirit of his Son' is in you, Wesley's words have already drawn an echo from your heart; and if they have left you cold, I do not know how you can imagine that you are a Christian at all.

One more thing must be added to show how great is the blessing of adoption — namely, this: that it is a blessing that *abides*. Social experts drum into us these days that the family unit needs to be stable and secure, and that any unsteadiness in the parent-child relationship takes its toll in strain, neurosis, and arrested development in the child himself. The depressions, randomnesses, and immaturities that mark the children of broken homes are known to us all. But things are not like that in God's family. There you have absolute stability and security; the parent is entirely wise and good, and the child's position is permanently assured. The very concept of adoption is itself a proof and guarantee of the preservation of the saints, for only bad fathers throw their sons out of the family, even under provocation; and God is not a bad father, but a good one. When one sees depression, randomness, and immaturity in Christians one cannot but wonder whether they have learned the health-giving habit of dwelling on the abiding security of the sons of God.

III

Our second point about adoption is that *the entire Christian life has to be understood in terms of it.* Sonship must be the controlling thought—the normative category, if you like—at every point. This follows from the nature of the case, and is strikingly confirmed by the fact that all our Lord's teaching on Christian discipleship is cast in these terms.

It is clear that, just as Jesus always thought of Himself as Son of God in a unique sense, so He always thought of His followers as children of His heavenly Father, members of the same divine family as Himself. Early in His ministry we find Him saying, 'Whosoever shall do the will of God, the same is my brother, and my sister, and mother' (Mark 3:35). And two evangelists note how after His resurrection He called His disciples His brothers. 'As they (the women) went to tell His *disciples*, behold, Jesus met them . . . Then said Jesus unto them, Be not afraid: go tell my *brethren* that they go into Galilee, and there shall they see Me' (Matthew 28: 9 f.). 'Go to my *brethren*, and say unto them, I ascend unto my Father, and your Father; and to my God, and your God. Mary Magdalene came and told the *disciples* that . . . He had spoken these things unto her' (John 20:17 f.). The writer to the Hebrews assures us that the Lord Jesus regards all those for whom He has died, and whom He makes into His disciples, as His brothers. 'The Son does not shrink from calling men his brothers, when he says, "I will proclaim thy name unto my brothers . . ." and again, "Here am I, and the children whom God has given Me" ' (Hebrews 2: 12 f., NEB). As our Maker is our Father, so our Saviour is our brother, when we come into the family of God.

Now, just as the knowledge of His unique sonship controlled Jesus's living of His own life on earth, so He insists that the knowledge of our adoptive sonship must control our lives too. This comes out in His teaching again and again, but nowhere more clearly than in His Sermon on the Mount. Often called the charter of God's kingdom, this Sermon could equally well be described as the royal family code, for the thought of the disciple's sonship to God is basic to all the main issues of Christian obedience with which the Sermon deals. This is worth showing in detail, especially since the point is so rarely given its proper weight in exposition.

First, then, adoption appears in the Sermon as the basis of

Christian conduct. It is often remarked that the Sermon teaches Christian conduct, not by giving a full scheme of rules and a detailed casuistry, to be followed with mechanical precision, but by indicating in a broad and general way the spirit, direction, and objectives, the guiding principles and ideals, by which the Christian must steer his course. It is often noted that this is an ethic of responsible freedom, quite different from the tax-consultant type of instruction which was the stock-in-trade of Jewish lawyers and scribes in our Lord's day. What is less often noticed it that it is precisely the kind of moral instruction that parents are constantly trying to give their children—concrete, imaginative, teaching general principles from particular instances, and seeking all the time to bring the children to appreciate and share the parents' own attitudes and view of life. The reason why the Sermon has this quality is not far to seek: it is because it is in truth instruction for the children of a family—God's family. This basic orientation comes out in three all-embracing principles of conduct which our Lord lays down.

Number one is the principle of *imitating the Father.* 'I say unto you, Love your enemies . . . that ye may be children of your Father which is in heaven . . . Be ye therefore perfect, even as your Father which is in heaven is perfect' (Matthew 5:44 f., 48). The children must show the family likeness in their conduct. Jesus is here spelling out 'Be ye holy, for I am holy'—and spelling it out in family terms.

Number two is the principle of *glorifying the Father.* 'Let your light so shine before men, that they may see your good works, and glorify your Father which is in heaven' (5:16). It is a fine thing for children to be proud of their father, and to want others too to see how wonderful he is, and to take care that they behave in public in a way that is a credit to him; and similarly, says Jesus, Christians must seek to behave among men in a way that brings praise to their Father in heaven. Their constant concern must be that which they are taught to voice at the outset of all their prayers—'Our Father . . . Hallowed be thy name' (6:9).

Number three is the principle of *pleasing the Father.* In 6:1–18, Jesus dwells on the need to be a single-minded God-pleaser in one's religion, and He states the principle thus, 'Beware of practising your piety before men in order to be seen by them; for then you will have no reward from your Father who is in heaven' (6:1, RSV). Such 'reward' is not, of course, a mercenary matter—it will be a reward within the family, an extra-love-token such as parents love to surprise their children with when the children have tried specially hard to please. The purpose of our Lord's promise of reward (verses 4, 6, 18) is not to make us think in terms of wages and a *quid pro quo*, but simply to remind us that our heavenly Father will notice, and show special pleasure, when we concentrate our efforts on pleasing Him, and Him alone.

Second, adoption appears in the Sermon as the basis of *Christian prayer*. 'After this manner therefore pray ye: Our Father . . .' (6:9). As Jesus always prayed to His God as Father ('Abba' in Aramaic, an intimate family word), so must His followers do. Jesus could say to His Father 'thou hearest me always' (John 11:41), and He wants His disciples to know that, as God's adopted children, the same is true of them. The Father is always accessible to His children, and is never too preoccupied to listen to what they have to say. This is the basis of Christian prayer.

Two things follow, according to the Sermon. First, prayer must not be thought of in impersonal or mechanical terms, as a technique for putting pressure on someone who otherwise might disregard you. 'When ye pray, use not vain repetitions, as the heathen do: for they think that they shall be heard for their much speaking. Be not ye therefore like unto them: for your Father knoweth what things ye have need of, before ye ask him' (Matthew 6:7 f.). Second, prayer may be free and bold. We need not hesitate to imitate the sublime 'cheek' of the child who is not afraid to ask his parents for anything, because he knows he can count completely on their love. 'Ask, and it shall be given you . . . every one that asketh receiveth . . . if ye then, being evil, know how to give good gifts unto your children, how much more shall your Father which is in heaven give good things to them that ask him?' (7:7–11).

Not, indeed, that our Father in heaven always answers His children's prayers in the form in which we offer them. Sometimes we ask for the wrong thing! It is God's prerogative to give *good* things, things that we have *need* of, and if in our unwisdom we ask for things that do not come under these headings God, like any good parent, reserves the right to say 'No, not that; it wouldn't be good for you—but have this instead'. Good parents never simply ignore what their children are saying, nor simply disregard their feelings of need, and neither does God; but often He gives us what we should have asked for, rather than what we actually requested. Paul asked the Lord Jesus graciously to remove his thorn in the flesh, and the Lord replied by graciously leaving it and strengthening Paul to live with it (2 Corinthians 12:7 ff.). The Lord knew best!—and to suggest that because Paul's prayer was answered this way it was not answered at all would be utterly wrong. Here is a source of much light on what is sometimes miscalled 'the problem of unanswered prayer'.

Third, adoption appears in the Sermon as the basis of *the life of faith*—that is, the life of trusting God for one's material needs as one seeks His kingdom and righteousness. It is needless, I hope, to make the point that one can live the life of faith without foregoing gainful employment—some are called to do this, no doubt, but to attempt it without specific guidance would be, not faith, but foolhardiness—there is a big difference! All Christians are, in fact, called to a life of faith, in the sense of following God's will at whatever cost and trusting Him for the consequences. But all are tempted, sooner or later, to put status and security, in human terms, before loyalty to God's call; and then, if they resist this temptation, they are at once tempted to worry about the likely effect of their stand—particularly when, as happened to the disciples to whom the Sermon was first preached, and as has happened to many more since, following Jesus has obliged them actually to forfeit some measure of security or prosperity which they could otherwise have expected to enjoy. On those thus tempted in the life of faith, Jesus brings the truth of their adoption to bear.

'Be not anxious for your life,' says the Lord, 'what ye shall eat, or what ye shall drink; nor yet for your body, what ye shall put on' (Matthew 6:25, RV). But, says someone, this is not realistic; how can I help worrying, when I face this, and this, and this? To which Jesus's reply is: your faith is too small; have you forgotten that God is your Father? 'Behold the fowls of the air . . . your heavenly Father feedeth them. Are ye not much better than they?' (verse 26). If God cares for the birds, whose Father He is not, is it not plain that He will certainly care for you, whose Father He is? The point is put positively in verses 31–33. 'Be not therefore anxious, saying, What shall we eat? or, What shall we drink? . . . your heavenly Father knoweth that ye have need of all these things. But seek ye first His'—your Father's—'kingdom and His righteousness, and all these things shall be added unto you.' 'We might have a crash,' said the small girl anxiously, as the family car threaded its way through traffic. 'Trust Daddy; he's a good driver,' said Mummy. The young lady was reassured, and relaxed at once. Do you trust your heavenly Father like that? If not, why not? Such trust is vital; it is in truth the mainspring of the life of faith, which without it becomes a life of at least partial unbelief.

IV

In an earlier chapter, we saw that the thought of *propitiation*, which appears verbally only four times in the New Testament, is none the less fundamentally important, as being the nucleus and focal point of the whole New Testament view of the saving work of Christ. Something similar is true here. The word 'adoption' (the Greek means 'instating as a son') appears only five times, and of these occurrences only three refer to the Christian's present relation to God in Christ (Romans 8:14; Galatians 4:5; Ephesians 1:5); yet the thought itself is the nucleus and focal point of the whole New Testament teaching on the Christian life. These two concepts, indeed, link together; were I asked to focus the New Testament message in three words, my proposal would be *adoption through propitiation*, and I do not expect ever to meet a richer or more pregnant summary of the gospel than that. Nor is it only in the four gospels that the thought of our God-given sonship, 'our fountain privilege' as John Owen calls it, is set forth as controlling thought and life. The epistles, too, are full of it. We shall be drawing our evidence chiefly from the epistles as we move on now to show that the truth of our adoption gives us the deepest insights that the New Testament affords into five further matters: first, the greatness of God's love; second, the glory of the Christian hope; third, the ministry of the Holy Spirit; fourth, the meaning and motives of what the Puritans called 'gospel holiness'; fifth, the problem of Christian assurance.

First, then, *our adoption shows us the greatness of God's grace.*

The New Testament gives us two yardsticks for measuring God's love. The first is the cross (see Romans 5:8; 1 John 4:8–10); the second is the gift of sonship. 'Behold, what manner of love the Father has bestowed upon us, that we should be called the sons of God!' (1 John 3:1, RV). Of all the gifts of grace, adoption is the highest. The gift of pardon for the past is great: to know that

> *Bearing shame and scoffing rude,*
> *In my place condemned He stood,*
> *Sealed my pardon with His blood*

is a never-ending source of wonder and joy.

> *Ransomed, healed, restored, forgiven,*
> *Who like me His praise should sing?*

So, too, the gift of immunity and acceptance now and for the future is great: when once Charles Wesley's ecstatic epitome of Romans 8 becomes yours—

> *No condemnation now I dread,*
> *Jesus, and all in Him, is mine;*
> *Alive in Him, my living Head,*
> *And clothed in righteousness divine,*
> *Bold I approach the eternal throne*
> *And claim the crown, through Christ my own—*

your spirit takes wings and flies, as some who read this chapter will surely know. But when you realise that God has taken you from the gutter, so to speak, and made you a son in His own house— you, a miraculously pardoned offender, guilty, ungrateful, defiant, perverse as you were—your sense of God's 'love beyond degree' is more than words can express. You will echo Charles Wesley's question

> *O how shall I the goodness tell,*
> *Father, which Thou to me hast showed?*
> *That I, a child of wrath and hell,*
> *I should be called a child of God.*

You are not likely, however, to feel, any more than He did, that you know how to give it an adequate answer.

In the ancient world, adoption was a practice ordinarily confined to the childless well-to-do. Its subjects, as we said earlier, were not normally infants, as today, but young adults who had shown themselves fit and able to carry on a family name in a worthy way. In this case, however, God adopts us out of free love, not because our character and record show us worthy to bear His name, but despite the fact that they show the very opposite. We are not fit for a place in God's family; the idea of His loving and exalting us sinners as He loves and has exalted the Lord Jesus sounds ludicrous and wild—yet that, and nothing less than that, is what our adoption means.

Adoption, by its very nature, is an act of free kindness to the person adopted. If you become a father by adopting a child, you do so because you choose to, not because you are bound to. Similarly, God adopts because He chooses to. He had no duty to do so. He need not have done anything about our sins save punish us as we deserved. But He loved us; so He redeemed us, forgave us, took us as His sons, and gave Himself to us as our Father.

Nor does His grace stop short with that initial act, any more than the love of human parents who adopt stops short with the completing of the legal process that makes the child theirs. The establishing of the child's status as a member of the family is only a beginning. The real task remains: to establish a genuinely filial relationship between your adopted child and yourself. It is this, above all, that you want to see. Accordingly, you set yourself to win the child's love by loving it. You seek to excite affection by showing affection. So with God. And throughout our life in this world, and to all eternity beyond. He will constantly be showing us, in one way or another, more and more of His love, and thereby increasing our love to Him continually. The prospect before the adopted sons of God is an eternity of love.

Once I knew a family in which the eldest child was adopted at a time when the parents thought they could have no children. When their natural-born children arrived later on, they diverted all their affection to them, and the adopted eldest was very obviously left out in the cold. It was painful to see, and, judging by the look on the eldest's face, it was painful to experience. It was, of course, a miserable failure in parenthood. But in God's family things are not like that. Like the prodigal in the parable, we may only find ourselves able to say, 'I have sinned . . . I am not worthy to be called Thy son; make me as one of Thy hired servants' (Luke 15:18 f.). But God receives us as sons, and loves us with the same steadfast affection with which He eternally loves His beloved only-begotten. There are no distinctions of affection in the divine family. We are all loved just as fully as Jesus is loved. It is like a fairy story — the reigning monarch adopts waifs and strays to make princes of them — but, praise God, it is not a fairy story: it is hard and solid fact, founded on the bedrock of free and sovereign grace. This, and nothing less than this, is what adoption means. No wonder that John cries, 'Behold, what manner of love . . .!' When once you understand adoption, your heart will cry the same.

Nor is this all.

Second, *our adoption shows us the glory of the Christian hope.*

New Testament Christianity is a religion of hope, a faith that looks forward. For the Christian, the best is always yet to be. But how can we form any notion of that which awaits us at the end of the road? Here, too, the doctrine of adoption comes to our help. To start with, it teaches us to think of our hope, not as a possibility nor yet as a likelihood, but as a guaranteed certainty, because it is a *promised inheritance*. The reason for adopting, in the first-century world, was specifically to have an heir to whom one could bequeath one's goods. So, too, God's adoption of us makes us His heirs, and so guarantees to us, as of right (we might say), the inheritance that He has in store for us. 'We are the children of God; and if children, then heirs; heirs of God, and joint-heirs with Christ' (Romans 8:16 f.). 'Thou art no more a servant, but a son; and if a son, then an heir of God through Christ' (Galatians 4:7). Our Father's wealth is immeasurable, and we are to inherit the entire estate.

Next, the doctrine of adoption tells us that the sum and substance of our promised inheritance is *a share in the glory of Christ*. We shall be made like our elder brother at every point, and sin and mortality, the double corruption of God's good work in the moral and spiritual spheres respectively, will be things of the past. 'Joint-heirs with Christ . . . that we may be . . . glorified together' (Romans 8:17). 'Beloved, now are we the sons of God, and it doth not yet appear what we shall be: but we know that, when He shall appear, we shall be like Him' (1 John 3:2). This likeness will extend to our physical being, as well as our mind and character; indeed, Romans 8:23 speaks of the bestowing of it on the physical side as itself our adoption, clearly using the word to mean the conveying of the inheritance which we were adopted to receive. 'We . . . which have the firstfruits of the Spirit . . . groan within ourselves, waiting for our adoption, to wit, the redemption of our body' (RV). This, the blessing of resurrection day, will make actual for us all that was implicit in the relationship of adoption, for it will introduce us into the full experience of the heavenly life now enjoyed by our elder brother. Paul dwells on the splendour of this event, assuring us that all creation, inarticulately yet really, is looking and longing for 'the revealing of the sons of God. For . . . the creation itself also shall be delivered from the bondage of corruption into the liberty of the glory of the children of God' (Romans 8:19 ff., RV). Whatever else this passage may imply (and it was not written, let us remember, to satisfy the natural scientist's curiosity), it clearly underlines the surpassing grandeur of what awaits us in the good plan of God. When we think of Jesus exalted in glory, in the fullness of the joy for which He endured the cross (a fact, let it be said, of which Christians should think often), we should always remind ourselves that everything He has will some day be shared with us, for it is our inheritance no less than His; we are among the 'many sons' whom God is bringing to glory (Hebrews 2:10), and God's promise to us, and His work in us, are not going to fail.

Finally, the doctrine of adoption tells us that the experience of heaven will be of a *family gathering*, as the great host of the re-deemed meet together in face-to-face fellowship with their Father-God and Jesus their brother. This is the deepest and clearest idea of heaven that the Bible gives us. Many scriptures point to it. 'Father, I desire that they also, whom thou hast given me, may be with me where I am, to behold my glory' (John 17:24 RSV). 'Blessed are the pure in heart, for they shall see God' (Matthew 5:8). 'We shall see Him as He is' (1 John 3:2). 'They shall see His face' (Revelation 22:4). 'Then face to face' (1 Corinthians 13:12). 'So shall we be for ever with the Lord' (1 Thessalonians 4:15). It will be like the day when the sick child is at last able to leave hospital, and finds father and the whole family waiting outside to greet him — a family occasion, if ever there was one. 'I see myself now at the end of my journey, my toilsome days are ended,' said Bunyan's Mr. Stand-fast, as he stood half-way into Jordan's water, 'the thoughts of what I am going to, and of the conduct that waits for me on the other side, doth lie as a glowing coal at my heart. . . . I have formerly lived by hear-say, and faith, but now I go where I shall live by sight, and shall be with Him, in whose company I delight myself.' What will make heaven to be heaven is the presence of Jesus, and of a reconciled divine Father who loves us for Jesus's sake no less than He loves Jesus Himself. To see, and know, and love, and be loved by, the Father and the Son, in company with the rest of God's vast family, is the whole essence of the Christian hope. As Richard Baxter put it in his poetical version of the covenant with God which his wife-to-be 'subscribed with a cheerful will' on April 10, 1660:

> *My knowledge of that life is small;*
> *The eye of faith is dim:*
> *But it's enough that Christ knows all;*
> *And I shall be with Him.*

If you are a believer, and so a son, this prospect satisfies you completely; if it does not strike you as satisfying, it would seem that as yet you are neither.

Third, *our adoption gives us the key to understanding the ministry of the Holy Spirit.*

Pitfalls and perplexities regarding the ministry of the Spirit abound among Christians today. The problem is not in finding correct verbal labels, but in knowing what it is in experience that corresponds to the work of God to which the labels refer. Thus, we are all aware that the Spirit teaches the mind of God, and glorifies the Son of God, out of the scriptures; also, that He is the agent of new birth, giving us an understanding so that we know God and a new heart to obey Him; also, that He indwells, sanctifies, and energises Christians for their daily pilgrimage; also, that assurance, joy, peace, and power are His special gifts. But many complain in puzzlement that these statements are to them mere formulae, not corresponding with anything they recognise in their own lives. Naturally, such Christians feel they are missing something vital, and ask anxiously how they may close the gap between the New Testament picture of life in the Spirit and their own felt barrenness in daily experience. Then, perhaps, in desperation they set themselves to seek a single transforming psychic event whereby what they feel to be their personal 'unspirituality barrier' may be broken for good and all. The event may be thought of as the 'Keswick experience', or 'full surrender', or 'baptism in the Holy Spirit', or 'entire sanctification', or 'sealing with the Spirit', or the gift of tongues, or (if we steer by Catholic rather than Protestant stars) a 'second conversion', or the prayer of quiet, or of union. Yet even if something happens which they feel able to identify with what they were looking for, they soon find that the 'unspirituality barrier' has not been broken after all, and so move on restlessly to something new. Many are caught in these toils today. What help is needed here? we ask. The light shed by the truth of adoption on the ministry of the Spirit gives the answer.

The cause of such troubles as we have described is a false, magical type of supernaturalism, which leads people to hanker after a transforming touch as from an electric impersonal power that will make them feel wholly free from the burdens and bondages of living with themselves and other people. They believe that this is the essence of genuine spiritual experience. They think the work of the Spirit is to give them experiences that are like LSD trips. (How unhelpful it is when evangelists actually promise this, and when drugtakers equate their fantasies with religious experience! Will our age never learn to distinguish things that differ?) In fact, however, this quest for an inward explosion rather than an inward communion shows deep misunderstanding of the Spirit's ministry. For the vital truth to be grasped here is that the Spirit is given to Christians as 'the Spirit *of adoption*', and in all His ministry to Christians He acts as the Spirit of adoption. As such, His task and purpose throughout is to make Christians realise with increasing clarity the meaning of their filial relationship with God in Christ, and to lead them into an ever deeper response to God in this relationship. Paul is pointing to this truth when he writes, 'Ye have received the Spirit of adoption, whereby we cry Abba, Father' (Romans 8:15). 'God hath sent forth the Spirit of His Son into your hearts, crying' — that is, prompting you to cry — 'Abba, Father' Galatians 4:6). Just as adoption itself is the key thought for unlocking, and the focal thought for unifying, the New Testament view of the Christian life, so a recognition that the Spirit comes to us as the Spirit of adoption is the key thought for unlocking, and the focal thought for integrating, all that the New Testament tells us about His ministry to Christians.

From the standpoint provided by this focal thought, we see that His work has three aspects. In the first place, He makes and keeps us conscious — sometimes vividly conscious, always conscious to some extent, even when the perverse part of us prompts us to deny this consciousness — that we are God's children by free grace through Jesus Christ. This is His work of giving faith, assurance, and joy. In the second place, He moves us to look to God as to a father, showing towards Him the respectful boldness and unlimited trust that is natural to children secure in an adored father's love. This is His work of making us cry 'Abba, Father' — the attitude described is what the cry expresses. In the third place, He impels us to act up to our position as royal children by manifesting the family likeness (*i.e.* conforming to Christ), furthering the family welfare (*i.e.* loving the brethren), and maintaining the family honour (*i.e.* seeking God's glory). This is His work of sanctification. Through this progressive deepening of filial consciousness and character, with its outworking in the pursuit of what God loves and the avoidance of what He hates, 'we are transformed by the Spirit of the Lord in ever-increasing splendour into His own image' (2 Corinthians 3:18, Phillips). So it is not as we strain after feelings and experiences, of whatever sort, but as we seek God Himself, looking to Him as our Father, prizing His fellowship, and finding in ourselves an increasing concern to know and please Him, that the reality of the Spirit's ministry becomes visible in our lives. This is the needed truth which can lift us out of the quagmire of non-spiritual views of the Spirit in which so many today are floundering.

Fourth, and following on from what we have just said, *our adoption shows us the meaning and motives of 'gospel holiness'.*

'Gospel holiness' is no doubt an unfamiliar phrase to some. It was Puritan shorthand for authentic Christian living, springing from love and gratitude to God, in contrast with the spurious 'legal holiness' that consisted merely of forms, routines, and outward appearances, maintained from self-regarding motives. We have here just two short points to make about 'gospel holiness'. First, what has already been said shows us its essential nature. It is simply a consistent living out of our filial relationship with God, into which the gospel brings us. It is just a matter of the child of God being true to type, true to his Father, to his Saviour, and to himself. It is the expressing of one's adoption in one's life. It is a matter of being a good son, as distinct from a prodigal or black sheep in the royal family. Second, the adoptive relationship, which displays God's grace so signally, itself provides the motive for this authentically holy living. Christians know that God 'predestinated us into the adoption of children by Jesus Christ unto Himself', and that this involved His eternal intention that 'we should be holy and without blame before him in love' (Ephesians 1:3 f.). They know that they are moving towards a day when this destiny will be fully and finally realised. 'We know that, when He shall appear, we shall be like Him; for we shall see Him as He is' (1 John 3:2).

What flows from such knowledge? Why, this, 'every man that hath this hope in him purifieth himself, even as he is pure' (verse 3). The children know that holiness is their Father's will for them, and that it is both a means, condition, and constituent of their happiness, here and hereafter; and because they love their Father they actively seek the fulfilling of His beneficent purpose. Paternal discipline exercised through outward pressures and trials helps the process along: the Christian up to his eyes in trouble can take comfort from the knowledge that in God's kindly plan it all has a positive purpose, to further his sanctification. In this world, royal children have to undergo extra training and discipline, which other children escape, in order to fit them for their high destiny. It is the same with the children of the King of Kings. The clue to understanding all His dealings with them is to remember that throughout his life He is training them for what awaits them, and chiselling them into the image of Christ. Sometimes the chiselling process is painful, and the discipline irksome; but then the Scripture reminds us—'Whom the Lord *loveth* he chasteneth, and scourgeth *every son whom he receiveth*. If ye endure chastening, *God dealeth with you as with sons* ... Now no chastening for the present seemeth to be joyous, but grievous; nevertheless afterward it yieldeth the peaceable fruit of righteousness ...' (Hebrews 12:6 f., 11). Only the man who has grasped this can make sense of Romans 8:28, 'All things work together for good to them that love God'; equally, only he can maintain his assurance of sonship against satanic assault as things go wrong. But he who has mastered the truth of adoption both retains assurance and receives blessing in the day of trouble: this is one aspect of faith's victory over the world. Meanwhile, however, the point stands that the Christian's primary motive for holy living is not negative, the hope (vain!) that hereby he may avoid chastening, but positive, the impulse to show his love and gratitude to his adopting God by identifying himself with the Father's will for him.

This throws light at once on the question of the place of God's law in the Christian life. Many have found it hard to see what claim the law can have on the Christian. We are free from the law, they say; our salvation does not depend on law-keeping; we are justified through the blood and righteousness of Jesus Christ. How, then, can it matter, or make any difference to anything, whether we keep the law henceforth or not? And since justification means the pardon of all sin, past, present, and future, and complete acceptance for all eternity, why should we be concerned whether we sin or not? Why should we think God is concerned? Does it not show an imperfect grasp of justification when a Christian makes an issue of his daily sins, and spends time mourning over them and seeking forgiveness for them? Is not a refusal to look to the law for instruction, or to be concerned about one's daily shortcomings, part of the true boldness of justifying faith?

The Puritans had to face these 'antinomian' ideas, and sometimes made heavy weather of answering them. If one allows it to be assumed that justification is the be-all and end-all of the gift of salvation, one will always make heavy weather of answering such arguments. The truth is that these ideas must be answered in terms, not of justification, but of adoption: a reality which the Puritans never highlighted quite enough. Once the distinction is drawn between these two elements in the gift of salvation, the correct reply becomes plain.

What is that reply? It is this: that, while it is certainly true that justification frees one for ever from the need to keep the law, or try to, as the means of earning life, it is equally true that adoption lays on one the abiding obligation to keep the law, as the means of pleasing one's new-found Father. Law-keeping is the family likeness of God's children; Jesus fulfilled all righteousness, and God calls us to do likewise. Adoption puts law-keeping on a new footing: as children of God, we acknowledge the law's authority as a rule for our lives, because we know that this is what our Father wants. If we sin, we confess our fault and ask our Father's forgiveness on the basis of the family relationship, as Jesus taught us to do — 'Our Father . . . forgive us our sins' (Luke 11:2, 4). The sins of God's children do not destroy their justification or nullify their adoption, but they mar the children's fellowship with their Father. 'Be ye holy, for I am holy' is our Father's word to us, and it is no part of justifying faith to lose sight of the fact that God, the King, wants His royal children to live lives worthy of their paternity and position.

Fifth, *our adoption gives the clue we need to see our way through the problem of assurance.*

Here is a tangled skein, if ever there was one! This topic has been in constant dispute in the Church ever since the Reformation. The Reformers, Luther in particular, used to distinguish between 'historical faith' — what Tyndale called 'story-faith', that is, belief of the Christian facts without response or commitment — and true saving faith. The latter, they said, is essentially assurance. They called it *fiducia*, 'confidence' — confidence, that is, first in the truth of God's promise of pardon and life to believing sinners, and second in its application to oneself as a believer. 'Faith', declared Luther, 'is a living deliberate confidence in the grace of God, so certain that for it one could die a thousand deaths, and such confidence . . . makes us joyous, intrepid, and cheerful towards God and all creation.' And he attacked 'that pernicious doctrine of the Papists, which taught that no man knows certainly whether he be in the favour of God or not; whereby they utterly defaced the doctrine of faith, tormented men's consciences, banished Christ right out of the Church, and denied all the benefits of the Holy Spirit'. At the same time, the Reformers recognised that *fiducia*, the assurance of faith, could exist in a man who under temptation felt sure that it did not exist in him, and that he had no hope in God. (If this sounds paradoxical to you, be thankful that you have never been exposed to the kind of temptation that makes this the actual state of your soul, as it was on occasion the actual state of Luther's, and many more in his time.)

The Roman Catholics could make nothing of this: in answer to the Reformers they reaffirmed the standard medieval view, that though faith hopes for heaven it can have no certainty of arriving there, and that to claim such certainty is presumption.

The Puritans of the next century made a point of teaching that what is essential in faith is not assurance of salvation, whether present or future, but vital repentance and commitment to Jesus Christ. Often they spoke of assurance as if it were something distinct from faith, which the believer would not ordinarily experience unless he specifically sought it.

Wesley in the eighteenth century re-echoed Luther's insistence that the witness of the Spirit, and the assurance resulting, is of the essence of faith, though he later qualified this by distinguishing between the faith of a *servant*, of which assurance is no part, and the faith of a *son*, of which it is. He seems to have come to think of his pre-Aldersgate Street experience as the faith of a servant — one on the borders of full Christian experience, seeking salvation and following on to know the Lord but not yet assured of his standing in grace. Like all later Lutherans, however — though not like Luther himself! — Wesley held that assurance relates to present acceptance by God only, and that there can be no present assurance of persevering.

Among evangelicals the debate continues, and continues to bewilder, too. What is assurance? And whom does God assure? — all believers, some, or none? When He assures, what does He assure of? And by what means is assurance given? The tangle is formidable, but the truth of adoption can help us unravel it.

If God in love has made Christians His children, and if He is perfect as a Father, two things would seem to follow, in the nature of the case.

First, the family relationship must be an abiding one, lasting for ever. Perfect parents do not cast off their children. Christians may act the prodigal, but God will not cease to act the prodigal's father.

Second, God will go out of His way to make His children feel His love for them, and know their privilege and security as members of His family. Adopted children need assurance that they belong, and a perfect parent will not withhold it.

Paul in Romans 8, the classic New Testament passage on assurance, confirms both inferences. First, he tells us that those whom God 'predestinated to be conformed to the image of his Son, that he might be the firstborn among many brethren' — those, in other words, whom God eternally resolved to take as sons in His family, alongside His only-begotten — 'he called . . . justified . . . glorified' (Romans 8: 29 f.). 'Glorified', we note, is in the past tense, though the event itself is still future; this shows that to Paul's mind the thing is as good as done already, being fixed in God's decree. Hence Paul's confidence in declaring, 'I am persuaded, that neither death, nor life, nor principalities, nor powers, nor things present, nor things to come, nor height, nor depth, nor any other creature, shall be able to separate us from the love of God' — the electing, redeeming, paternal love of God — 'which is in Christ Jesus our Lord' (verses 38 f.).

Second, Paul tells us that here and now 'the Spirit . . . beareth witness with our spirit, that we are the children of God; and if children, then heirs' (verses 16 f.). The statement is inclusive: though Paul had never met the Romans, he felt able to take it for granted that if they were Christians, then they would know this inner witness of the Spirit to their happy status as sons and heirs of God. Well did James Denney once observe that whereas assurance is a sin in Romanism, and a duty in much of Protestantism, in the New Testament it is simply a fact.

We note that in this verse witness to our adoption is borne from two distinct sources: our spirit (that is, our conscious self), and God's Spirit, Who bears witness *with* our spirit, and so *to* our spirit. (This point is not affected if, with the Revised Standard Version, we re-punctuate, and render, 'When we cry, "Abba! Father!" it is the Spirit himself bearing witness with our spirit...' What it means then is that the filial cry, and the filial attitude it expresses, is evidence that the dual witness is a reality in the heart.)

What is the nature of this dual witness? Robert Haldane's analysis, which distils the essence of more than two centuries of evangelical exposition, can hardly be improved upon. The witness of our spirit, he writes, becomes a reality as 'the Holy Spirit enables us to ascertain our sonship, from being conscious of, and discovering in ourselves, the true marks of a renewed state.' This is *inferential* assurance, being a conclusion drawn from the fact that one knows the gospel, trusts Christ, brings forth works meet for repentance, and manifests the instincts of a regenerate man.

But [continues Haldane] to say that this is all that is signified by the Holy Spirit's testimony, would be to fall short of what is affirmed in this text; for in that case the Holy Spirit would only help the conscience to be a witness, but could not be said to be a witness Himself... The Holy Spirit testifies to our spirit in a distinct and immediate testimony, and also with our spirit in a concurrent testimony. This testimony, although it cannot be explained, is nevertheless felt by the believer; it is felt by him, too, in its variations, as sometimes stronger and more palpable, and at other times more feeble and less discernible... Its reality is indicated in Scripture by such expressions as those of the Father and the Son coming unto us, and making their *abode* with us — Christ *manifesting* Himself to us, and *supping* with us — His giving us the *hidden manna*, and the *white stone*, denoting the communication to us of the knowledge of an acquittal from guilt, and a *new name* written, which no man knoweth saving he that receiveth it. 'The love of God is shed abroad in our hearts by the Holy Ghost, which is given unto us' (*Romans*, p. 363).

This is *immediate* assurance, the direct work of the Spirit in the regenerate heart, coming in to supplement the God-prompted witness of our own spirit (*i.e.* of our own self-consciousness and self-knowledge as believers). While this dual witness can be temporarily clouded through divine withdrawal and satanic assault, every whole-hearted Christian who is not grieving and quenching the Spirit by unfaithfulness ordinarily enjoys both aspects of the witness, more or less, as his abiding experience; as Paul's present tense ('beareth witness with our spirit') makes clear.

So the truth about assurance comes out like this: Our heavenly Father intends His sons to know His love for them, and their own security in His family. He would not be the perfect Father if He did not want this, and if He did not act to bring it about. His action takes the form of making the dual witness that we have described part of the regular experience of His children. Thus He leads them to rejoice in His love. The dual witness is itself a gift—the crowning element in the complex gift of faith, the element whereby believers gain 'feeling knowledge' that their faith, and adoption, and the hope of heaven, and the infinite sovereign love of God to them, are all 'really real'. Of this dimension of faith's experience one has to say, as Mr. Squeers said of Nature, that it is 'more easier conceived than described'—'more easily felt than tell't', as a Scots lady is supposed to have put it, rather more grammatically and whimsically; yet all Christians ordinarily enjoy it to some extent, for it is in truth part of their birthright. Being prone to self-deception, we do well to test our assurance by applying the doctrinal and ethical criteria which 1 John provides for this very purpose (see 1 John 2:3, 29; 3:6–10, 14, 18–21; 4:7 f., 15 f.; 5:1–4, 18), and by this means the inferential element in our assurance will be strengthened and the vividness of assurance as a whole may vastly increase. The source of assurance, however, is not our inferences as such, but the work of the Spirit, apart from as well as through our inferences, convincing us that we are God's children and that the saving love and promises of God apply directly to us.

What, then, of the historic disputes? The Romanists were wrong: viewed in the light of adoption and the fatherhood of God, their denial of both preservation and assurance becomes a ludicrous monstrosity. What sort of a father is it that never tells His children individually that He loves them, but proposes to throw them out of the family unless they behave? The Wesleyan and Lutheran denial of preservation is similarly mistaken. God is a better father than this denial allows for: He *keeps* His children in faith and grace, and will not let them slip from His hand. The Reformers and Wesley were right to say that assurance is integral to faith; the Puritans, however, were also right to lay more stress than either on the fact that Christians who grieve the Spirit by sin, and who fail to seek God with all their heart, must expect to miss the full fruition of this crowning gift of the double witness, just as careless and naughty children stop their parents' smiles and provoke frowns instead. Some gifts are too precious for careless and naughty children, and this is a gift which our heavenly Father will, to some extent at least, hold back if He sees us to be in a state where it would spoil us, by making us think our Father did not care whether we lived holy lives or not.

V

It is a strange fact that the truth of adoption has been little regarded in Christian history. Apart from two last-century books, now scarcely known (R. S. Candlish, *The Fatherhood of God*, R. A. Webb, *The Reformed Doctrine of Adoption*), there is no evangelical writing on it, nor has there been at any time since the Reformation, any more than there was before. Luther's grasp of adoption was as strong and clear as his grasp of justification, but his disciples held to the former and made nothing of the latter. The Puritan teaching on the Christian life, so strong in other ways, was notably deficient here, which is one reason why legalistic misunderstandings of it so easily arise. Perhaps the early Methodists, and later Methodist saints like Billy Bray, 'the King's Son', with his unforgettable approach to prayer—'I must talk to Father about this'—came closest to the life of sonship as the New Testament depicts it. There is certainly more to make of adoption in Christian teaching today.

Meanwhile, the immediate message to our hearts of what we have studied in the present chapter is surely this: do I, as a Christian, understand myself? Do I know my own real identity? My own real destiny? *I am a child of God. God is my Father; heaven is my home; every day is one day nearer. My Saviour is my brother; every Christian is my brother too.* Say it over and over to yourself first thing in the morning, last thing at night, as you wait for the bus, any time when your mind is free, and ask that you may be enabled to live as one who knows it is all utterly and completely true. For this is the Christian's secret of—a happy life?—yes, certainly, but we have something both higher and profounder to say. This is the Christian's secret of a *Christian* life, and of a *God-honouring* life: and these are the aspects of the situation that really matter. May this secret become fully yours, and fully mine.

To help us realise more adequately who and what, as children of God, we are, and are called to be, here are some questions by which we do well to examine ourselves again and again.

Do I understand my adoption? Do I value it? Do I daily remind myself of my privilege as a child of God?

Have I sought full assurance of my adoption? Do I daily dwell on the love of God to me?

Do I treat God as my Father in heaven, loving, honouring, and obeying Him, seeking and welcoming His fellowship, and trying in everything to please Him, as a human parent would want His child to do?

Do I think of Jesus Christ, my Saviour and my Lord, as my brother too, bearing to me not only a divine authority but also a divine-human sympathy? Do I think daily how close He is to me, how completely He understands me, and how much, as my kinsman-redeemer, He cares for me?

Have I learned to hate the things that displease my Father? Am I sensitive to the evil things to which He is sensitive? Do I make a point of avoiding them, lest I grieve Him?

Do I look forward daily to that great family occasion when the sons of God will finally gather in heaven before the throne of God, their Father, and of the Lamb, their brother and their Lord? Have I felt the thrill of this hope?

Do I love my Christian brothers, with whom I live day by day, in a way that I shall not be ashamed of when in heaven I think back over it?

Am I proud of my Father, and of His family, to which by His grace I belong?

Does the family likeness appear in me? If not, why not?

God humble us; God instruct us; God make us His own true sons.

CHAPTER 20

Thou our Guide

I

To many Christians, guidance is a chronic problem. Why? Not because they doubt that divine guidance is a fact, but because they are sure it is. They know that God can guide, and has promised to guide, every Christian believer. Books, and friends, and public speakers, tell them how guidance has worked in the lives of others. Their fear, therefore, is not that no guidance should be available for them, but that they may miss the guidance which God provides through some fault of their own. When they sing:

> *Guide me, O thou great Jehovah,*
> *Pilgrim through this barren land;*
> *I am weak, but Thou art mighty,*
> *Hold me with Thy powerful hand:*
> *Bread of heaven*
> *Feed me now and evermore,*

they have no doubt that God is able both to lead and to feed, as they ask. But they remain anxious, because they are not certain of their own receptiveness to the guidance God offers.

Not all, however, have yet come so far. In our day, as we have frequently noted already, knowledge of God has been obscured — turned, in effect, into ignorance of God — by the twisting of our thoughts about God. Thus, the reality of God's rule, God's speech, God's independence, God's moral goodness, even God's personality, has been queried not only outside the Church but inside it also. This has made it hard for many to believe that divine guidance can exist at all. How can it, if God is not the sort of being who can, or will, give it?—and that is what, in one way or another, all these suggestions imply. It is worth while, therefore, to recall at this point some of the basic truths which divine guidance presupposes.

II

Belief that divine guidance is real rests upon two foundation-facts: first, the reality of God's *plan* for us; second, the ability of God to *communicate* with us. On both these facts the Bible has much to say.

Has God a plan for individuals? Indeed He has. He has formed an 'eternal purpose' (literally, a 'plan of the ages'), 'a plan for the fulness of time', in accordance with which he 'accomplishes all things according to the counsel of his will' (Ephesians 3:11, 1:10, 11, RSV). He had a plan for the redemption of His people from Egyptian bondage, when He guided them through the sea and the desert by means of a pillar of cloud by day and a pillar of fire by night. He had a plan for the return of His people from Babylonian exile, where He guided by setting Cyrus on the throne and 'stirring up his spirit' (Ezra 1:1) to send the Jews home to build their temple. He had a plan for Jesus (see Luke 18:31, 22:24, etc.); Jesus's whole business on earth was to do His Father's will (John 4:34; Hebrews 10:7, 9). God had a plan for Paul (see Acts 21:14,22: 14, 26:16–19; 1 Timothy 1:16); in five of his letters Paul announces himself as an apostle 'by the will of God'. God has a plan for each of His children.

But can God communicate His plan to us? Indeed He can. As man is a communicative animal, so his Maker is a communicative God. He made known His will to and through the Old Testament prophets. He guided Jesus and Paul. Acts records several instances of detailed guidance (Philip being sent to the desert to meet the Ethiopian eunuch, 8:26, 29; Peter being told to accept the invitation of Cornelius, 10:19 f.; the church at Antioch being charged to send Paul and Barnabas as missionaries, 13:2; Paul and Silas being called into Europe, 16:6–10; Paul being instructed to press on with his Corinthian ministry, 18:9 f.): and though guidance by dreams, visions, and direct verbal messages must be judged exceptional and not normal, even for the apostles and their contemporaries, yet these events do at least show that God has no difficulty in making His will known to His servants.

Moreover, Scripture contains explicit promises of divine guidance, whereby we may know God's plan for our action. 'I will instruct you and teach you the way you should go; I will counsel you with my eye upon you,' says God to David (Psalm 32:8,

RSV). Isaiah 58:11 contains the assurance that if the people repent and obey 'the Lord will guide you continually'. Guidance is a main theme in Psalm 25, where we read, 'Good and upright is the Lord; therefore he instructs sinners in the way. He leads the humble in what is right, and teaches the humble his way . . . Who is the man that feareth the Lord? Him will he instruct in the way that he should choose' (verses 8, 9, 12, RSV). So in Proverbs 3:6, 'In all thy ways acknowledge him, and he shall direct thy paths.'

In the New Testament, the same expectation of guidance appears. Paul's prayer that the Colossians 'might be filled with the knowledge of his will in all wisdom and spiritual understanding', and Epaphras' prayer that they might 'stand perfect . . . in all the will of God' (Colossians 1:9, 4:12), clearly assume that God is ready and willing to make His will known. 'Wisdom' in Scripture always means knowledge of the course of action that will please God and secure life, so that the promise of James 1:5 – 'if any of you lacks wisdom, let him ask of God who gives to all men generously and without reproaching, and it will be given him' (RSV) – is in effect a promise of guidance. 'Let your minds be remade and your whole nature thus transformed,' counsels Paul. 'Then you will be able to discern the will of God, and to know what is good, acceptable and perfect' (Romans 12:2, NEB).

Other lines of biblical truth come in here to confirm this confidence that God will guide. First, Christians are God's sons; and if human parents have a responsibility to give their children guidance in matters where ignorance and incapacity would spell danger, we should not doubt that in the family of God the same applies. 'If ye then, being evil, know how to give good gifts unto your children, how much more shall your Father which is in heaven give good gifts to them that ask him?' (Matthew 7:11).

Again, Scripture is God's Word, 'profitable' (we read) 'for teaching, for reproof, for correction, and for training in righteousness, that the man of God may be complete, equipped for every good work' (2 Timothy 3:16, RSV) 'Teaching' means comprehensive instruction in doctrine and ethics, the work and will of God; 'reproof', 'correction', and 'training in righteousness' signify the applying of this instruction to our disordered lives; 'readiness for every good work' – that is, a life set to go God's way – is the promised result.

Again, Christians have an indwelling Instructor, the Holy Spirit. 'You have been anointed by the Holy One . . . the anointing which you received from him abides in you . . . his anointing teaches you about everything, and is true, and is no lie . . .' (1 John

2:20, 27, RSV). Doubt as to the availability of guidance would be a slur on the faithfulness of the Holy Spirit to His ministry. It is notable that in Acts 8:29, 10:19, 13:2, 16:6, and most strikingly in the decree of the Jerusalem council—'it seemed good to the Holy Ghost, and to us . . .' (15:28)—the giving of guidance is specifically ascribed to the Spirit.

Again, God seeks His glory in our lives, and He is glorified in us only when we obey His will. It follows that, as a means to His own end, He must be ready to teach us His way, so that we may walk in it. Confidence in God's readiness to teach those who desire to obey underlies all Psalm 119. In Psalm 23: 3, David proclaims the reality of God giving guidance for His own glory—'He guideth me in the paths of righteousness *for his name's sake*' (RV).

So we might go on; but the point is sufficiently established. It is impossible to doubt that guidance is a reality intended for, and promised to, every child of God. Christians who miss it thereby show only that they did not seek it as they should. It is right, therefore, to be concerned about one's own receptiveness to guidance, and to study how to seek it.

III

Earnest Christians seeking guidance often go wrong about it. Why is this? Often the reason is that their notion of the nature and method of divine guidance is distorted. They look for a will-o'-the-wisp; they overlook the guidance that is ready to hand, and lay themselves open to all sorts of delusions. Their basic mistake is to think of guidance as essentially *inward prompting by the Holy Spirit, apart from the written Word*. This idea, which is as old as the false prophets of the Old Testament and as new as the Oxford Group and Moral Re-Armament, is a seed-bed in which all forms of fanaticism and folly can grow.

How do thoughtful Christians come to make this mistake? What seems to happen is this. They hear the word 'guidance', and think at once of a particular class of 'guidance problems'—on which, perhaps, the books they have read, and the testimonies they have heard tended to harp exclusively. This is the class of problems concerned with what we may call 'vocational choices—choices, that is, between competing options, all of which in themselves appear lawful and good. Examples are: should I contemplate marriage, or not? should I marry this person, or not? should we aim at having another child? should I join this church, or that one? should I serve God in the land of my upbringing, or abroad? which of the professions open to me should I follow? which of the jobs open to me in my profession should I take? is my present sphere of work the right one to stay in? what claim has this person, or cause, on my care, energies, and generosity? which claims on my voluntary service time should have priority?—and so forth. Naturally, because they shape our lives so decisively, and mean so much for joy or sorrow, we think a lot about 'vocational choices', and it is right that we should. But what is not right is to jump to the conclusion that, in the last analysis, all guidance problems are of this one type. Here, as it seems, is the root of the mistake.

Two features about divine guidance in the case of 'vocational choices' are distinctive. Both follow from the nature of the situation itself. First, these problems cannot be resolved by a direct application of biblical teaching. All one can do from Scripture is circumscribe the lawful possibilities between which the choice has to be made. (No biblical text, for instance, told the present writer to propose to the lady who is now his wife, or to seek ordination, or to start his ministry in England, or to buy his large old car.) Second, just because Scripture cannot decide one's choice directly, the factor of God-given prompting and inclination, whereby one is drawn to commit oneself to one set of responsibilities rather than another, and finds one's mind settled in peace as one contemplates them, becomes decisive. The basis of the mistake which we are trying to detect is to assume, first, that all guidance problems have these same two characteristics, and, second, that all life should be treated as a field in which this kind of guidance should be sought.

The consequences of this mistake among earnest Christians have been both comic and tragic. The idea of a life in which the inward voice of the Spirit decides and directs everything sounds most attractive, for it seems to exalt the Spirit's ministry and to promise the closest intimacy with God; but in practice this quest for super-spirituality leads only to frantic bewilderment or lunacy. Hannah Whitall Smith (Mrs R. Pearsall Smith), that shrewd and common-sensical Quaker lady, saw much of this, and wrote of it instructively in her 'fanaticism papers' (published posthumously by Ray Strachey, first as *Religious Fanaticism* [1928], then as *Group Movements of the Past and Experiments in Guidance* [1934]). There she tells of the woman who each morning, having consecrated the day to the Lord as soon as she woke, 'would then ask Him whether she was to get up or not,' and would not stir till 'the voice' told her to dress. 'As she put on each article she asked the Lord whether she was to put it on, and very often the Lord would tell her to put on the right shoe and leave off the other; sometimes she was to put on both stockings and no shoes; and sometimes both shoes and no stockings; it was the same with all the articles of dress . . .' Then there was the invalid who, when her hostess, visiting her, left money by accident on the dressing-table, had 'an impression . . . that the Lord wanted her to take that money in order to illustrate the truth of the text that "all things are yours" '—which she did, and hid it under her pillow, and prevaricated when her hostess came back for it, and was eventually thrown out as a thief. Here, too, we meet the 'quiet refined lady rather past middle age' who explained that ' "there have been times when, in order to help my friends to receive the Baptism of the Holy Spirit, I have felt distinctly led of the Lord to have them get into bed with me and lie back to back without any night-gown between" ' (*Group Movements*, pp. 184, 245, 198). These pathetic stories are sadly typical of what ensues once the basic mistake about guidance has been made.

What conduct of this sort shows is failure to grasp that the fundamental mode whereby our rational Creator guides His rational creatures is by rational understanding and application of His written Word. This mode of guidance is fundamental, both because it limits the area within which 'vocational' guidance is needed and given, and also because only those who have attuned themselves to it, so that their basic attitudes are right, are likely to be able to recognise 'vocational' guidance when it comes. In their uncritical acceptance of non-rational and non-moral impulses as coming from the Holy Spirit, Mrs. Smith's friends were forgetting that decent modest dress, respect for property, and recognition that sensuality is not spiritual, were already matters of scriptural requirement (1 Timothy 2:9; 1 Peter 4:15; Ephesians 4:19–22). But the true way to honour the Holy Spirit as our guide is to honour the Holy Scriptures through which He guides us. The fundamental guidance which God gives to shape our lives—the instilling, that is, of the basic convictions, attitudes, ideals, and value-judgments, in terms of which we are to live—is not a matter of inward promptings apart from the Word but of the pressure on our consciences of the portrayal of God's character and will in the Word, which the Spirit enlightens us to understand and apply to ourselves.

The basic form of divine guidance, therefore, is the presentation to us of positive ideals as guidelines for all our living. 'Be the kind of person that Jesus was'; 'seek this virtue, and this one, and this, and practise them up to the limit'; 'know your responsibilities— husbands, to your wives; wives, to your husbands; parents, to your children; all of you, to all your fellow-Christians and all your fellow-men; know them, and seek strength constantly to discharge them'—this is how God guides us through the Bible, as any student of the Psalms, the Proverbs, the prophets, the Sermon on the Mount, and the ethical parts of the epistles will soon discover. 'Depart from evil, and do good' (Psalm 34:14, 37:27)—this is the highway along which the Bible is concerned to lead us, and all its admonitions are concerned to keep us on it. Be it noted that the reference to being 'led by the Spirit' in Romans 8:14 relates, not to inward 'voices' or any such experience, but to mortifying known sin, and not living after the flesh!

Only within the limits of *this* guidance does God prompt us inwardly in matters of 'vocational' decision. So never expect to be guided to marry an unbeliever, or elope with a married person, as long as 1 Corinthians 7:39 and the seventh commandment stand! The present writer has known divine guidance to be claimed for both courses of action. Inward inclinations were undoubtedly present, but they were quite certainly not from the Spirit of God, for they went against the Word. The Spirit leads within the limits which the Word sets, not beyond them. 'He guideth me *in the paths of righteousness*'—but not anywhere else.

IV

Even with right ideas about guidance in general, however, it is still easy to go wrong, particularly in 'vocational' choices. No area of life bears clearer witness to the frailty of human nature—even regenerate human nature. The work of God in these cases is to incline first our judgment and then our whole being to the course which, of all the competing alternatives, He has marked out as best suited for us, and for His glory and the good of others through us. But the Spirit can be quenched, and we can all too easily behave in a way which stops this guidance getting through. It is worth listing some of the main pitfalls.

First, unwillingness to *think*. It is false piety, super-supernaturalism of an unhealthy and pernicious sort, that demands inward impressions that have no rational base, and declines to heed the constant biblical summons to *'consider'*. God made us thinking beings, and He guides our minds as in His presence we think things out—not otherwise. 'O that they were *wise* . . . that they would *consider* . . .' (Deuteronomy 32:29).

Second, unwillingness to *think ahead*, and weigh the long-term consequences of alternative courses of action. 'Think ahead' is part of the divine rule of life no less than of the human rule of the road. Often we can only see what is wise and right (and what is foolish and wrong) as we dwell on its long-term issues. 'O that they were *wise . . .* that they would consider *their latter end.*'

Third, unwillingness to *take advice.* Scripture is emphatic on the need for this. 'The way of the foolish is right in his own eyes; but he that is wise hearkeneth unto counsel' (Proverbs 12:15, RV). It is a sign of conceit and immaturity to dispense with taking advice in major decisions. There are always people who know the Bible, human nature, and our own gifts and limitations, better than we do, and even if we cannot finally accept their advice, nothing but good will come to us from carefully weighing what they say.

Fourth, unwillingness to *suspect oneself.* We dislike being realistic with ourselves, and we do not know ourselves at all well; we can recognise rationalisations in others and quite overlook them in ourselves. 'Feelings' with an ego-boosting, or escapist, or self-indulging, or self-aggrandising base, must be detected and discredited, not mistaken for guidance. This is particularly true of sexual, or sexually conditioned, feelings. As a biologist-theologian has written:

> The joy and general sense of well-being that often (but not always) goes with being 'in love' can easily silence conscience and inhibit critical thinking. How often people say that they 'feel led' to get married (and probably they will say 'the Lord has so clearly guided'), when all they are really describing is a particularly novel state of endocrine balance which makes them feel extremely sanguine and happy (O. R. Barclay, *Guidance,* p. 29 f.).

We need to ask ourselves *why* we 'feel' a particular course to be right, and make ourselves give reasons—and we shall be wise to lay the case before someone else whose judgment we trust, to give his verdict on our reasons. We need also to keep praying), 'Search me, O God, and know my heart; try me, and know my thoughts; and see if there be any wicked way in me, and lead me in the way everlasting' (Psalm 139: 23 f.). We can never distrust ourselves too much.

Fifth, unwillingness to *discount personal magnetism.* Those who have not been made deeply aware of pride and self-deception in themselves cannot always detect these things in others, and this has from time to time made it possible for well-meaning but deluded men with a flair for self-dramatisation to gain an alarming domination over the minds and consciences of others, who fall under their spell and decline to judge them by ordinary standards. And even when a gifted and magnetic man is aware of the danger and tries to avoid it, he is not always able to stop Christian people treating him as an angel, or a prophet, construing his words as guidance for themselves, and blindly following his lead. But this is not the way to be led by God. Outstanding men are not, indeed, necessarily wrong, but they are not necessarily right, either! They, and their views, must be respected, but may not be idolised. 'Prove (test) all things; hold fast that which is good' (1 Thessalonians 5: 21).

Sixth, unwillingness to *wait*. 'Wait on the Lord' is a constant refrain in the Psalms, and it is a necessary word, for God often keeps us waiting. He is not in such a hurry as we are, and it is not His way to give more light on the future than we need for action in the present, or to guide us more than one step at a time. When in doubt, do nothing, but continue to wait on God. When action is needed, light will come.

V

But it does not follow that right guidance will be vindicated as such by a trouble-free course thereafter. Here is another cause of deep perplexity for Christian people. They have sought guidance and believe it has been given. They have set off along the road which God seemed to indicate. And now, as a direct result, they have run into a crop of new problems which otherwise would not have arisen—isolation, criticism, abandonment by their friends, practical frustrations of all sorts. At once they grow anxious. They recall the prophet Jonah who, when told to go east and preach at Nineveh, took a ship going north to Tarshish instead, 'away from the presence of the Lord' (Jonah 1:3 RSV), and was caught in a storm, humiliated before unbelievers, thrown overboard and swallowed by a great fish in order to bring him to his senses. Is their own present experience of the rough side of life (they ask themselves) a sign from God that they are themselves like Jonah, off track, following the path of self-will rather than the way of God?

It may be so, and the wise man will take occasion from his new troubles to check his original guidance very carefully. Trouble should always be treated as a call to consider one's ways. But trouble is not necessarily a sign of being off track at all: for as the Bible declares in general that 'many are the afflictions of the righteous' (Psalm 34:19), so it teaches in particular that following God's guidance regularly leads to upsets and distresses which one would otherwise have escaped. Examples abound. God guided Israel by means of a fiery cloudy pillar that went before them (Exodus 13:21 f.); yet the way by which he led them involved the nerve-shredding cliff-hanger of the Red Sea crossing, long days without water and meat in 'that great and terrible wilderness' (Deuteronomy 1:19, cf. 31–33), and bloody battles with Amalek, Sihon, and Og (Exodus 17:8; Numbers 21:21 ff., 32 ff.), and we can understand, if not excuse, Israel's constant grumbling (see Exodus 14:10 ff., 16:3, Numbers 11:4 ff., 14:3 ff., 20:3 ff., 21:5 ff.). Again, Jesus's disciples were twice caught by night in bad weather on the Sea of Galilee (Mark 4:37, 6:48), and both times the reason why they were there was the command of Jesus himself (see Mark 4:35, 6:45). Again, the apostle Paul crossed to Greece 'concluding' from his dream of the man of Macedonia 'that God had called us for to preach the gospel unto them' (Acts 16:10), and before long he was in gaol at Philippi. Later he 're-solved in the Spirit to . . . go to Jerusalem' (19:21 RSV), and told the Ephesian elders whom he met on his way, 'I am going to Jerusalem, bound in the Spirit, not knowing what shall befall me there; except that the Holy Spirit testifies to me in every city that imprisonment and afflictions await me' (20:22 f. RSV). So it proved to be: Paul found trouble on the grand scale through following divine guidance.

Nor is this all. For a final example and proof of the truth that following God's guidance brings trouble, look at the life of the Lord Jesus himself. No human life has ever been so completely guided by God, and no human being has ever qualified so comprehensively for the description 'a man of sorrows'. Divine guidance set Jesus at a distance from his family and fellow-townsmen, brought him into conflict with all the nation's leaders, religious and civil, and led finally to betrayal, arrest, and the cross. What more can Christians expect, while they abide in the will of God? 'A disciple is not above his teacher, nor a servant above his master . . . If they have called the master of the house Beelzebub, how much more will they malign those of his household' (Matthew 10:24 f., RSV).

By every human standard of reckoning, the cross was a *waste* — the waste of a young life, a prophet's influence, a leader's potential. We know the secret of its meaning and achievement only from God's own statements. Similarly, the Christian's guided life may appear as a waste — as with Paul, spending years in prison because he followed God's guidance to Jerusalem, whereas he might otherwise have been evangelising Europe the whole time. Nor does God always tell us the why and wherefore of the frustrations and losses which are part and parcel of the guided life.

The early experience of Elisabeth Elliot, widow and biographer of a martyred missionary husband, strikingly illustrates this. Confident of God's guidance, she went to an Ecuador tribe to reduce their language to writing so that the Bible might be translated for them. The only person who could or would help her was a Spanish-speaking Christian who lived with the tribe, but within a month he was shot dead in an argument. She struggled on with virtually no help for eight months more. Then she moved to another field, leaving her full file of linguistic material with her colleagues so that they could carry on where she had left off. Within a fortnight she heard that the file had been stolen. No copy existed; all her work was wasted. That, humanly speaking, was the end of the story. She comments:

> I simply had to bow in the knowledge that God was his own interpreter. . . . We must allow God to do what he wants to do. And if you are thinking that you know the will of God for your life and you are anxious to do that, you are probably in for a very rude awakening because nobody knows the will of God for his entire life . . . (quoted from *Eternity*, January 1969, p. 18).

This is right. Sooner or later, God's guidance, which brings us out of darkness into light, will also bring us out of light into darkness. It is part of the way of the cross.

VI

If I found I had driven into a bog, I should know I had missed the road. But this knowledge would not be of much comfort if I then had to stand helpless watching the car sink and vanish: the damage would be done, and that would be that. Is it the same when a Christian wakes up to the fact that he has missed God's guidance and taken the wrong way? Is the damage irrevocable? Must he now be put off course for life? Thank God, no. Our God is a God who not merely restores, but takes up our mistakes and follies into His plan for us and brings good out of them. This is part of the wonder of His gracious sovereignty. 'I will restore to you the years that the locust has eaten . . . and ye shall eat in plenty, and be satisfied, and praise the name of the Lord your God, that hath dealt wondrously with you' (Joel 2: 25 f.). The Jesus who restored Peter after his denial, and corrected his course more than once after that (see Acts 10, Galatians 2:11–14), is our Saviour today and He has not changed. God makes not only the wrath of man to turn to His praise but the misadventures of Christians too.

Recently a letter came from a minister who has felt obliged to leave his congregation and denomination, and who now, like Abraham, goes out not knowing whither. In his letter, he quoted from a hymn by Charles Wesley on the sovereignty and security of God's guidance. This is the note on which we would close. Guidance, like all God's acts of blessing under the covenant of grace, is a sovereign act. Not merely does God will to guide us in the sense of showing us His way, that we may tread it; He wills also to guide us in the more fundamental sense of ensuring that, whatever happens, whatever mistakes we may make, we shall come safe home. Slippings and strayings there will be, no doubt, but the everlasting arms are beneath us; we shall be caught, rescued, restored. This is God's promise; this is how good He is. Thus it appears that the right context for discussing guidance is one of confidence in the God who will not let us ruin our souls. Our concern, therefore, in this discussion should be more for His glory than for our security—for that is already taken care of. And our self-distrust, while keeping us humble, must not cloud the joy with which we lean on 'the Lord Protector'—our faithful covenant God. Here is the verse from Wesley:

> *Captain of Israel's host and Guide*
> *Of all who seek the land above,*
> *Beneath Thy shadow we abide,*
> *The cloud of Thy protecting love;*
> *Our strength, Thy grace; our rule, Thy Word;*
> *Our end, the glory of the Lord.*

And here is the conclusion of the matter, in the words of Joseph Hart:

> *'Tis Jesus, the first and the last,*
> *Whose Spirit shall guide us safe home;*
> *We'll praise Him for all that is past,*
> *And trust Him for all that's to come.*

CHAPTER 21

These Inward Trials

I

A certain type of ministry of the gospel is *cruel*. It does not mean to be, but it is. It means to magnify grace, but what it does is rather the opposite. It scales down the problem of sin, and loses touch with the purpose of God. The effect is twofold: first, to depict the work of grace as less than it really is; second, to leave people with a gospel that is not big enough to cover the whole area of their need. Isaiah once pictured the misery of inadequate resources in terms of short beds and narrow blankets (Isaiah 28:20) — a sure recipe for long-term discomfort and discontent, with a chance of serious illness thrown in. To such unhappiness, in the spiritual realm, this kind of ministry exposes all who take it seriously. Its prevalence ia a major hindrance to knowledge of God and growth in grace at the present time. We hope we may do service to some by exposing it, and trying to show where it falls short.

What kind of ministry is this? The first thing to say is that, sad as it may seem, it is an *evangelical* ministry. Its basis is acceptance of the Bible as God's Word and its promises as God's assurances. Its regular themes are justification by faith through the cross, new birth through the Spirit, and new life in the power of Christ's resurrection. Its aim is to bring people to new birth and from there to lead them on into the fullest possible experience of resurrection life. It is in every sense a ministry of the gospel. Its errors are not the errors of those whose ministry strays from the central evangelical message. They are errors to which only an evangelical ministry could ever be exposed. This must be stressed at the start.

But if it is a doctrinally sound evangelical ministry, whatever can go wrong with it? How can anything be seriously amiss with it, when its message and aims are so scriptural? The answer is that a ministry which is wholly concerned with gospel truths can still go wrong by giving those truths *an inaccurate application*. Scripture is full of truth that will heal souls, just as a chemist's shop is stocked with remedies for bodily disorders; but in both cases a misapplication of what, rightly used, will heal, will have a disastrous effect. If, instead of dabbing iodine on, you drink it, the effect will be the reverse of curative! — and the doctrines of new birth and new life can be misapplied too, with unhappy results. That is what seems to happen in the case under discussion, as we shall see.

II

The type of ministry that is here in mind starts by stressing, in an evangelistic context, the difference that becoming a Christian will make. Not only will it bring a man forgiveness of sins, peace of conscience, and fellowship with God as his Father; it will also mean that, through the power of the indwelling Spirit, he will be able to overcome the sins that previously mastered him, and the light and leading that God will give him will enable him to find a way through problems of guidance, self-fulfilment, personal relations, heart's desire, and such like, which had hitherto defeated him completely. Now, put like that, in general terms, these great assurances are scriptural and true — praise God, they are! But it is possible so to stress them, and so to play down the rougher side of the Christian life — the daily chastening, the endless war with sin and Satan, the periodic walk in darkness — as to give the impression that normal Christian living is a perfect bed of roses, a state of affairs in which everything in the garden is lovely all the time, and problems no longer exist — or, if they come, they have only to be taken to the throne of grace, and they will melt away at once. This is to suggest that the world, the flesh, and the devil, will give a man no serious trouble once he is a Christian; nor will his circumstances and personal relationships ever be a problem to him; nor will he ever be a problem to himself. Such suggestions are mischievous, however, because they are false.

Of course, an equally lop-sided impression can be given the other way. You can so stress the rough side of the Christian life, and so play down the bright side, as to give the impression that Christian living is for the most part grievous and gloomy — hell on earth, in hope of heaven hereafter! No doubt this impression has from time to time been given; no doubt the ministry we are examining here is partly a reaction against it. But it must be said that of these two extremes of error, the first is the worse, just to the extent that false hopes are a greater evil than false fears. The second error will, in the mercy of God, lead only to the pleasant surprise of finding that Christians have joy as well as sorrow. But the first, which pictures the normal Christian life as trouble-free, is bound to lead to bitter disillusionment sooner or later.

Our assertion is that, in order to appeal compellingly to human wistfulness, the type of ministry we are examining allows itself to promise at this point more than God has undertaken to perform in this world. This, we hold, is the first feature that marks it out as cruel. It buys results with false hopes. To be sure, the cruelty is not that of malice. It is prompted rather by irresponsible kindness. The preacher wants to win his hearers to Christ; therefore he glamorises the Christian life, making it sound as gay and carefree as he can, in order to allure them. But the absence of a bad motive, and the presence of a good one, does not in any way reduce the damage which his exaggerations do.

For what happens, as ministers know all too well, is this. While tough-minded listeners who have heard this kind of thing before take the preacher's promises with a pinch of salt, a few serious seekers will believe him absolutely. On this basis, they are converted; they experience the new birth; and they advance into their new life joyfully certain that they have left all the old headaches and heartaches behind them. And then they find that it is not like that at all. Long-standing problems of temperament, of personal relations, of felt wants, of nagging temptations, are still there — sometimes, indeed, intensified. God does not make their circumstances notably easier; rather the reverse. Dissatisfaction over wife, or husband, or parents, or in-laws, or children, or colleagues, or neighbours, recurs. Temptations and bad habits which their conversion experience seemed to have banished for good reappear. As the first great waves of joy rolled over them during the opening weeks of their Christian experience, they had really felt that all problems had solved themselves, but now they see that it was not so, and that the trouble-free life which they were promised has not materialised. Things which got them down before they were Christians are threatening to get them down again. What are they to think now?

The truth here is that the God of whom it was said, 'he shall feed his flock like a shepherd; he shall gather the lambs in his arms' (Isaiah 40:11), is very gentle with very young Christians, just as mothers are with very young babies. Often the start of their Christian career is marked by great emotional joy, striking providences, remarkable answers to prayer, and immediate fruitfulness in their first acts of witness; thus God encourages them, and establishes them in 'the life'. But as they grow stronger, and are able to bear more, He exercises them in a tougher school. He exposes them to as much testing by the pressure of opposed and discouraging influences as they are able to bear—not more (see the promise, 1 Corinthians 10:13), but equally not less (see the admonition, Acts 14:22). Thus He builds our character, strengthens our faith, and prepares us to help others. Thus He crystallises our sense of values. Thus He glorifies Himself in our lives, making His strength perfect in our weakness. There is nothing unnatural, therefore, in an increase of temptations, conflicts, and pressures, as the Christian goes on with God—indeed, something would be wrong if it did not happen. But the Christian who has been told that the normal Christian life is unshadowed and trouble-free can only conclude, as experiences of inadequacy and imperfection pile in upon him, that he must have lapsed from normal. 'Something's gone wrong,' he will say, 'it isn't working any more!' And his question will be: how can it be made to 'work' again?

III

The second cruel feature of the ministry we have in mind appears at this point. Having created bondage—for such it is—by leading young Christians to regard all experiences of frustration and perplexity as signs of sub-standard Christianity, it now induces further bondage by the strait-jacket of a remedy by which it proposes to dispel these experiences. It insists on diagnosing the 'struggle', which it equates with 'defeat', as a relapse caused by failure to maintain 'consecration' and 'faith'. At first (so it is suggested) the convert was fully surrendered to his new-found Saviour; hence his joy; but since then he has grown cold or careless, or compromised his obedience in some way, or ceased to sustain moment-by-moment trust in the Lord Jesus, and that is why his experience is now as it is. The remedy, therefore, is for him to find, and confess, and forsake, his defection; to reconsecrate himself to Christ, and maintain his consecration daily; and to learn the habit, when problems and temptations come, of handing them over to Christ to deal with for him. If he does this (it is affirmed) he will find himself once more, in the theological as well as the metaphorical sense, on top of the world.

Now it is true that if the Christians grow careless towards God, and slip back into ways of deliberate sin, their inward joy and rest of heart grows less, and discontent of spirit comes to mark them more and more. Those who through union with Christ are 'dead to sin' (Romans 6:1)—done with it, that is, as the ruling principle of their lives—cannot find in sinning even that limited pleasure which it gave them before they were reborn. Nor can they indulge in wrong ways without imperilling their enjoyment of God's favour—God will see to that! 'Because of the iniquity of his covetousness I was angry, I smote him, I hid my face and was angry; but he went on backsliding . . .' (Isaiah 57:15, RSV). That is how God reacts when His children lapse into wrong ways. Unregenerate apostates are often cheerful souls, but backsliding Christians are always miserable. So that the Christian who finds himself asking:

> *Where is the blessedness I knew*
> *when first I saw the Lord?*

ought certainly to ask himself, before he goes any further, whether there have been particular wilful

> *sins that made Thee mourn,*
> *And drove Thee from my breast.*

If so, then the remedy prescribed above is, at least in broad principle, the right one.

But it may not be so; and sooner or later a time will come for every Christian when it is not so. Sooner or later, the truth will be that God is now exercising His child—His consecrated child—in the ways of adult godliness, as He exercised Job, and some of the psalmists, and the addressees of the epistle to the Hebrews, by exposing them to strong attacks from the world, the flesh, and the devil, so that their powers of resistance might grow greater, and their character as men of God become stronger. As we said above, all the children of God undergo this treatment—it is part of the 'chastening of the Lord' (Hebrews 12:15, echoing Job 5:17; Proverbs 3:11), to which He subjects every son whom He loves. And if *this* is what is happening to the perplexed Christian, then the proposed remedy will be disastrous.

For what does it do? It sentences devoted Christians to a treadmill life of hunting each day for non-existent failures in consecration, in the belief that if only they could find some such failures to confess and forsake they could recover an experience of spiritual infancy which God means them now to leave behind. Thus it not only produces spiritual regression and unreality; it sets them at cross-purposes with their God, who has taken from them the carefree glow of spiritual babyhood, with its huge chuckles and contented passivity, precisely in order that He may lead them into an experience that is more adult and mature. Earthly parents enjoy their babies, but are, to say the least, sorry if their growing children want to be babies again, and they hesitate to let them return to babyish ways. It is exactly so with our heavenly Father. He wants us to grow in Christ, not to stay babes in Christ. But the teaching we have in view here sets us against God at this point, and sets before us a return to babyhood as our supreme good. Again, this is *cruelty*, just as the old Japanese habit of binding girls' feet and forcing them permanently out of shape was cruelty, and the fact that the motive is kindness is neither here nor there. The *least* effect of accepting the proposed remedy will be arrested spiritual development—the emergence of a childish, grinning, irresponsible, self-absorbed breed of evangelical adults. The *worst* effects, among sincere and honest believers, will be morbid introspection, hysteria, mental breakdown, and loss of faith, at any rate in its evangelical form.

IV

What, basically, is wrong with this teaching? It is open to criticism from many angles. It fails to grasp New Testament teaching on sanctification and the Christian warfare. It does not understand the meaning of growth in grace. It does not understand the operations of indwelling sin. It confuses the Christian life on earth with the Christian life as it will be in heaven. It misconceives the psychology of Christian obedience (Spirit-prompted activity, *not* Spirit-prompted passivity). But the basic criticism must surely be that it loses sight of *the method and purpose of grace*. Let us try to expound this.

What is *grace*? In the New Testament, grace means God's love in action towards men who merited the opposite of love. Grace means God moving heaven and earth to save sinners who could not lift a finger to save themselves. Grace means God sending His only Son to descend into hell on the cross so that we guilty ones might be reconciled to God and received into heaven. '(God) hath made him to be sin for us, who knew no sin, that we might be made the righteousness of God in him' (2 Corinthians 5:21).

The New Testament knows both a *will* of grace and a *work* of grace. The former is God's eternal plan to save; the latter is God's 'good work in you' (Philippians 1:6), whereby He calls men into living fellowship with Christ (1 Corinthians 1:9), raises them from death to life (Ephesians 2:1–6), seals them as His own by the gift of His Spirit (Ephesians 1:13 f.), transforms them into Christ's image (2 Corinthians 3:18), and will finally raise their bodies in glory (Romans 8:30; 1 Corinthians 15:47–54). It was fashionable among Protestant scholars some years ago to say that grace means God's loving attitude as distinct from His loving work, but that is an unscriptural distinction. In (for instance) 1 Corinthians 15:10 — 'by the *grace* of God I am what I am: and his *grace* which was bestowed upon me was not in vain: but I laboured more abundantly than they all: yet not I, but the *grace* of God which was with me'—the word 'grace' clearly denotes God's loving work in Paul, whereby He made him first a Christian and then a minister.

What is the *purpose* of grace? Primarily, to restore man's relationship with God. When God lays the foundation of this restored relationship, by forgiving our sins as we trust His Son, He does so in order that henceforth we and He may live in fellowship, and what He does in renewing our nature is intended to make us capable of, and actually to lead us into, the exercise of love, trust, delight, hope, and obedience Godward—those acts which, from our side, made up the reality of fellowship with God, who is constantly making Himself known to us. This is what all the work of grace aims at—an ever deeper knowledge of God, and an ever closer fellowship with Him. Grace is God drawing us sinners closer and closer to Himself.

How does God in grace prosecute this purpose? Not by shielding us from assault by the world, the flesh, and the devil, nor by protecting us from burdensome and frustrating circumstances, nor yet by shielding us from troubles created by our own temperament and psychology; but rather by exposing us to all these things, so as to overwhelm us with a sense of our own inadequacy, and to drive us to cling to Him more closely. This is the ultimate reason, from our standpoint, why God fills our lives with troubles and perplexities of one sort and another—it is to ensure that we shall learn to hold Him fast. The reason why the Bible spends so much of its time reiterating that God is a strong rock, a firm defence, and a sure refuge and help for the weak, is that God spends so much of His time bringing home to us that we are weak, both mentally and morally, and dare not trust ourselves to find, or to follow, the right road. When we walk along a clear road feeling fine, and someone takes our arm to help us, as likely as not we shall impatiently shake him off; but when we are caught in rough country in the dark, with a storm getting up and our strength spent, and someone takes our arm to help us, we shall thankfully lean on him. And God wants us to feel that our way through life is rough and perplexing, so that we may learn thankfully to lean on Him. Therefore He takes steps to drive us out of self-confidence to trust in Himself — in the classical scriptural phrase for the secret of the godly man's life, to 'wait on the Lord'.

This truth has many applications. One of the most startling is that God actually uses our sins and mistakes to this end. He employs the educative discipline of failures and mistakes very frequently. It is striking to see how much of the Bible deals with men of God making mistakes, and God chastening them for it. Abraham, promised a son, but made to wait for him, loses patience, makes the mistake of acting the amateur providence, and begets Ishmael—and is made to wait for thirteen more years before God speaks to him again (Genesis 16:16–17:1). Moses makes the mistake of trying to save his people by acts of self-assertion, throwing his weight about, killing an Egyptian, insisting on sorting out the Israelites' private problems for them—and finds himself banished for many decades to the backside of the desert, to bring him to a less vainglorious mind. David makes a run of mistakes—seducing Bathsheba and getting Uriah killed, neglecting his family, numbering the people for prestige—and in each case is chastened bitterly. Jonah makes the mistake of running away from God's call—and finds himself inside a great fish. So we might go on. But the point to stress is that the human mistake, and the immediate divine displeasure, were in no case the end of the story. Abraham learned to wait God's time. Moses was cured of his self-confidence (indeed his subsequent diffidence was itself almost sinful! —see Exodus 4:14). David found repentance after each of his lapses, and was closer to God at the end than at the beginning. Jonah prayed from the fish's belly, and lived to fulfil his mission to Nineveh. God can bring good out of the extremes of our own folly; God can restore the years that the locust has eaten. They say that those who never make mistakes never make anything; certainly, these men made mistakes, but through their mistakes God taught them to know His grace, and to cleave to Him in a way that would never have happened otherwise. Is your trouble a sense of failure? the knowledge of having made some ghastly mistake? Go back to God; His restoring grace waits for you.

V

Unreality in religion is an accursed thing. Unreality is the curse of the kind of teaching that we have challenged in this article. Unreality towards God is the wasting disease of much modern Christianity. We need God to make us realists about both ourselves and Him. Perhaps there is a word for us in the famous hymn in which John Newton describes the passage into the kind of realism that we have been seeking to induce.

These Inward Trials

I asked the Lord, that I might grow
  In faith, and love, and every grace;
Might more of His salvation know,
  And seek more earnestly His face.

I hoped that in some favoured hour
  At once He'd answer my request,
And by His love's constraining power
  Subdue my sins, and give me rest.

Instead of this, He made me feel
  The hidden evils of my heart;
And let the angry powers of hell
  Assault my soul in every part.

Yea more, with His own hand He seemed
  Intent to aggravate my woe;
Crossed all the fair designs I schemed,
  Blasted my gourds, and laid me low.

'Lord, why is this?' I trembling cried,
  'Wilt thou pursue Thy worm to death?'
''Tis in this way,' the Lord replied,
  'I answer prayer for grace and faith.

These inward trials I employ
  From self and pride to set thee free;
And break thy schemes of earthly joy,
  That thou may'st seek thy all in me.'

CHAPTER 22

The Adequacy of God

I

Paul's letter to Rome is the high peak of Scripture, however you look at it. Luther called it 'the clearest gospel of all'. 'If a man understands it', wrote Calvin, 'he has a sure road opened for him to the understanding of the whole Scripture.' Tyndale, in his Preface to Romans, linked both thoughts, calling Romans 'the principal and most excellent part of the New Testament, and most pure Euangelion, that is to say glad tidings and that we call gospel, and also a light and a way in unto the whole Scripture.' All roads in the Bible lead to Romans, and all views afforded by the Bible are seen most clearly from Romans, and when the message of Romans gets into a man's heart there is no telling what may happen.

What do you look for in the Bible? The wise man has his eye open for several things, and Romans is supreme on them all.

Is it *doctrine*—truth about God, taught by God—that you are after? If so, you will find that Romans gives you all the main themes integrated together: God, man, sin, law, judgment, faith, works, grace, creation, redemption, justification, sanctification, the plan of salvation, election, reprobation, the person and work of Christ, the work of the Spirit, the Christian hope, the nature of the church, the place of Jew and Gentile in God's purpose, the philosophy of church and world history, the meaning and message of the Old Testament, the significance of baptism, the principles of personal piety and ethics, the duties of Christian citizenship — *et cetera*!

But the wise man also reads the Bible as a book of *life*, showing by exposition and example what it means to serve God and not to serve Him, to find Him and to lose Him in actual human experience. What has Romans to offer here? The answer is: the fullest cross-section of the life of sin and the life of grace, and the deepest analysis of the way of faith, that the Bible gives anywhere. (On sin, see chapters 1–3, 5–7, 9; on grace, see chapters 3–15; on faith, see chapters 4, 10, 14.)

Another way of reading the Bible, much commended by modern scholars, is as the book of the *church*, where the God-given faith and self-understanding of the believing fellowship is voiced. From this standpoint, Romans, just because it is the classic statement of the gospel by which the church lives, is also the classic account of the church's identity. What is the church? It is the true seed of faithful Abraham, Jew and non-Jew together, chosen by God, justified through faith, and freed from sin for a new life of personal righteousness and mutual ministry. It is the family of a loving heavenly Father, living in hope of inheriting His entire fortune. It is the community of the resurrection, in which the powers of Christ's historic death and present heavenly life are already at work. And nowhere is this presented so fully as in Romans.

The wise man also reads the Bible as *God's personal letter* to each of his spiritual children, and therefore to him as much as to anyone. Read Romans this way, and you will find that it has unique power to search out and deal with things that are so much part of you that ordinarily you do not give them a thought—your sinful habits and attitudes; your instinct for hypocrisy; your natural self-righteousness and self-reliance; your constant unbelief; your moral frivolity, and shallowness in repentance; your half-heartedness, worldliness, fearfulness, despondency; your spiritual conceit and insensitiveness. And you will also find that this shattering letter has unique power to evoke the joy, assurance, boldness, liberty and ardour of spirit which God both requires of and gives to those who love him.

It was said of Jonathan Edwards that his doctrine was all application, and his application was all doctrine. Romans is supremely like that.

No man verily can read it too oft or study it too well [wrote Tyndale] for the more it is studied the easier it is, and the more groundly (i.e., deeply) it is searched the preciouser things are found in it, so great treasury of spiritual things lieth hid therein . . . Wherefore let every man without exception exercise himself herein diligently, and record (i.e., remember) it night and day continually, until he be full acquainted therewith.

Not every Christian, however, appreciates the magnificence of Romans, and there is a reason for this. A man who touched down on the top of Everest in a helicopter (could such a thing be) would not at that moment feel anything like what Hillary and Tensing felt when they stood on the same spot *after climbing the mountain.* Similarly, the impact of Romans upon you will depend on what has gone before. The law that operates is that the more you have dug into the rest of the Bible, the more you are exercised with the intellectual and moral problems of being a Christian, and the more you have felt the burden of weakness and the strain of faithfulness in your Christian life, the more you will find Romans saying to you. John Chrysostom had it read aloud to him once a week; you and I could do a lot worse than that.

Now, as Romans is the high peak of the Bible, so chapter 8 is the high peak of Romans. It is, says the Puritan commentator Edward Elton,

as the Honey combe, most full of heavenly sweetnesse and soul comfort . . . our conceits and apprehensions of comfort are but dreams, till we attain some true feeling of God's love to us in Christ Jesus powred (i.e., poured) and shed abroad in our hearts by the Holy Ghost given unto us: that once gained, it fills our hearts with joy unspeakable and glorious, and it makes us more than conquerours . . . And where find we this ground of comfort more plainly and pithily deciphered than in this chapter? (Epistle Dedicatory before *The Triumph of a true Christian Described,* Elton's exposition of Romans 8).

'Comfort' is of course used here in the old strong sense of that which encourages and nerves, not in the modern sense of that which tranquillises and enervates. The quest for 'comfort' in the modern sense is self-indulgent, sentimental and unreal, and the modern religion of 'I-go-to-church-for-comfort' is not Christianity; but Elton is talking of Christian assurance, which is a different thing.

Here again, however, the Everest principle operates. You will not penetrate the secret of Romans 8 by studying the chapter on its own. The way into Romans 8 is through Romans 1–7, and the impact of Romans 8 upon you will reflect what it has cost you to come to terms with what those chapters say. Only if you have come to know yourself as a lost and helpless sinner (chapters 1–3), and with Abraham to trust the divine promise that seems too good to be true—in your case, the promise of acceptance because Jesus, your covenant Head, died and rose (chapters 4–5); only if, as a new man in Christ, you have committed yourself to total holiness and then found in yourself that the flesh is at war with the spirit, so that you live in contradiction, never fully achieving the good your purposed nor avoiding all the evil you renounced (chapters 6–7); only if, on top of this, 'losses and crosses' are upon you (illness, strain, accident, shock, disappointment, unfair treatment — see chapter 8:18–23, 35–39); only then will Romans 8 yield up its full riches and make its great power known.

In Romans 8 we find Paul restating in a vastly expanded form what he had already said in Romans 5:1–11. He is not ordinarily a repetitive man: why did he go back on his tracks here? Why did he write Romans 8 at all? The short answer — not as silly as it sounds — is: because he had just written Romans 7! In Romans 7:7 he had raised the question, is the law sin? The answer he had to give was: no, but the law is a source of sinning, for it actually foments what it forbids, and so stirs up the impulse to disobey that the more a man sets himself to keep the law the more he finds himself transgressing it. To show this in the quickest and vividest way, he had described his own experience of it. He had told how, before he was a Christian, 'sin, finding opportunity in the commandment, deceived me and by it killed me' (verse 11, RSV); and he had gone on (verse 14–25) to review the present, in which, Christian and apostle though he now is, 'I can will what is right, but I cannot do it . . . I delight in the law of God, in my inmost self, but I see in my members another law at war with the law of my mind and making me captive to the law of sin which dwells in my members . . .' (verses 18, 22 f., RSV). As he described this, his reaction had welled up spontaneously: 'Wretched man that I am! Who will deliver me from this body of death?' (verse 24). The question was rhetorical, for he knew that total deliverance from sin through Christ would certainly be his one day, through 'the redemption of our body' (8:23); but for the present, as he had gone on to say, he had to bear the bitter experience of being unable to attain the perfection he sought, because the law which required it — the law in which, as a regenerate man, he delighted, verse 22 — was powerless to induce it. 'So then, I of myself (i.e., in my inmost self, the real 'me') serve the law (i.e., command) of God with my mind, but with my flesh I serve the law (i.e., principle) of sin' (verse 25, RSV).

Paul has made his point; now he pauses. What has he done? He has shared with his readers what the law tells him about himself, and so reminded them what the law has to say about them.

The law speaks not of privilege and achievement, but only of failure and guilt. For sensitive Christians, therefore, who know how God hates sin, to be diagnosed by the law is a miserable and depressing experience. The writing of these verses had clouded Paul's own joy, and as a good pastor, always thinking of the effect his words would have, he knew that the reading of them would spread the gloom. But he does not think it right to leave the Roman Christians contemplating the sad side of their experience and feeling as if they were back under the law. Instead, he sees need to remind them at once that what is decisive is not what the law says about them, but what the gospel says. So, by a logic both evangelical and pastoral — evangelical, because the gospel demands the last word; pastoral, because pastors must always 'work . . . for your joy' (2 Cor. 1:24) — Paul now picks up again the theme of Christian assurance and develops it as forcibly as he can, from 'no condemnation' at the start to 'no separation' at the close. Romans 8 does not 'get Christians out of Romans 7' in the sense of pointing to a present possibility of no longer having in us imperfection for the law to detect; this was Alexander Whyte's point when he told his congregation, 'you'll not get out of the seventh of Romans while I'm your minister' — and the point is true. But in the sense of directing Christians to the assurances that God gives them in the gospel, and teaching them to rejoice in 'sovereign grace o'er sin abounding', as an antidote to the wretchedness that comes from being measured by the law, Romans 8 'gets Christians out of Romans 7' in a very thorough way.

What does Romans 8 contain? It falls into two parts of unequal length. The first thirty verses set forth *the adequacy of the grace of God* to deal with a whole series of predicaments — the guilt and power of sin (verses 1–9); the fact of death (verses 6–13); the terror of confronting God's holiness (verse 15); weakness and despair in face of suffering (verses 17–25); paralysis in prayer (verses 26 f.); the feeling that life is meaningless and hopeless (verses 28–30). Paul makes his point by dwelling on four gifts of God given to all who by faith are 'in Christ Jesus'. The first is *righteousness* — 'no condemnation' (verse 1). The second is *the Holy Spirit* (verses 4–27). The third is *sonship* — adoption into the divine family in which the Lord Jesus is the firstborn (verses 14–17, 29). The fourth is *security*, now and for ever (verses 28–30). This composite endowment — a status, plus a dynamic, plus an identity, plus a safe-conduct — is more than enough to support a Christian whatever his trouble.

Then in verses 31–39 Paul calls on his readers to react to what he has said. 'What then shall we say to these things?' (verse 31). He goes on to spell out the reaction which is his and should also be ours, and as he does so his theme shifts slightly and becomes *the adequacy of the God of grace.* Interest moves from the gift to the Giver, from the thought of deliverance from evil to the thought of God being to each Christian what He said He would be to Abraham — 'thy *shield, and thy exceeding great reward*' (Genesis 15:1). If verses 1–30 are saying, 'Thou shalt guide me with Thy counsel, and afterward receive me to glory,' verses 31–39 are saying: 'Whom have I in heaven but Thee? and there is none upon earth that I desire beside Thee. My flesh and my heart faileth: but God is the strength of my heart, and my portion for ever' (Psalm 73:24-26). It is this reaction that we shall now explore.

II

'What then shall we say to these things?' The 'we' here is not the royal 'we' nor the literary 'we'; the New Testament knows neither of these idioms. It is rather the inclusive, hortatory 'we' of Christian preaching, which means 'I, and I hope you, and all believers with us'. The thought behind 'what shall we say?' is: 'I know what I shall say; will you say it too?'

In asking his readers to speak, Paul calls on them first to think. He wants them to work out with him how 'these things' bear on their present state — in other words, to apply the fact to themselves. Though he does not know them personally (nor us who read him in the twentieth century), he knows that what determines their state is two factors common to all real Christians everywhere in every age. The first is *commitment to all-round righteousness.* Romans 8:31–39 assumes that its readers are yielded to God as 'slaves of righteousness' (6:13, 18), and are seeking to do the will of God with no half measures. The second factor is *exposure to all-round pressures.* Romans 8:31–39 treats material hardship and human hostility as the common lot of Christians; it is 'we', not just Paul, who face 'tribulation, distress, persecution, famine, nakedness (the ultimate in deprivation), peril, sword' (verse 35). As Paul had taught the converts of his first missionary journey, '*through many tribulations* we must enter the kingdom of God' (Acts 14:22, RSV). Some trouble (not all) can perhaps be dodged for the moment (not for good) by trimming one's spiritual sails, but Paul knows that those set on what the Puritans called 'universal obedience' have to swim against the world's stream all the way, and are constantly made to feel it.

So Paul pictures his readers; and we recognise ourselves in his mirror. Here is the Christian troubled by the memory of a moral lapse; the Christian whose integrity has lost him a friend or a job; the Christian parent whose children are disappointing him (or her); the Christian woman going through 'the change'; the Christian made to feel an outsider at home or at work because of his faith; the Christian burdened by the death of someone he feels should have lived, or the continued life of a senile relative or a mongol child who he feels should have died; the Christian who feels God cannot care for him, or life would be less rough; and many more. But it is precisely people like this—people, in other words, like us—whom Paul is challenging. 'What shall *we* say to these things? Think—think—*think*!'

What does Paul want to happen to us? He wants us to possess our possessions (to use a sometimes abused phrase). Our unpossessed possessions are not, as is sometimes thought, techniques of sinlessness, but the peace, hope and joy in God's love which are the Christian's birthright. Paul knows that 'emotional thinking' under life's pressures—that is, the rationalising of reactions—forfeits these possessions: hence his demand for a reaction, not now to *those* things, but to '*these* things' set out in verses 1–30. Think of what you know of God through the gospel, says Paul, and apply it. Think against your feelings; argue yourself out of the gloom they have spread; unmask the unbelief they have nourished; take yourself in hand, talk to yourself, make yourself look up from your problems to the God of the gospel; let *evangelical* thinking correct *emotional* thinking. By this means (so Paul believes) the indwelling Holy Spirit, whose ministry it is to assure us that we are God's sons and heirs (verse 15 f.), will lead us to the point where Paul's last triumphant inference—'I am sure that neither death, nor life . . . nor anything else in all creation, will be able to separate us from the love of God in Christ Jesus our Lord' (verses 38 f., RSV)—will evoke from us the response: 'And so am I! hallelujah!' For in this response, as Paul knows, lies the secret of the 'more-than-conquerors' experience, which is the victory that overcomes the world and the Christian's heaven on earth.

'What then shall we say to these things?' Paul's model answer consists of four thoughts, each focused in a further question. (Questions, after all, make people think!) 'If God is for us, who is against us? . . . Will He not also give us all things with Him (Christ)? Who shall bring any charge against God's elect? Who shall separate us from the love of Christ?' The recurring keyword of the first three thoughts is 'for' (Greek, *huper*, 'on behalf of'): 'God is *for* us . . . He delivered up His Son *for* us all . . . Christ intercedes *for* us.' The fourth thought is a conclusion from the first three together: 'nothing can ever separate us from the love of God to us which is in Christ Jesus our Lord.' We shall look at these thoughts in order.

III

1 'If God is for us, who is against us?' The thought here is that *no opposition can finally crush us.* To convey this thought, Paul sets before us the adequacy of God as our *sovereign protector*, and the decisiveness of His *covenant commitment* to us.

'If *God* is for us . . .' Who is God? Paul speaks of the God of the Bible and of the gospel, the Lord Jehovah, 'a God merciful and gracious, slow to anger and abounding in steadfast love and faithfulness' (Exodus 34:6 RSV), the God whom 'the only-begotten Son, who is in the bosom of the Father, hath declared' (John 1:18). This is the God who has spoken to announce His sovereignty: 'I am God, and there is no other; I am God, and there is none like Me, declaring the end from the beginning and from ancient times things not yet done, saying, "My counsel shall stand, and I will accomplish all My purpose"' (Isaiah 46:9 f., RSV). This is the God who showed His sovereignty by bringing Abraham out of Ur, Israel out of captivity in Egypt and later in Babylon, and Jesus out of the grave: and who shows the same sovereignty still every time He raises a sinner to spiritual life out of spiritual death. This is the God of Romans, the God whose wrath 'is revealed from heaven against all ungodliness and unrighteousness of men' (1:18), yet who 'commendeth His love towards us, in that, while we were yet sinners, Christ died for us' (5:8). This is the God who calls, justifies and glorifies those whom from eternity He 'predestinated to be conformed to the image of His Son' (8:29). This is the God of the first Anglican article, the 'one living and true God, everlasting . . . of infinite power, wisdom and goodness; the Maker and Preserver of all things both visible and invisible.' This is (be it added) the God whose ways we have been studying in this book.

'If God'—this God—'is *for us*'—what does that mean? The words 'for us' declare God's *covenant commitment*. The goal of grace, as we have seen, is to create a love-relationship between God and us who believe, the kind of relationship for which man was first made, and the bond of fellowship by which God binds Himself to us is His covenant. He imposes it unilaterally, by promise and command. We see Him doing this in His words to Abraham in Genesis 17: 'I am the Almighty God . . . I will establish my

237

covenant between me and thee and thy seed ... to be a God unto thee, and to thy seed after thee ... I will be their God ... thou shalt keep my covenant therefore ...' (verses 1 f., 7 ff.). Galatians 3 and 4 show that all who put faith in Christ, Gentile no less than Jew, are incorporated through Christ into the seed of Abraham, which is the covenant company. Once established, the covenant abides, for God keeps it in being. As Father, Husband and King (these are the human models in terms of which His covenant relationship is presented), God is faithful to His promise and purpose, and the promise itself — the promise to be 'your God', 'a God unto thee' — is a comprehensive promise which, when unpacked, proves to contain within itself all the 'exceeding great and precious promises' in which God has pledged Himself to meet our needs. This covenant relationship is the basis of all biblical religion: when worshippers say '*my* God', and God says '*my* people', covenant language is being talked. And the words 'God is for us' are also covenant language; what is being proclaimed here is God's undertaking to uphold and protect us when men and things are threatening, to provide for us as long as our earthly pilgrimage lasts, and to lead us finally into the full enjoyment of Himself, however many obstacles may seem at present to stand in the way of our getting there. The simple statement, 'God is for us', is in truth one of the richest and weightiest utterances that the Bible contains.

What does it mean for a man when he is able to say: 'God is for me'? The answer is seen in Psalm 56, where the declaration: 'God is for me' (verse 9) is the hinge on which everything turns. The psalmist has his back to the wall ('my enemies trample upon me all day long, for many fight against me proudly' [verse 2, RSV; cf. verses 5 f.]). But the knowledge that God is on his side brings a note of triumph into his prayer. First, it assures him that God has not forgotten or overlooked his need. 'Thou hast kept count of my tossings; put thou my tears in thy bottle (for preservation!). Are they not in thy book (permanently recorded)?' (verse 8, RSV). Second, it gives him confidence that 'when I cry unto thee, then shall mine enemies turn back' (verse 9). Third, it gives a basis for the trust that quells panic. 'When I am afraid, I put my trust in thee ... in God I trust without a fear. What can flesh do to me?' (verse 4, RSV). Whatever 'flesh' — or 'man', as it is put in verse 11 — may do to the psalmist from the outside, so to speak, in the deepest sense they cannot touch him, for his real life is the inward life of fellowship with a loving God, and the God who loves him will preserve that life whatever happens.

The Adequacy of God

Incidentally, Psalm 56 also helps answer the question, who are the 'us' when God is 'for'? The psalmist displays three qualities which together mark out the true believer. First, he *praises*, and what he praises is God's *word* (verses 4, 10) — that is, he attends to God's revelation and venerates God in it and according to it, rather than indulging his own unchecked theological fancies. Second, he *prays*, and the desire that prompts his prayer is for communion with God as life's goal and end — 'that I may walk before God' (verse 13). Third, he *pays* — pays his vows, that is, of faithfulness and thanksgiving (verses 12 f.). The praising, praying, thankful, faithful man has on him the marks of a child of God.

What, now, was Paul's purpose in asking his question? He was (and is) countering *fear* — the timid Christian's fear of the forces which he feels are massed against him, the forces, we might say of 'him', or 'her', or 'them'. Paul knows that there is always some person, or group of persons, whose ridicule, displeasure, or hostile reaction the Christian feels unable to face. Paul knows that sooner or later this becomes a problem for every Christian, including those who before conversion did not care what anyone said or thought about them, and he knows how inhibiting and desolating such fear can be. But he knows too how to answer it. Think! says Paul in effect. God is for you: you see what that means: now reckon up who is against you, and ask yourself how the two sides compare. (Note, the translation 'who *can be* against us' is wrong, and misses Paul's point; what he asks for is a realistic review of the opposition, human and demonic, not a romantic pretence that it does not exist. Opposition is a fact: the Christian who is not conscious of being opposed had better watch himself, for he is in danger. Such unrealism is no requirement of Christian discipleship, but is rather a mark of failure in it.) Are you afraid of 'them'? Paul asks. You need not be, any more than Moses needed to be afraid of Pharaoh after God had said to him: 'Certainly I will be with thee' (Exodus 3:12). Paul is calling on his readers to make the kind of calculation that Hezekiah made: 'Do not be afraid or dismayed before the king of Assyria and all the horde that is with him, for there is one greater with us than with him . . . with us is the LORD our God, to help us and to fight our battles' (2 Chronicles 32:7 f., RSV). Toplady, who is the poet of Christian assurance in the same sense as Watts is the poet of God's sovereignty and Charles Wesley the poet of the new creation, voices the realisation to which Paul's question seeks to lead us as follows:

A sovereign protector I have,
Unseen, yet for ever at hand;
Unchangeably faithful to save,
Almighty to rule and command.
He smiles, and my comforts abound;
His grace as the dew shall descend,
And walls of salvation surround
The soul He delighted to defend.

Grasp this, says Paul; hold on to it; let this certainty make its impact on you in relation to what you are up against at this very moment; and you will find in thus knowing God as your sovereign protector, irrevocably committed to you in the covenant of grace, both freedom from fear and new strength for the fight.

IV

2 'He who did not spare His own Son but gave Him up for us all, will He not also give us all things with Him?' The thought expressed by Paul's second question is that *no good thing will finally be withheld from us.* He conveys this thought by pointing to the adequacy of God as our *sovereign benefactor*, and to the decisiveness of His *redeeming work* for us.

Three comments will bring out the force of Paul's argument.

Note, first, what Paul implies about the *costliness* of our redemption. 'He did not spare His own Son.' In saving us, God went to the limit. What more could He have given for us? What more had He to give? We cannot know what Calvary cost the Father, any more than we can know what Jesus felt as He tasted the penalty due to our sins. 'We may not know, we cannot tell what pains He had to bear.' Yet we can say this: that if the measure of love is what it gives, then there never was such love as God showed to sinners at Calvary, nor will any subsequent love-gift to us cost God so much. So if God has already commended His love towards us in that while we were yet sinners Christ died for us (cf. 5:8), it is believable, to say the least, that He will go on to give us 'all things' beside. Most Christians know the fearful feeling that God may not have anything more for them beyond what they have already received, but a thoughtful look at Calvary should banish this mood.

But this is not all. Note, second, what Paul implies about the *effectiveness* of our redemption. 'God,' he says, 'gave Him up *for us all'* — and this fact is itself the guarantee that 'all things' will be given us, because they all come to us as the direct fruit of Christ's death. We have just said that the greatness of God's giving on the cross makes His further giving (if the words may be allowed) natural and likely, but what we must note now is that the unity of God's saving purpose makes such further giving necessary, and therefore certain.

At this point the New Testament view of the cross involves more than is sometimes realised. That the apostolic writers present the death of Christ as the ground and warrant of God's offer of forgiveness, and that men enter into forgiveness through repentance and faith in Christ, will not be disputed. But does this mean that, as a loaded gun is only potentially explosive, and an act of pulling the trigger is needed to make it go off, so Christ's death achieved only a possibility of salvation, needing an exercise of faith on man's part to trigger it off and make it actual? If so, then it is not strictly Christ's death that saves us at all, any more than it is loading the gun that makes it fire; strictly speaking, we save ourselves by our faith, and for all we know, Christ's death might not have saved anyone, since it might have been the case that nobody believed the gospel. But that is not how the New Testament sees it. The New Testament view is that the death of Christ has actually saved 'us all' — all, that is to say, whom God foreknew, and has called and justified, and will in due course glorify. For our faith, which from man's point of view is the means of salvation, is from God's point of view part of salvation, and is as directly and completely God's gift to us as is the pardon and peace of which faith lays hold. Psychologically, faith is our own act, but the theological truth about it is that it is God's work in us: both our faith, and our new relationship with God as believers, and all the divine gifts that are enjoyed within this relationship, were alike secured for us by Jesus's death on the cross. For the cross was not an isolated event; it was, rather, the focal point in God's eternal plan to save His elect, and it ensured and guaranteed first the calling (i.e., the bringing to faith, through the gospel in the mind and the Holy Spirit in the heart), and then the justification, and finally the glorification, of all for whom, specifically and personally, Christ died.

Now we see why the Greek of this verse says literally (and so the AV renders it), *how shall He not* with Him also give us all things? It is simply impossible for Him not to do this, for Christ and 'all things' go together as ingredients in the single gift of eternal life and glory, and the giving of Christ for us, to remove the 'sin barrier' by substitutionary atonement, has effectively opened the door to our being given all the rest. The saving purpose of God, from eternal election to final glory, is one, and it is vital for both our understanding and our assurance that we should not lose sight of the links that bind together its various stages and parts. Which leads to our next point.

Note, third, what Paul implies about the *consequences* of our redemption. God, he says will with Christ give us 'all things'. What does that cover? Calling, justification, glorification (which in verse 30 includes everything from the new birth to the resurrection of the body) have already been mentioned, and so throughout the chapter has the many-sided ministry of the Holy Spirit. Here is wealth indeed, and from other Scriptures we could add to it. We could, for instance, dwell on our Lord's assurance that when disciples seek first 'the kingdom of God and His righteousness', then 'all these things' (their material necessities) will be providentially supplied (Matthew 6:33) — a truth to which he pointed again, startlingly, when he said, 'there is no one who has left house or brothers or sisters or mother or father or children or lands for my sake and for the gospel, who will not receive a hundredfold now in this life, houses and brothers and sisters and mothers and children and lands, with persecutions (!), and in the age to come eternal life' (Mark 10:30, RSV). Or we could dwell on the thought that 'all things' means all the good, not that *we* can think of, but that *God* can think of, as infinite wisdom and power guide His generosity. But we shall come closest to Paul's mind if we understand this phrase as prompted, like the 'therefore' of verse 1, by Paul's special brand of pastoral logic, which counters by anticipation wrong inferences that his readers might otherwise draw. The wrong inference which he was countering in verse 1 (and which we shall see him counter again in verse 33) was that the Christian's sins of infirmity may endanger God's continued acceptance of him; the wrong inference that he is countering here is that following Christ will mean the loss of things worth having, uncompensated by any corresponding gain — which, if true, would make Christian discipleship, like the Roundheads in *1066 and All That,* 'right but repulsive'. Paul's assurance that with Christ God will give us 'all things' corrects this inference by anticipation, for it proclaims the adequacy of God as our sovereign benefactor, whose way with His servants leaves no ground for any sense or fear of real personal impoverishment at any stage. Let us work this out.

The Christian, like Israel at Sinai, faces the exclusive claim of the first commandment. God said to Israel: 'I am the LORD thy God, which have brought thee out of the land of Egypt, out of the house of bondage. *Thou shalt have no other gods before me'* (Exodus 20:2 f.; RV renders the last words 'beside Me'). This command, like all the Decalogue, was couched in negative form, because it came as a summons to stop living in the old way and make a fresh start. Its background was the polytheism of Egypt, which the Israelites knew already, and that of Canaan, which was to confront them very shortly. Polytheism, the worship of many gods, was in fact universal throughout the ancient Near East. The idea behind it was that every god's power was limited by the power of his fellows. The corn-god, or the fertility-god, for instance, could never exercise the functions of the storm-god, or the god of the seas. A god who made his home in one particular shrine or sacred grove or tree, could only act to help men on his own home ground; elsewhere, other gods were supreme. Therefore, it was not enough to worship one god only; one needed, so far as possible, to get on good terms with them all, or else one would constantly be exposed to the ill-will of gods whom one had neglected, with consequent loss of the good things that it was the special prerogative of those neglected deities to bestow. It was the pressure of these ideas that in after years made the temptation to the Israelites to worship 'other gods' so strong. No doubt in Egypt they had come to take the polytheistic outlook for granted, however much or little they may have joined in worshipping the gods of the Egyptians. But the first commandment clamped down absolutely upon this way of thinking and behaving. 'Thou shalt have no other gods beside Me.'

Note, now, how God deals with this question of dividing allegiance between Himself and 'other gods'. He puts it to Israel as an issue, not of theology, but of loyalty; a matter not of the mind simply, but of the heart. Elsewhere in Scripture, notably in the Psalms and Isaiah, we find Him telling His people explicitly that to worship pagan gods is madness, because they are in fact no gods; but He is not making that point here. For the moment He leaves open the question whether other gods have any existence or not. He frames the first commandment, not to settle that issue, but to settle the question of loyalty. God does not say: there are no other gods beside Me for you to have; He simply says: you shall have no other gods but Me. And He grounds His claim on the fact that He is their God who brought them out of Egypt. It is as if He said: by saving you from Pharaoh and his hosts 'by a mighty hand and a stretched out arm', by signs and wonders, by the Passover and the crossing of the Red Sea, I gave you a sample of what I can do for you, and showed you clearly enough that anywhere, at any time, against any foe, under any privation whatsoever, I can protect you, provide for you, and give you all that makes up true life. You need no god but Me; therefore you are not to be betrayed into looking for any god but Me, but you are to serve Me, and Me alone.

In other words, in the first commandment God told Israel to serve Him exclusively, not only because they owed it to Him, but also because He was worthy of their entire and exclusive trust. They were to bow to His absolute authority over them on the basis of confidence in His complete adequacy for them. And, clearly, these two things needed to go together; for they could hardly have been whole-hearted in serving Him to the exclusion of other gods if they had doubted His all-sufficiency to provide whatever they might need,

Now, if you are a Christian, you know that you, too, are being claimed in the same way. God did not spare His Son, but delivered Him up for you; Christ loved you, and gave Himself for you, to save you out of the spiritual Egypt of bondage to sin and Satan. The first commandment, in its positive form, is put to you by Christ Himself—'you shall love the Lord your God with all your heart, and with all your soul, and with all your mind. This is the great and first commandment' (Matthew 22:37 f.). The claim rests on the right of both creation and redemption, and it cannot be evaded.

You know what kind of life it is that Christ calls you, as His disciple, to live. His own example and teaching in the gospels (to look no further in the book of God than that) make it abundantly clear. You are called to go through this world as a pilgrim, a mere temporary resident, travelling light, and willing, as Christ directs, to do what the rich young ruler refused to do, give up material wealth and the security it provides, and live in a way that involves you in poverty, and loss of possessions. Having your treasure in heaven, you are not to budget for treasure on earth, nor for a high standard of living—you may well be required to forgo both. You are called to follow Christ, carrying your cross. What does that mean? Well, the only persons in the ancient world who carried a cross were condemned criminals going out to execution; they, like our Lord Himself, were made to carry the cross on which they were to be crucified. So that what Christ means is that you must accept for yourself the position of such a person in the sense that you renounce all future expectations from society and learn to take it as a matter of course if your fellow-men give you the cold shoulder and view you with contempt and disgust, as an alien sort of being. You may often find yourself treated in this fashion if you are loyal to the Lord Jesus Christ.

Again: you are called to be a meek man, not always standing up for your rights, nor concerned to get your own back, nor troubled in your heart by ill-treatment and personal slights (though, if you are normally sensitive, these things are bound to hurt you at the top level of consciousness); but you are simply to commit your cause to God and leave it to Him to vindicate you if and when He sees fit. Your attitude to your fellow-men, good and bad, nice and nasty, both Christians and unbelievers, is to be that of the Good Samaritan towards the Jew in the gutter—that is to say, your eyes must be open to see others' needs, both spiritual and material; your heart must be ready to care for needy souls when you find them; your mind must be alert to plan out the best way to help them; and your will must be set against the trick that we are all so good at—'passing the buck', going by on the other side and contracting out of situations of need where sacrificial help is called for.

None of this, of course, is strange to any of us. We know what kind of life Christ calls us to; we often preach and talk to each other about it. But do we live it? Well, look at the churches. Observe the shortage of ministers and missionaries, especially men; the luxury goods in Christian homes; the fund-raising problems of Christian societies; the readiness of Christians in all walks of life to grumble about their salaries; the lack of concern for the old and lonely, or indeed for anyone outside the circle of 'sound believers'. We are unlike the Christians of New Testament times. Our approach to life is conventional and static; theirs was not. The thought of 'safety first' was not a drag on their enterprise as it is on ours. By being exuberant, unconventional, and uninhibited in living by the gospel they turned their world upside down, but you could not accuse us twentieth-century Christians of doing anything like that. Why are we so different? Why, compared with them, do we appear as no more than half-way Christians? Whence comes the nervous, dithery, take-no-risks mood that mars so much of our discipleship? Why are we not free enough from fear and anxiety to allow ourselves to go full stretch in following Christ?

One reason it seems is that in our heart of hearts we are afraid of the consequences of going the whole way into the Christian life. We shrink from accepting burdens of responsibility for others because we fear we should not have strength to bear them. We shrink from accepting a way of life in which we forfeit material security because we are afraid of being left stranded. We shrink from being meek because we are afraid that if we do not stand up for ourselves we shall be trodden down and victimised, and end up among life's casualties and failures. We shrink from breaking with social conventions in order to serve Christ because we fear that if we did, the established structure of our life would collapse all round us, leaving us without a footing anywhere. It is these half-conscious fears, this dread of insecurity, rather than any deliberate refusal to face the cost of following Christ, which make us hold back. We feel that the risks of out-and-out discipleship are too great for us to take. In other words, we are not persuaded of the adequacy of God to provide for all the needs of those who launch out wholeheartedly on to the deep sea of unconventional living in obedience to the call of Christ. Therefore, we feel obliged to break the first commandment just a little, by withdrawing a certain amount of our time and energy from serving God in order to serve mammon. This, at bottom, seems to be what is wrong with us. We are afraid to go all the way in accepting the *authority* of God, because of our secret *uncertainty* as to His adequacy to look after us if we do.

Now let us call a spade a spade. The name of the game we are playing is *unbelief*, and Paul's 'He will give us *all things*' stands as an everlasting rebuke to us. Paul is telling us that there is no ultimate loss or irreparable impoverishment to be feared; if God denies us something, it is only in order to make room for one or other of the things He has in mind. Are we, perhaps, still assuming that a man's life consists, partly at any rate, in the things he possesses? But that is to budget for discontent, and to block the blessing—for Paul's 'all things' is not a plethora of material possessions, and the passion for possessions has to be cast out of us in order to let the 'all things' in. For this phrase has to do with knowing and enjoying God, and not with anything else. The meaning of 'He will give us all things' can be put thus: one day we shall see that nothing—literally nothing—which could have increased our eternal happiness has been denied us, and that nothing—literally nothing—that could have reduced that happiness has been left with us. What higher assurance do we want than that?

Yet when it comes to cheerful self-abandonment in Christ's service we dither. Why? Out of unbelief, pure and simple. Do we fear that God lacks *strength* or *wisdom* for fulfilling His declared purpose? But it is He who made the worlds, and rules them, and ordains all that takes place, from the careers of Pharaoh and

Nebuchadnezzar to the fall of a sparrow. Or do we fear that He is *infirm of purpose*, and that as good men with good intentions sometimes let down their friends, so our God may fail to carry out His good intentions towards us? But Paul states it as a fact that (following the RSV of Romans 8:28) 'in *everything* God works for good with those who love Him': and who are you to suppose that you will be the first exception, the first person to find God wavering and failing to keep His word? Do you not see how you dishonour God by such fears? Or do you doubt His *constancy*, suspecting that He has 'emerged' or 'developed' or 'died' in the interim between Bible times and our own (modern men have explored all these ideas), and that now He is no longer quite the God with whom the saints of Scripture had to do? But 'I the Lord do not change', and 'Jesus Christ is the same yesterday and today and for ever' (Malachi 3:6; Hebrews 13:8, RSV).

Have you been holding back from a risky, costly course to which you know in your heart God has called you? Hold back no longer. Your God is faithful to you, and adequate for you. You will never need more than He can supply, and what He supplies, both materially and spiritually, will always be enough for the present. 'No good thing does the LORD withhold from those who walk uprightly' (Psalm 84:11, RSV). 'God is faithful, and He will not let you be tempted beyond your strength, but with the temptation will also provide the way of escape, that you may be able to endure it' (1 Corinthians 10:13, RSV). 'My grace is sufficient for thee, for my strength is made perfect in weakness' (2 Corinthians 12:8). Think on these things!—and let your thoughts drive out your inhibitions is serving your Master.

V

3 'Who shall bring any charge against God's elect? It is God who justifies; who is to condemn?' The thought expressed by Paul's third question is that *no accusation can ever disinherit us*. He conveys this thought by pointing to the adequacy of God as our *sovereign champion*, and to the decisiveness of His *justifying verdict* upon us.

Paul wrote the two previous verses to counter the Christian's fear of *opposition* and *privation* among men; he writes this verse to counter fear of *rejection* by God. There are two sorts of sick consciences, those that are not aware enough of sin and those that are not aware enough of pardon, and it is to the second sort that Paul is ministering now. He knows how easily the conscience of a Christian under pressure can grow morbid, particularly when that

Christian's nose is rubbed as Romans 7:14–25 would rub it in the reality of continued sin and failure. Paul knows too how impossible it is for Christian hope to rejoice a man's heart while doubts of his security as a justified believer still remain. So, as the next stage in his outline of what Christians should say to 'these things', Paul speaks directly to the fear (to which no Christian is a total stranger) that present justification may be no more than provisional, and may one day be lost by reason of the imperfections of one's Christian life. Paul does not for a moment deny that Christians fail and fall, sometimes grievously, nor does he question that (as all true Christians know, and as his own words in Romans 7 reveal) the memory of sins committed after becoming a Christian is far more painful than are any thoughts of one's moral lapses, however gross, before that time. But Paul denies emphatically that any lapses now can endanger our justified status. The reason, he says in effect, is simple: nobody is in a position to get God's verdict reviewed! The NEB rendering puts Paul's point well: 'Who will be the accuser of God's chosen ones?' Paul's wording enforces the point in several ways.

First, Paul brings in a reminder of God's *grace in election*. 'Who shall bring any charge against *God's elect*?' Remember, says Paul, that those whom God justifies now were chosen from eternity for final salvation, and if their justification were at any stage revoked God's plan for them would be entirely overthrown. So loss of justification is inconceivable on that score.

Second, Paul brings in a reminder of God's *sovereignty in judgment*. 'It is God who justifies; who is to condemn?' If it is God, Maker and Judge of all, who passes the justifying sentence — that is, who declares that you have been set right with His law and with Himself, and are not now liable to death for your sins, but are accepted in Christ — and if God has passed this sentence in full view of all your shortcomings, justifying you on the explicit basis and understanding that you were not righteous, but ungodly (cf. Romans 4:5), then nobody can ever challenge the verdict, not even 'the accuser of the brethren' himself. Nobody can alter God's decision over His head — there is only one Judge! — and nobody can produce new evidence of your depravity that will make God change His mind. For God justified you with (so to speak) His eyes open. He knew the worst about you at the time when He accepted you for Jesus's sake; and the verdict which He passed then was, and is, final.

In the Bible world, judgment was a royal prerogative, and the royal judge, in whom the powers of legislature, judiciary, and executive came together, was expected, once he had settled what a person's rights were, to take action to see that he got them. Thus the king became champion and protector of those whom he justified in judgment. This is the background of Paul's thought here: the sovereign Lord who justified you will take active steps to see that the status He has given you is maintained and enjoyed to the full. So loss of justification is inconceivable on this score also.

Third, Paul brings in a reminder of Christ's *effectiveness in mediation*. It is best, with the RSV, to read the reference to Christ as a question. 'Who is to condemn? Is it Christ Jesus, who died, yes, who was raised from the dead, who is at the right hand of God, who indeed intercedes for us?' All that Paul says serves to show that the idea of Christ condemning us is absurd. He *died* — to save us from condemnation, by bearing the penalty of our sins as our substitute. He *rose* and was *exalted* — 'to be a Prince and a Saviour, for to give repentance to Israel, and forgiveness of sins' (Acts 5:31). Now, by virtue of His enthroned presence at the Father's right hand, He *intercedes* with authority for us — that is, He intervenes in our interest to ensure that we receive all that He died to procure for us. Shall He now condemn us? — He, the Mediator, who loved us and gave Himself for us, and whose constant concern in heaven is that we should enjoy the full fruits of His redemption? The idea is grotesque and impossible. Once more, therefore, it appears that loss of justification is inconceivable; and so the troubled Christian must tell himself, as from God. Once more it is Toplady who puts the right words into his mouth, in a hymn entitled 'Faith Reviving':

> *From whence this fear and unbelief?*
> *Hath not the Father put to grief*
> *His spotless Son for me?*
> *And will the righteous Judge of men*
> *Condemn me for that debt of sin*
> *Which, Lord, was charged on Thee?*

> *Complete atonement Thou hast made,*
> *And to the utmost farthing paid*
> *Whate'er Thy people owed;*
> *Nor can His wrath on me take place,*
> *If sheltered in Thy righteousness*
> *And sprinkled with Thy blood.*

If Thou hast my discharge procured,
And freely in my room endured
The whole of wrath divine,
Payment God cannot twice demand,
First at my bleeding Surety's hand,
And then again at mine.

Turn then, my soul, unto Thy rest;
The merits of Thy great High Priest
Have bought Thy liberty;
Trust in His efficacious blood,
Nor fear thy banishment from God,
Since Jesus died for thee!

VI

4 'Who shall separate us from the love of Christ?' The climactic thought to which Paul rises in his fourth question is that *no separation from Christ's love can ever befall us.* He conveys this by setting before us God, the Father and the Son, as our *sovereign keeper,* and by making plain the decisiveness of *divine love* in settling our destiny.

We studied the love of God in an earlier chapter, and we need not therefore dwell on it here. The crucial point, on which Paul's reasoning turns, is already familiar ground—namely, that whereas human love, for all its power in other ways, cannot ensure that what is desired for the beloved will actually happen (as multitudes of star-crossed lovers and heartbroken parents know), divine love is a function of omnipotence, and has at its heart an almighty purpose to bless which cannot be thwarted. This sovereign resolve is referred to here as both 'the love of Christ' and 'the love of God, which is in Christ Jesus our Lord' (verses 35, 39); and the double description reminds us both that the Father and the Son (together with the Holy Spirit, as the previous part of the chapter showed) are one in loving sinners, and also that the love which elects, justifies, and glorifies is love 'in Christ Jesus', love knowable only by those to whom Christ Jesus is 'our Lord'. The love Paul speaks of is love that saves, and the New Testament will not allow any man to suppose that this divine love embraces him unless he has come as a sinner to Jesus and has learned to say to Jesus with Thomas, 'My Lord and my God!' But once a man has truly given himself up to the Lord Jesus (so Paul is telling us) he never need feel the uncertainty of the cartoonists' lady who murmurs as she puffs at her thistledown, 'he loves me—he loves me not—' For it is the

Christian's privilege to know for certain that God loves him immutably, and that nothing can at any time part him from that love, or come between him and the final enjoyment of its fruits.

This is what Paul is proclaiming in the triumphant declaration of verses 38 f., in which the very heartbeat of Christian assurance is heard: 'I am convinced' – 'persuaded', AV; 'sure', RSV; 'absolutely convinced', Phillips – 'that there is nothing in death or life, in the realm of spirits or superhuman powers, in the world as it is or the world as it shall be, in the forces of the universe, in heights or depths – nothing in all creation that can separate us from the love of God in Christ Jesus our Lord' (NEB). Here Paul displays God's adequacy – His 'all-sufficiency', to use the old word – in at least two ways. First, God is adequate as our *keeper*. 'Nothing . . . can separate us from the love of God,' because the love of God holds us fast. Christians 'are kept by the power of God through faith unto salvation' (1 Peter 1:5), and the power of God keeps them believing as well as keeping them safe through believing. Your faith will not fail while God sustains it; you are not strong enough to fall away while God is resolved to hold you. Then, second, God is adequate as our *end*. Human love-relationships – between child and parent, or wife and husband, or friend and friend – are ends in themselves, having their value and joy in themselves, and the same is true of our knowledge of the God who loves us, the God whose love is seen in Jesus. Wrote Paul: 'I count everything sheer loss, because all is far outweighed by the gain of knowing Christ Jesus my Lord, for whose sake I did in fact lose everything. I count it so much garbage, for the sake of gaining Christ . . . All I care for is to know Christ, to experience the power of His resurrection, and to share His sufferings, in growing conformity with His death, if only I may finally arrive at the resurrection from the dead . . . I press on, hoping to take hold of that for which Christ once took hold of me . . . forgetting what is behind me, and reaching out for what lies ahead, I press towards the goal to win the prize which is God's call to the life above, in Christ Jesus' (Philippians 3:8–14, NEB). As the hymn puts it, 'Christ is the path, and Christ is the prize.' The purpose of our relationship with God in Christ is the perfecting of the relationship itself. How could it be otherwise, when it is a love-relationship? So God is adequate in this further sense, that in knowing Him fully we shall find ourselves fully satisfied, needing and desiring nothing more.

Once more, Paul is countering fear – fear, this time, of the unknown, whether in terms of unprecedented suffering (verses 35 f.)

or of a horrific future ('the world as it shall be') or of cosmic forces which one cannot measure or master ('height' and 'depth' in verse 39 are technical astrological terms for mysterious cosmic powers). The focus of fear is the effect these things might have on one's fellowship with God, by overwhelming both reason and faith and so destroying sanity and salvation together. In an age like ours (not so different in this respect from Paul's!) all Christians, especially the more imaginative, know something of this fear. It is the Christian version of the existentialist *angst* at the prospect of personal destruction. But, says Paul, we must fight this fear, for the bogey is unreal. Nothing, literally nothing, can separate us from the love of God: 'in all these things we are more than conquerors through Him that loved us' (verse 37). When Paul and Silas sat in the stocks in the Philippian gaol, they found themselves so exultant that at midnight they began to sing, and this is how those who know God's sovereign love will always find themselves when the harrowing things are actually upon them. Once again it is Toplady, in a hymn called 'Full Assurance', who finds words to spell out what is involved.

> *The work which His goodness began*
> *The arm of His strength will complete;*
> *His promise is Yea and Amen,*
> *And never was forfeited yet;*
> *Things future, nor things that are now,*
> *Not all things below nor above*
> *Can make Him His purpose forego,*
> *Or sever my soul from His love.*
>
> *My name from the palms of His hands*
> *Eternity will not erase;*
> *Impressed on His heart it remains*
> *In marks of indelible grace;*
> *Yes, I to the end shall endure,*
> *As sure as the earnest is given;*
> *More happy, but not more secure,*
> *The glorified spirits in heaven!*

VII

The climax of our book has now been reached. We set out to see what it means to know God. We found that the God who is 'there' for us to know is the God of the Bible, the God of Romans, the

God revealed in Jesus, the Three-in-One of historic Christian teaching. We realised that knowing Him starts with knowing about Him, so we studied His revealed character and ways and came to know something of His goodness and severity, His wrath and His grace. As we did so, we learned to re-evaluate ourselves as fallen creatures, not strong and self-sufficient as we once supposed, but weak, foolish and indeed bad, heading not for Utopia but for hell unless grace intervenes. Also, we saw that knowing God involves a personal relationship whereby you give yourself to God on the basis of His promise to give Himself to you. Knowing God means asking His mercy, and resting on His undertaking to forgive sinners for Jesus's sake. Further, it means becoming a disciple of Jesus, the living Saviour who is 'there' today, calling the needy to Himself as He did in Galilee in the days of His flesh. Knowing God, in other words, involves *faith* — assent, consent, commitment — and faith expresses itself in prayer and obedience. 'The best measure of a spiritual life', said Oswald Chambers, 'is not its ecstasies, but its obedience.' Good king Josiah 'judged the cause of the poor and needy . . . *was not this to know me?* saith the Lord' (Jeremiah 22:16). Now, finally, and on the basis of all that went before, we learn that a man who knows God will be more than conqueror, and will live in Romans 8, exulting with Paul in the adequacy of God. And here we have to stop, for this is as high in the knowledge of God as any man can go this side of glory.

Where has all this led us? To the very heart of biblical religion. We have been brought to the point where David's prayer and profession in Psalm 16 may become our own. 'Preserve me, O God, for in Thee I take refuge. I say to the Lord, "Thou art my Lord; I have no good apart from Thee." . . . The Lord is my chosen portion and my cup; thou holdest my lot . . . I bless the Lord who gives me counsel . . . I keep the Lord always before me; because He is at my right hand, I shall not be moved. Therefore my heart is glad . . . Thou dost show me the path of life; in Thy presence there is fulness of joy; in Thy right hand are pleasures for evermore' (RSV). Then one may say with Habakkuk in face of economic ruin, or any other deprivation: 'Although the fig tree shall not blossom, neither shall fruit be in the vines; the labour of the olive shall fail, and the fields shall yield no meat; the flock shall be cut off from the fold, and there shall be no herd in the stalls: *yet I will rejoice in the Lord, I will joy in the God of my salvation.* The Lord God is my strength . . .' (Habakkuk 3:17 f.) Happy the man who can say these things and mean them!

Again: we have been brought to the point where we can grasp

the truth in descriptions of the Christian life in terms of 'victory' and 'Jesus satisfies'. Used naïvely, this language could mislead — for the 'victory' is not yet the end of the war, nor can faith in the Triune God be reduced to 'Jesusolatry'. None the less, these phrases are precious, for they point to the link between knowedge of God on the one hand and human fulfilment on the other. When we speak of the adequacy of God, it is this link that we highlight and the link is of the essence of Christianity. Those who know God in Christ have found the secret of true freedom and true manhood. But it would take another book to go into that!

Finally: we have been brought to the point where we both can and must get our life's priorities straight. From current Christian publications you might think that the most vital issue for any real or would-be Christian in the world today is church union, or social witness, or dialogue with other Christians and other faiths, or refuting this or that -ism, or developing a Christian philosophy and culture, or what have you. But our line of study makes the present-day concentration on these things look like a gigantic conspiracy of misdirection. Of course, it is not that; the issues themselves are real and must be dealt with in their place. But it is tragic that, in paying attention to them, so many in our day seem to have been distracted from what was, is, and always will be the true priority for every human being — that is, learning to know God in Christ. 'Thou hast said, "Seek ye my face." My heart says to Thee, "Thy face, Lord, do I seek"' (Psalm 27:8, RSV). If this book moves any of its readers to identify more closely with the psalmist at this point, it will not have been written in vain.

Biblical Passages Discussed